Subject Control
in Online Catalogs

Subject Control in Online Catalogs

Robert P. Holley
Editor

The Haworth Press
New York • London

Subject Control in Online Catalogs has also been published as *Cataloging & Classification Quarterly*, Volume 10, Numbers 1/2 1989.

The Haworth Press, Inc., 10 Alice Street, Binghamton, NY 13904-1580
EUROSPAN/Haworth, 3 Henrietta Street, London WC2E 8LU England

Library of Congress Cataloging-in-Publication Data

Subject control in online catalogs / Robert P. Holley, editor.
    p. cm.
    Also published as v. 10, no. 1/2 1989 of Cataloging & classification quarterly.
    Includes bibliographical references.
    ISBN 0-86656-793-3
    1. Catalogs, On-line — Subject access. 2. On-line bibliographic searching. 3. Subject cataloging — Data processing. 4. Machine-readable bibliographic data. 5. Catalogs, Subject. I. Holley, Robert P.
Z699.35.S92S83 1989
025.3'132 — dc20
            89-19953
            CIP

Subject Control in Online Catalogs

CONTENTS

ALL HAWORTH BOOKS & JOURNALS
ARE PRINTED ON CERTIFIED
ACID-FREE PAPER

ABOUT THE EDITOR

Robert P. Holley, PhD, MLS, MPhil, is Associate Dean of Libraries, Wayne State University, Detroit, Michigan. He has been concerned about subject access to information throughout his library career. Dr. Holley's articles on subject analysis and classification have appeared in various publications. He was a member (1979-1983) and then Chair (1981-1983) of the American Library Association RTSD CCS Subject Analysis Committee. A charter member of the Standing Committee of the IFLA Section on Classification and Indexing, he served as its chair from 1985-1989.

Preface

Now as we complete our first decade of online catalog use, the time has come to evaluate where we are and where we are going in providing adequate subject access to our users. We began the decade by wondering about the importance of subject searching over known item searching in online catalogs. User preference for subject searching is now a given—the shortcomings and potential strategies for improvement in online subject access are the new issues. As the euphoria over online subject access in any form falls aside, we must confront barriers to access from different systems and interfaces, inadequate cross references and online user assistance, outdated terminology, incomplete or inconsistent indexing, and problems in subject heading displays. We have automated our card catalogs without rethinking subject cataloging practice in light of the power and changed environment of computer retrieval. Even with Boolean and keyword searching capabilities and online authority control, we find ourselves and our users disatisfied with the resulting subject retrieval. Is the problem in the system, in unrealistic expectations, or most seriously, in current subject cataloging practice?

This volume presents a balanced exposition of the issues in subject control in online catalogs. It addresses subject access both from the eyes of the library practitioner and the library theoretician. Practical topics such as the importance of public service/technical service communication in subject cataloging are interspersed with research issues such as the promise of artificial intelligence in improving subject retrieval.

As you read the articles in this volume, you will no doubt agree with some assertions and disagree vehemently with others. Is *LCSH* in form and content a dinosaur heading for extinction in the era of online subject access? Do we need a subject code? What are the online navigational and browsing devices that will replace serendipitous thumbing through the card catalog drawers and roaming through the stacks? The authors challenge catalogers, public services librarians, automation staff, researchers and library management to understand the online catalog environment and take bold steps in developing principles and strategies for subject access to meet this new environment.

Joan S. Mitchell
Carnegie Mellon University

Subject Access in the Online Catalog

Robert P. Holley

THE QUESTIONS

Will the online catalog revolutionize subject access to information? The analyses of online catalog transaction logs indicate that patrons enter many more subject searches than had been anticipated. Are they finding what they are looking for, has the computer reduced the frustrations of the card catalog, or has so little changed that the wealth of subject information in library collections remained untapped? Since they were based upon card catalogs, should librarians scrap the current subject access systems and begin anew?

The online catalog has not been available for a long enough time to give definitive answers to these questions, but articles in this volume show progress to date and make suggestions for future research.

SOME ANSWERS

Doris Cruger Dale provides a summary of previous writing on the subject in her annotated bibliography, "Subject Access in Online Catalogs: An Overview Bibliography." She divides the 55 items from 1978 to 1988 into general discussions of the topic, research studies, and glimpses of the future.

Now that the online catalog is a reality, researchers have begun to test various hypotheses on its functioning, on patron use, and on possibilities for future improvements. Elaine Broadbent with her "The Online Catalog: Dictionary, Classified, or Both?" asks whether enough linkage occurs between subject headings and classification that the online catalog can function even as a partial and

3

imperfect classified catalog without significant additional cataloging effort.

Carolyn O. Frost considers a different possibility for enhanced searching in her study "Title Words as Entry Vocabulary to *LCSH*: Correlation Between Assigned *LCSH* Terms and Derived Terms from Titles in Bibliographic Records with Implications for Subject Access in Online Catalogs." She studies how often online catalog users would encounter records with the same word or words in the title and in the subject heading. She also sorts her results by classification number to give the differences between disciplines.

Allyson Carlyle establishes a firm methodological base of matching studies in "Marching *LCSH* and User Vocabulary in the Library Catalog." She discusses previous matching studies, establishes rigorously defined matching categories, and tests her categories against a sample from the UCLA online catalog transaction logs. She discovers that user-selected terms at least partially match *LCSH* in a very high percentage of cases.

Keyword searching with Boolean operators was impossible in the traditional online catalog. Will it deliver its promised benefits in online systems? A team of librarians from Brigham Young University, Randy J. Olsen, John O. Christensen, Kal A. Larsen, and Kayla Willey, investigated this question when their library was selected as a test site for keyword searching in the NOTIS online catalog. Their "Implementing NOTIS Keyword/Boolean Searching: A Case Study" shows mixed results. While keyword searching will require increased computer capacity for unrestricted use at Brigham Young University, students, though content with the new search tool, are not adept at using its sophisticated features and will require much more training than for the basic NOTIS online catalog.

Nancy J. Williamson continues her ongoing research on classification with "The Role of Classification in Online Systems." She examines classification's use in online databases where she discovers, perhaps contrary to expectations, that online database providers are inherently conservative about offering search enhancements. In addition, North American librarians often do not make the necessary distinctions between classification as a subject retrieval tool and the call number as a location device. Her conclusion that systems designers confuse ease of use with effectiveness can apply to the online public catalog.

Research can serve only as the beginning point for the policy decisions to be made in the next few years about subject access in the online catalog. A recurring theme in three articles is the need to adapt the online catalog to user behavior rather than the other way around. Are catalogers the appropriate guardians of the library's principal finding tool?

Paul R. Murdock in "Cataloging Catalysis: Toward a New Chemistry of Conscience, Communication and Conduct in the Online Catalog" makes an impassioned plea for increased communication between public services and technical services librarians. He also represents the public library perspective where patrons are more likely to come into the library with current terminology encountered in the media than with a scholarly vocabulary.

Constance McCarthy gives "A Reference Librarian's View of the Online Subject Catalog." She worries that catalogers may be too tolerant of the current inadequacies in subject access in the online catalog. She is especially concerned about the consistency of Library of Congress subject headings. Books on the same subject should receive the same subject headings, and related subject headings should have all the necessary links. As a possible answer to the complexities of the subject heading system, she proposes the appointment of subject specialists at the Library of Congress to monitor the assignment of subject headings.

Simone Klugman draws upon her extensive experience as a reference librarian and online searcher at the University of California, Berkeley in the paper on "Failures in Subject Retrieval." She sounds the cautionary note that the new features to improve the online catalog have added so much complexity that they often hinder rather help patrons access. While the card catalog was forgiving of user ignorance in its unified alphabetical sequence, many online catalogs require patrons to recognize differences among searching commands and among types of subject headings.

Since most online catalogs have been designed for access to general library collections, they may not serve the needs of specialized users. Alva T. Stone considers this problem from the viewpoint of "Subject Searching in Law Library OPACs." Government agency names and titles of laws pose special problems for the law library user. Subject headings and policies, which may make sense for the general collection, create problems for subject access to specialized legal materials.

Many Americans focus exclusively upon Library of Congress subject headings when they think of subject access and forget that other alternatives exist. Three papers in this volume present an international perspective. Mary Dykstra deals with "PRECIS in the Online Catalog." Though PRECIS was designed for the computer manipulation of printed headings, it has functioned impressively in online catalogs, in part because it incorporates the results of two decades of research in analytico-synthetic classification and takes advantage of the international standardization of thesaurus design and construction.

Paule Rolland-Thomas and Gérard Mercure treat an issue that American libraries face in areas with large Spanish-speaking populations. Since Canada is bilingual by law at the federal level, their paper considers the special problems of "Subject Access in a Bilingual Online Catalogue." Results to date are disappointing, though the DOBIS implementation at the National Library of Canada and Canadian Workplace Automation Research Center's ISIR/SIRI with its online bilingual thesaurus offer some hope. They also remind English speakers that theirs is the only major Western European language which does not require accents to make distinctions in meaning.

Suzanne Jouguelet reports on "Subject Access in Online Catalogs: Developments in France." France has two subject headings systems; one is a modified version of *LCSH*. Many French homes have access to online catalogs because the French government has supported development of a widely available telecommunications network through MINITEL with it 3,600,000 installations. American librarians may find this description of online catalogs both surprisingly similar and refreshingly different.

Finally, one contribution looks towards the future of American subject access in general as Lois Mai Chan asks the question: "A Subject Cataloging Code?" Would it be worth the effort at this time? If so, who should be responsible? Should experiences with

AACR-II make librarians fearful or hopeful about similar work with subject headings?

THE FUTURE

Except for their belief in the value of subject access to information, the authors in this volume would certainly disagree on many points. Most share the belief that radical change will not occur in the near future. The weight of at least a billion individual bibliographic records in online systems around the country favors continued use of *LCSH*, the Dewey Decimal Classification, and the Library of Congress Classification.

As some suggest, the solution may be the innovative use of existing subject data with strategies that go beyond keyword access and Boolean operators. Perhaps the computer can help unskilled searchers master the intricacies of the current system without hours of training. The ultimate solution, however, may be to devise a completely new subject access system, built upon a strong theoretical base which takes into account both searcher behavior and computerization including expert systems and artificial intelligence.

Various actors will play a part in this future. Theoreticians, pragmatic researchers, and interested practitioners will continue to write and to speak on subject access. The ALA RTSD CCS Subject Analysis Committee tackles both theoretical and practical issues with frequent use of ad hoc subcommittees on specific concerns. Many of the specialized library associations also have committees with subject access as part of their charge.

The Library of Congress as keeper of *LCSH* and the Library of Congress Classification will continue its dominant role. Will it successfully balance its internal and external responsibilities? Positive signs include the availability of *LCSH* in machine readable form and the proposed MARC format for classification. The recent merger with OCLC provides Forest Press with a firm financial base to better serve Dewey users around the world.

As three papers in this volume show, Americans should not neglect international developments. Especially in classification, important work with implications for American subject access occurs around the world. The IFLA Section on Classification and Indexing, established in 1981, focuses greater attention on subject access within this international organization. The International Federation for Documentation is also active with its Working Group for Classification.

The search for perfect subject access will never be complete. The future will bring continued study and debate. May this volume serve as a small step forward.

Failures in Subject Retrieval

Simone Klugman

SUMMARY. Finding books by subject in large libraries is a difficult task at the best of times. Since users seldom think of their topic in terms of library subject headings, they encounter problems in finding matches. Online catalogs have helped somewhat by allowing keyword searching and Boolean combinations. They have also perpetuated some problems (lack of authority control and of cross references) and created new ones, namely requiring users to acquire complex skills. Libraries need to look carefully at the MARC format and at enhanced and enriched subject approaches. Machine-generated links and leads can provide more paths and wider access to subject information.

MATCHMAKERS NEEDED: APPLY WITHIN

On a recent visit to another campus (UCLA), I felt the disorientation that most library users must experience when they are not well acquainted with the physical environment, the catalogs system, and even the topic that they are investigating. In my case, this triple handicap was only slightly alleviated by the fact that I am used to libraries and to navigating in online waters. I was trying to help my daughter get started on a library school assignment by identifying some books for her to consult. The topic was: "Should libraries collect books for current needs or should they buy materials for which there is presently little demand, in order to satisfy some hypothetical future need?" I remember my feeling of relief at seeing the familiar MELVYL screens. (The Melvyl Online Catalog is a union catalog for all nine campuses). Even though I was interested

Simone Klugman is Social Sciences Bibliographer, Reference Librarian and Online Searcher at the Main Library, University of California, Berkeley, Berkeley, CA 94720.

in exploring ORION, UCLA'S own online catalog, and knew that it would be a more direct route to finding local books, MELVYL's friendly countenance exercised an undeniable pull, to be dispelled as soon as I noticed a rather user-hostile sign proclaiming that usage should be limited to five minutes when others were waiting. At least with card catalogs, you could hide in a corner with your drawer and trust that no one would be hunting you. I tried various subject headings (here I had the jump over the novice library patron): "Collection Development" and "Book Selection" proved far too general. I then explored "Libraries — Aims and Objectives" and found myself looking at books on library management. Since Melvyl allows keyword-in-title searching, I experimented with "library philosophy" and "library principles" in their truncated possibilities. I also browsed through various "library" and "libraries" headings, stumbled around, noted some call numbers for possible further exploration and far exceeded my allotted five minutes. Here I was, an experienced librarian, using a familiar tool, duplicating the blind groping of countless library users and not making a satisfactory connection to books I knew must exist in the collection.

Surveys have shown that subject searching accounts for about half of all catalog use.[15] Before the advent of online catalogs at Berkeley, subject access to books followed the standard library practice, through subject headings listed in *Library of Congress Subject Headings* and used in the subject card catalog. All attempts to match users' natural language with controlled vocabulary were the uni-directional ones which consisted in initiating them into the mysteries of library terminology. This behavior modification was achieved through bibliographic instruction in its many guises: one-on-one or group teaching, brochures, and slide tapes. It was also done more formally through a Library School course offered to undergraduates called Methods of Library Use, popularly known as Bib I. Figure 1 represents the first page of a brochure prepared by Berkeley reference librarians in pre-online times. Since Berkeley is primarily a closed stacks library, it also prided itself on its public shelflist; and librarians encouraged patrons to browse the cards in known call number areas. When our records first started to be computerized, a modest change in access was inaugurated with a microfiche keyword-in-title list. In those days it was an accepted credo

How to Find Books By Subject

Two subject catalogs must be used in conjunction when you are searching for books by subject in the Main Library of the University of California, Berkeley:

- **Catalog 1: Subjects** is the *card* catalog located on the 2nd floor of the Main Library, just outside the Reference Room. It lists books acquired by the libraries through 1980; after which no new cards were added.

- **Catalog 2: Subjects** is on *microfiche*. It lists materials cataloged after 1980, and is located in all libraries on campus. It is distinguished from other microfiche catalogs by a green stripe across the top.

Books throughout the library system are listed in these two catalogs under terms, called *subject headings*, which describe their subject content.

Subject headings are sometimes the words that come first to mind. For example, CHILDREN'S LITERATURE, MIGRANT LABOR, PHOTOGRAPHY. On the other hand, they may be different from what is expected. For example:

Subject	Subject heading used
World War I	EUROPEAN WAR, 1914–1918
World War II	WORLD WAR, 1939–1945
American Indians	INDIANS
	INDIANS OF NORTH AMERICA
	INDIANS OF SOUTH AMERICA
Rapid Transit	LOCAL TRANSIT

Cross references in both Catalogs 1 and 2 will often direct you from terms that are not used to terms that are. For example, in **Catalog 1: Subjects**, you will find the following:

Abstract art

see

Art, Abstract

FIGURE 1

that readers adapted to libraries and not vice versa. It is only recently that the whole subject headings structure and indeed the MARC format itself have come under criticism from many directions. David Henige[7] points out numerous inaccuracies in headings as well as inconsistencies in cross references and facetiously suggests euthanasia as the answer. Marcia Bates,[2] citing a 1979 study of OCLC records, notes that the "the average number of subject headings assigned per document by the Library of Congress and large academic libraries is only 1.4." Michael Simonds[19] echoes the same complaint. The construction of those headings has also come under fire. In a paper presented at Online 87, Marcia Bates[1] describes subject headings as a pre-coordinated string of headings and subdivisions dating from the nineteenth century and designed for an alphabetical linear listing. The language thus created is an artificial, cumbersome, and stilted one. A library user looking for books on English as a second language would not normally think of looking under a convoluted phrase like: "English Language—Textbooks for Foreigners- French." Sometimes the headings are unnecessarily pedantic in their insistence on official nomenclature. The average reader interested in the Greens Party may not be aware that the "real" name of the party is "Gruemen." *LCSH* was not intended for the library user. Until the latest edition, it contained puzzling symbols (x, xx, sa) and incomprehensible jargon (what is indirect?). It is not even considered a bona fide thesaurus because it does not follow international standards of hierarchical relationships.[5] Even the rationale of "one place to look" which is used to justify this edifice no longer holds true. Terminology changes; new subjects evolve or grow out of old ones. Well meaning librarians keep tinkering with and doctoring the headings. According to Dykstra,[5] the whole "related terms" structure is wobbly because librarians are adding extra rooms and extensions without consideration of the integrity of the original building.

In general, catalogers look upon a book as a physical object to be labeled. They assign subject headings to fit the book as a whole and leave many informative portions in obscurity. The user, on the other hand, is trying to look through the container, to determine its contents, and is having a hard time extrapolating from these labels. Carol Mandel,[13] in a study of library catalogs, analyzes failure and asks the question: "Should library catalogs provide access to parts of books?" In addition and because of the prevalence of copy cataloging, subject headings in large library catalogs represent, as one of my colleagues expressed it, "a diachronic sampling of subject cataloging as practiced by many different libraries and librarians of various degrees of skill and sophistication over many decades." When new terminology appears, catalogers do not generally go back and change earlier headings; "Near East" and "Middle East" coexist. It is not clear to many why there are still headings starting with "Negroes" as well as "Blacks" and "Afroamericans." Sometimes a heading splits into two or more like an amoeba, and they must all be used if the original concept is to be retrieved. "Nurses and Nursing" some years ago was divided into "Nurses" and "Nursing." Our catalogs have numerous entries under all three. Main headings and subdivisions live peacefully, if illegally, in the same database. Thus, one can encounter "Iran — Politics and Government" in one neighborhood but also stumble across "Politics and Culture — Iran" in another. It is not only the headings themselves which are unsynchronized. Catalogers vary considerably in the way they assign headings and even the same person may not always use the same term when indexing several documents. As a result, any topic can and usually is represented by a splendid variety of headings. At the Reference Desk, we often advise patrons to look under the most specific term; but at Berkeley our catalogs contain records from many provenances. The specificity levels of our headings vary accordingly. The Library of Congress headings are often very precise and specific. On the other hand, OCLC or RLIN libraries may assign some very broad and vague terms to very similar books. The construction of headings (subdivided, inverted, or phrase) does not seem to follow a logical pattern; or, if there originally was one, it has long ceased to be apparent. There are probably very similar books under "Art — France" and "Art, French." At the same time we use "French drama," "French fiction," and "French periodicals" in the non-inverted form. When we observe how our users approach our catalogs with very amorphous and fluid thoughts about their topic and realize that we are requiring them to match those elusive thoughts with a set of ambiguous, imprecise and unreliable terminology, we cannot help coming to the conclusion that a successful match is very unlikely. Even when they have somehow stumbled upon some relevant books, they have no way of assessing how many other good books were missed.

A CHIP OFF THE OLD BOOK

By the time our card catalog was closed (December 1980) and *AACR-II* implemented, the confusion to users was compounded. Not only did they have to contend with three kinds of catalogs (cards, multiple microfiche sets, and an emerging online catalog); but they also needed to remember different strategies for each one, mainly because the new headings conformed to *AACR-II* but the old ones were not changed. At Berkeley, the transition from cards to online was lengthy and turbulent. Already in the late seventies, automated records were being created and made available on microfiche. For several years, they overlapped with the card catalog. With the pressure to produce the records rapidly, there was dissatisfaction because they did not always adhere to the quality control criteria used earlier for the card catalog. At the same time, a budding online catalog was emerging. The Melvyl Online Catalog (hereafter called Melvyl) was being developed as a nine campus union catalog by the statewide Division of Library Automation and was slated to serve as the nucleus for each campus' future online catalog. The microfiche lists were viewed as an interim tool to be phased out when Melvyl grew into a sizable database and became the "real" catalog. By the mid-eighties, however, it was becoming increasingly apparent that Berkeley's reliance on Melvyl was not well founded. At that time, Melvyl was plagued with storage problems which resulted in a much slowed response time. We also began to realize that we were not in a position to influence Melvyl's record loading priorities. But, most importantly, Melvyl was not set up to perform some crucial local functions such as the editing and maintenance of records, the processing of circulation transactions, and an eventual acquisition module. Thus Gladis was born as a complementary local system to Melvyl. Gladis has enabled us to perform these tasks and became the conduit for records flowing from both RLIN and OCLC to merge into a single Berkeley database and then from there to be transmitted to Melvyl. In 1986 Gladis' public interface was created. Over the next year, the microfiche catalogs gradually disappeared; and users were confronted with two online catalogs: Melvyl and Gladis. In those days Gladis was only an embryo of a catalog and needed to be nurtured and fashioned into a useful gateway to our collection. In March 1986, a Catalog Planning Retreat was convened to identify our concerns, to express our needs for improvement, and to plan for their phased implementation. Of the many problems identified, "searchability" was one of the most important ones. Out of this conference, a task force was created. It meets regularly with the Head of the Systems Office and works out the best ways of developing an effective catalog. Another result of this retreat was the creation of an experimental mode to try out new features and to solicit online comments from staff. Gladis is at this stage essentially what Hildreth calls a "first generation online catalog" in that it is still closely patterned after the card catalog's linear approach. Right now it can be searched only in an "exact phrase" mode, which includes automatic truncation, and by call number. Figure 2 shows a Gladis "welcome screen" and a "help subject" screen. A caution at the bottom of the screen reminds users that names as subjects cannot be searched by the SU (subject) index because in the present Gladis configuration only topical and geographical subjects are searched by the SU index. This leaves out a huge category of material. The Gladis Task Force has identified this as a serious flaw and on a high priority list for change. It is practically impossible for patrons and librarians alike to remember that books about the Catholic Church, the Peace Corps, the Bauhaus Movement or the Bible with all its subdivisions such as concordances, to name but a few glaring examples, are not retrievable by the SU index. Figure 3 shows the task force's recommendation for a Gladis subject search which would include all possible subjects no matter which MARC tag they happen to be wearing. Another cause of difficulty is the fact that Gladis headings are listed in strict alphabetical order whether they are subdivided, inverted, or phrase headings. This causes splits with headings separated by many intervening terms. It is also not apparent to users that when they have found the heading "AIDS (Disease)—California," for instance, they need to continue browsing because a few screens later they may encounter "AIDS (Disease)—Law and Legisla-

FIGURE 2

WELCOME TO GLADIS

The University of California at Berkeley's Online Library Catalog

****
For library hours type NEWS SPRING HOURS. Type NEWS INSTRUCTION to find out
when instruction in how to use the online catalogs will be offered.
****

Enter one of these two-letter codes, then press the RETURN key:

FI FIND (to do a search)

HE HELP (for online help)
NE NEWS (for online news)
CO COMMENTS (to send the library your comments)
ST START or STOP (returns you to this screen)

===> help subject
You can search GLADIS for material on particular topics and geographic
locations using standardized terms for them called "subject headings" (SU).
To search by a subject heading, type the search statement:
                FIND SU [subject heading] <RETURN>

EXAMPLES: FIND SU AFRICA--BIBLIOGRAPHY [double hyphens are optional]
             F SU psycholinguistics
             f su nuclear power plants

WHEN SEARCHING BY SUBJECT HEADING, REMEMBER:
-- Subject headings are standardized descriptors assigned to items cataloged
   by the Library. If you do not find anything under your subject, you may
   need to consult the list of "Library of Congress Subject Headings," or ask
   a librarian for help. Type up to 130 characters of a subject term.
-- Do not use SU when searching for a PERSON'S NAME AS A SUBJECT; instead
   use Personal Name (PN). When searching for an ORGANIZATION'S NAME AS A
   SUBJECT, use Corporate/Conference Name (CN).

COMMANDS: FIND SU [subject heading]
             HELP GLOSSARY = list of help screens
             HELP COMMANDS = list of commands;   OR type and other command

17

FIGURE 3

Subject Search

```
                          -Auth:100     Bib:600, 696        Personal Subject Index
                      --!
                      !
                  --!  -Auth:400, 490                       Personal Subject Reference
                  !                                         Index
          PSU---!
          !       --!  -Auth:150                            Topical Subject Index
          !       !
          !       !    Bib:650, 690
          !   TSU---!
          !   !     --!  -Auth:450, 495                     Topical Subject Reference
          !   !                                             Index
          !   !       -Auth:151                             Geographical Subject Index
          !   !     --!
   SU-----!  GSU---!  Bib:651, 691
                   !
                    --!  -Auth:451, 496                     Geographical Subject Reference
                                                            Index
```

Corporate Subject Index

--|
--|
CSU--|--Auth:110, 111
--| Bib:610, 697, 611, 698
--|

Corporate Subject Reference
Index

--Auth:410, 411, 491

Title Subject Index

--Auth:130/Bib: 630, 699

--|
USU--|

Title Subject Reference
Index

--Auth:$t (100, 110, 111),
$t¹ (400, 490, 410, 411, 491)/
Bib:$t (600, 610, 611,
        696, 697, 698)
Auth:430, 493/Bib:630, 699

¹Except when the 1xx of the authority record is a 130.

19

tion—California" or "AIDS (Disease)—Political Aspects—California." Chronological subdivisions (for instance, period subdivisions under the subdivision "History") are interfiled with topical subdivisions creating a fragmented display that lacks organizational integrity. A typical user has no patience with these subtleties and will usually walk away either empty-handed or with only part of the picture. We have not yet been able to supply a rational approach to the online catalog that will yield predictable and consistent results.

When Melvyl first entered our lives, several years ago, it was greeted with great enthusiasm; and even its problems were seen as solvable.[11] A euphoric Aladdin's lamp syndrome seemed to take possession of librarians. Online catalogs were seen as saviors, especially for subject searching. The features embraced with the greatest eagerness were those that were previously beyond the scope of library catalogs: keyword searching, Boolean logic, and limiting capabilities. It no longer mattered whether the subject heading was "Art, Abstract" or "Abstract Art." We could experiment with such innovations as "find subject dogs or title dogs." We could easily find books about two topics: "find su Roosevelt and su Kennedy." Among the many books of Nobel prizes, we could isolate the few which dealt with women ("find su Nobel prizes and su women"). A great bonus was the ability to truncate a term when exact terminology was not known. In addition, Melvyl came equipped with limiting features (by language and by dates). We all hailed its "browse" command which featured a display of subject headings by keywords: "Browse su Librarians" would result in a list of 381 headings beginning with "Afroamerican Librarians" and ending with "Women Librarians." The ability to retrieve bits of information embedded in larger chunks of writing was justifiably acclaimed as revolutionary because it was the first break in the linear concept in which our catalogs had been imprisoned for so long. It also looked like the catalog was beginning to adapt to users' ideas of how catalogs worked. For the first time, we had improved the catalog instead of insisting on improving the user. A new species had appeared in the evolutionary chain. Such enthusiasm, inevitably, could not be sustained. We have gradually realized, as Holley points out,[10] that we cannot count on the computer to solve our subject cataloging problems. When Melvyl was a static prototype, it was easy to notice and rejoice in its admirable qualities. But Melvyl started growing to the point where it is now the largest on-line catalog in the nation. In response to users' suggestions, it has developed more and more sophisticated features. These two factors soon became as much a handicap as they had originally seemed to be a blessing. That the size of the database was negating some of its best features soon became apparent when searches involving Bool-ean operators became "long searches" or simply impossible searches. We can no longer combine two large headings such as South Africa and Israel, for instance, or browse under all the subdi-visions of headings like France or Germany. By trying so hard to improve its features, Melvyl became so sophisticated a system that it is no longer self-evident to users. In spite of 500 "show" screens and as many "explain" screens, many patrons only skim its surface and remain unaware of its unexplored depths. It is easy to walk up to Melvyl and obtain some results, but no one masters all its intrica-cies unless they are pointed out or taught in structured catalog in-struction sessions. During some periods response time is too slow, and the waiting becomes tedious.

Online catalogs are now ubiquitous. Practically every library has closed its card catalog and has or is moving towards an online sys-tem. It is time to examine in more detail how this affects user suc-cess in finding material by subject. From my vantage point as refer-ence librarian, online catalog instructor, and online searcher, it looks as if our patrons still face many difficulties.

HAS ANYONE SEEN ALADDIN'S LAMP?

Basically the problems users face are threefold: Organizational problems (which system to use; how does it work?); subject cata-loging problems; and problems inherent in the online structure.

Organizational Problems

a. The transition, often a very lengthy one, from one system to another with many in-between phases has resulted in co-existing tools for retrieval which often leave users bewildered; at Berkeley these are: a closed card catalog; two online catalogs and the vague memory of an all but vanished microfiche catalog. As Hildreth[8] says: "We may have to adapt to a continuing state of mutability."

b. In the age of Dobis, Gladis, Notis and Tomus, each with his or her own searching structure, patrons have to learn a new protocol everywhere they go. The lack of standardization between various systems, which exists in the online industry as a whole, requires people to cope with various ways of searching; and transfer of skills is not guaranteed. Even catalogs like Gladis and Melvyl, which try to use the same commands, are dissimilar enough to leave users perplexed; where they are similar but not identical, they can be downright misleading. For instance, in Gladis, periodicals are integrated in the catalog and are searched by the TI (title) index. In Melvyl, they constitute a separate file and are searched by the PE (periodicals) index. In Gladis, SU means exact subject heading; in Melvyl, SU means keywords-in-subject; and an exact subject heading is searched with the XS index. To compound the confusion in the FIND mode Melvyl interprets SU as keywords; but in the DISPLAY mode a request to display SU will result in a listing of exact subject headings. People coming from nearby institutions like Stanford or other campuses like UCLA may have learned other techniques on SOCRATES or on ORION, but their expertise will not necessarily help them and might even lead them to assume analogies which do not in fact exist. Pauline Cochrane[4] surveyed five different OPACs, each with a different user interface and display screens. At least card catalogs had a certain reassuring universality. Librarians deal in information semiotics. Much of what we transmit to our users requires them to understand symbols (call numbers, shelving locations, etc.) In the online age we require them not only to interpret symbols but to become adept at using them in the guise of commands. Unfortunately we are no longer giving the same message. Are we becoming the keepers of local, esoteric, and mysterious codes?

Problems Endemic to Our Subject Cataloging

The problem of matching user vocabulary to library terminology has already been mentioned. It has been perpetuated online. As Michael Simonds[19] puts it: "The MARC record does not provide adequate access to the material it has been used to catalog." And it is the MARC format which forms the basis of most online catalogs. Simonds also points out that the Boolean kind of retrieval is only effective where there is a multiplicity of subject headings and cannot be used successfully with the limited subject access inherent in the MARC format.

In online catalogs, inconsistencies in subject cataloging produce invisible split files. The problem of discovering the right heading is aggravated by the paucity of "see" and "see also" references. Take the following true situation: A student is looking for books on adolescent drug abuse. "Find SU drug abuse — adolescents" produces 0 results. When he retreats to: "Find SU drug — abuse," he is confronted with 1,974 books. A librarian intervenes and eventually redirects him to: "Find SU youth — drug abuse." This heading was discovered only by trial and error because neither the catalog nor *LCSH* offered any guidance in the matter. Far too often searches result in this kind of fuzzy outcome and require skill, patience, and multi level strategies (searching by keywords, displaying tracings) to focus properly.

One way to alleviate the terminology deficiency is to supplement subject searching by providing access to the library's classification scheme. On Gladis it is possible to browse up and down the online shelflist. It is a technique that librarians recommend. Call numbers, though not immutable, have a somewhat greater degree of stability than linguistic nomenclature and are also more likely to be used consistently across similar libraries. The following is a good example of muddled terminology which could have been remedied by call number searching: A student needs to locate books on Japanese film. He knows about headings for "Japanese Art," "Japanese Drama" and "Japanese Fiction" and naively imagines that there should therefore be one for "Japanese Film" as well. He is quickly disabused of this notion. Going to *LCSH* (10th edition), he finds "Film Adaptation," "Film Makeup," "Film Posters" and a great many more references to moving pictures. Switching now to "Moving Pictures," he hits upon what looks like the perfect heading: "Moving Pictures, American, French, etc." Armed with this new knowledge, the student returns to Gladis and confidently types in "Find SU Moving pictures, Japanese," again with no results.

Amazingly undaunted, he now tries: "Find SU Moving pictures" and is rewarded with one of Gladis' rare cross references. Gladis switches him to "Motion Pictures." Thus encouraged the student asks Gladis to find "Motion Pictures, Japanese." She professes to having never heard of it. No one knows whether he ever discovered the subdivision "Japan" under "Motion Pictures." The student, shouting incoherently, was last seen running out of the library. It is rumored that he has joined the AALH (American Association of Library Haters). Had this hapless student started out with "Find call number PN1993.5 J" he would have struck oil immediately.

Lest we rejoice in call number searching too soon, Lois Mai Chan[3] points out that because classification collocates materials in ways different from those provided by the alphabetical keyword or subject heading approach, "it has been demonstrated that . . . different records can be retrieved." However she goes on to say: "the current one call number per-item policy will have an adverse effect on recall in online searching."

Problems Inherent in the Online Format

a. *Equipment*: There must be as many terminals as there are people using the catalog. With the card catalog a greater dispersion was possible. People also tend to stay longer at terminals since more fumbling and adjusting occurs. Interruptions can happen because of malfunction or down time. Beyond these obvious drawbacks, somewhat alleviated by the possibility of dial-up access, other more subtle obstacles face users.

b. *Serendipity*: Not all learning is deliberate and targeted. Sometimes we do not know what we are going to find until we find it. Bumping into things is not as easily achieved online as in the card catalog where the eye sometimes lights upon something unforseen. Online catalogs are also much more intolerant of the slightest inexactitude or variant spelling and are quick to come back with negative results where a manual scan would often be successful. A certain initial vagueness has been replaced by the necessity to be specific much sooner. How are we going to build the element of fortuitousness into our online catalogs?

c. *Default Screens*: It is ironic that the electronic format, theoretically liberating by having escaped the confines of the 3 × 5 card, in reality provides a default display in most systems that is even more restricted. Particularly serious in the context of subject searching is the absence of tracings in the short format. In order to see subject headings and be able to recycle them into a new strategy, the user has to request the long format. In Melvyl (s)he can also request a display of subject headings only, but most users do not discover this on their own. Our terminal screens require so much space for instructions that the bibliographic information is often abbreviated and more limited than what appears on a catalog card.

d. *User Skills*: That wonderful and uniquely American achievement, the dictionary card catalog, allowed readers to open drawers and simply look by whatever they happened to remember about a book. They did not need to be aware that they were in fact looking by title, author, subject, or series. Like Moliere's Mr. Jourdain, who spoke in prose all his life and did not know it, they never labeled the process they were going through. But much more is needed to successfully query a terminal. Besides skill, dexterity, and concentration, it takes a certain understanding of how the machine operates. Even the simplest menu-driven system requires that you read and follow instructions. In a command mode, you must preface a search by a qualifier and therefore are forced to analyze your thought processes and to translate them into the right machine commands to accomplish your mission. In most research libraries, the labels you are required to apply to this transaction can be very baffling and involve a whole set of terms that you never suspected existed: corporate names, series, not to mention uniform titles. The more complex the refinements, the more learning there is to do. "An online catalog outfitted with a multitude of sophisticated searching features is virtually useless if the searcher cannot communicate with the system effectively."[9] In the advanced Melvyl instruction sessions, students are delighted to be shown the "tricks of the trade"; but they seldom discover them on their own. How many people really know how the system processes Boolean operators? It is therefore not uncommon to come upon searches like this one: "Find su motivation and needs or values." The "dangling or" phenomenon is not something ordinary people are likely to understand without help. Most users do not discover by themselves how to

truncate effectively or especially how to turn off an implicit truncation. Nor do they know when to use exact indexes and when to use
keyworded ones. If you don't realize that the following command:
"find SU latin poetry" on Melvyl will also retrieve books on Latin
American poetry, the results of your search might look very puzzling to you. One student who keyed in the following: "Find Su
French Revolution" did retrieve some books but not as many as
expected and not exactly on target. When he was shown the subject
heading of those books, he was surprised to see that it read as follows: United States—History—Revolution—French participation.

Some online catalogs have great potential for helping users discover their materials, but they have not yet been primed by catalogers with the right "open sesame" vocabulary nor enriched by
systems people with intelligent, human-like features that anticipate
needs and lead people to solutions. At this stage they require much
more teaching than card catalogs ever did.

FROM PAST IMPERFECT TO FUTURE PERFECT?

Some organizational problems will eventually disappear when
retrospective conversion is achieved and when more people have
remote access to online catalogs. It is hard to predict how soon
standardization will occur. Hildreth[9] points out that proposed standards for a common language, developed by a committee of the
National Information Standards Organization, are being reviewed
for adoption.

Much effort has been expended in studying ways to enrich subject access. Pauline Atherton Cochrane[18] has been a pioneer in this
area with her research involving the use of back-of-books indexes
combined with table of contents information. She and many others
have also advocated automatic displays of broader, narrower, and
related terms as well as linkage with logical outlines (classified
lists) to help users select appropriate terms or be guided to relevant
call number areas. As early as 1980, Jeff Pemberton[16] in a *Database*
editorial suggested using book indices and table of contents information to widen and deepen subject access. Karen Markey,[14] in a
Council on Library Resources sponsored survey, points out that users feel very positive about online catalogs; 80% expressed satisfac-

tion with the experience. Nevertheless, her findings also show that subject access needs enriching by multiple entry points and the use of "related-word-lists." Carol Mandel,[13] with her use of "failure analysis" as a technique to study automated information retrieval, discusses free text searching, the use of the PRECIS indexing system as a supplement to *LCSH*, and the possibility of providing access to parts of books. Marcia Bates[1] believes that the ideal indexing system does not exist and that we should therefore generate a variety of terms taken from title words or other free text identifiers. Information systems, she says, should be generous: any reasonable English language word or phrase should get the searcher started and linked to explanatory, guiding material. She also favors using descriptors rather than subject headings in online files. Descriptors are usually short, are intended to describe the concepts within the document, can be liberally applied, and can be post-coordinated by the searcher. In the "wouldn't it be nice" category, we can also dream about such things as using blurbs on book jackets (that great shortcut to a book's contents) by making every word therein searchable or persuading publishers to provide us with book annotations, akin to the little digests that come with children's books. It should even be possible to provide an online index to the classification scheme.

Some of these ideas might seem utopian given the investment that most research libraries have in the present "MARC cum *LCSH*" edifice and at a time when much money and energy are being poured into retrospective conversion. Lest we become too discouraged however, it must be pointed out that some modest improvements are already discernible. In the RLIN Archives and Manuscripts Collection file (AMC), the online format was used to greatly multiply the headings assigned to documents. In indexing a collection of papers, it is not unusual to have as many as from forty to one hundred headings covering every possible name or topic for which information is available in the collection. This kind of generosity was not possible in pre-online times. CITE, an online catalog at the National Library of Medicine, requests feedback from the searcher about relevant terminology in displayed items, automatically incorporates the searcher's feedback in the ongoing search strategy, retrieves additional items, and ranks output on a best match of searched terms basis.[14] Paperchase, the catalog of Beth

Israel Hospital, has a feature which suggests headings to the user based on analysis of headings common to items retrieved through free text searching. The system, rather than the user, does the analyzing.[6] Melvyl is beginning to generate automatic suggestions for 0 result subject searches. Figure 4 shows an unsuccessful subject search: "Find SU underclass" with the suggestion to redo the search in the title word index and to type HELP for more information. At this point, more help is provided by amplifying and fleshing out the original suggestion. The system explains how to display subject headings retrieved by the title search and how to reuse them in a new search by subject.

The Gladis task force is very concerned with improving subject searching. One of its proposals involves an alternative to the bewildering array of search tags that a user must remember. This involves the creation of an ALL index. The ALL index will retrieve matches from all searchable fields without the patron having to know in which index his/her terms would be found. (See Figure 5.) This is analogous to default searching on BRS where, unless a qualifier is added to the search formulation, every available area of the document is searched. Dialog has solved the problem by designating subject rich fields as the default searchable area: descriptors, identifiers, and keywords in title and abstract. The sophisticated searcher still has the option of using more precise tags, but the average user now has a simpler path to follow. Other possible improvements would be building in automatic plurals, adjusting for variant spelling (labor vs labour), and providing right and left truncation.

Although this section started out by examining ways in which subject access could be enriched, it has imperceptibly shifted to a consideration of various system improvements. That is because the two are inextricably tied together. Much of the improvement must come from a combination of better and more thoughtful cataloging with system-provided links between the various parts of the document. Systems improvements, however, can also be directed towards "understanding" the user.

Until recently, many online catalog producers seem to have been mesmerized by the user-friendliness concept. We have produced catalogs with friendly names that greet you with a relentless cordiality. We should perhaps ask ourselves whether user-friendly amiability constitutes user-useful effectiveness. A shoe salesman may be the very epitome of friendliness and ask you to call him Fred; but if he can't find any shoes in your size, then he is user-useless in spite of his smile and eager manner.

In online catalogs, we need to combine an inviting interface with novel features not available in the linear world of card catalogs. To a certain extent, we have already done so; but in the process we have created an environment where much participation and involvement are required of the user. The power of the computer might be used to gradually teach this user to be a better participant. This involves studying typical user/catalog transactions and programming the computer to anticipate behavior and respond appropriately. Melvyl has an intelligent TI (title) index which sometimes works as TW (Title words) and at other times as XT (exact title). It came about because many patrons were not differentiating between the two concepts. Therefore, if the searcher has used connecting words (on, to, in, for, with, etc.) Melvyl translates TI into exact title and tells the searcher so. If, however, the words seem unconnected, then Melvyl assumes that they are keywords. In that way, a beginner has a greater chance of success without initial knowledge about the system but can learn gradually if he is curious enough to do so. This is a very modest beginning towards artificial intelligence. As new developments occur in this field, more of these kinds of features can be built in. A new concept in AI known as the "intelligent agent" is appearing on the horizon.[6] This person-inside-the-computer is built around a "user expectancy model" which recognizes elements of user behavior and reacts accordingly. A system of this kind can spot an inexpert searcher by certain characteristics in his search technique and allow this bumbler to stumble around without penalties. It should also gradually guide him to better techniques. At the same time, this agent will recognize a smart user, reward him with more leads, and allow him to perceive how his query fits in the total scheme of things. An illusion may thus be created of an understanding system which keeps on asking questions until it knows what the searcher needs and leads him to it.

We can also benefit from other developments such as CD ROM and hypertext which employ novel features such as screen manipu-

FIGURE 4

* The official subject headings assigned to materials may not be the same
  as terms you have chosen to describe your subject.

A good strategy is to search your terms again in the TITLE WORD (TW) index.
Then type DISPLAY LONG or DISPLAY SU to see the official subject headings.
For example, F TW BODY LANGUAGE retrieves materials with the official
heading "Nonverbal Communication".

* Ask a reference librarian for "Library of Congress Subject Headings" or for
  "Medical Subject Headings", to help identify your exact subject heading.

* Use truncation if your subject terms can have different endings. For
  example: Cinema# retrieves cinema, cinematic, cinematography, etc.

You can now: Begin a new search. For more information, type EXPLAIN FIND.
              Type EXPLAIN COMMANDS for other commands you can use.
              Type END to end your session.

-> f tw underclass

Search request: F TW UNDERCLASS
Search result: 15 records at all libraries

Type D to display results, or type HELP.

-> d su

Search request: F TW UNDERCLASS
Search result: 15 records at all libraries

Type HELP for other display options.

1.
Subjects: Afro-Americans -- Illinois -- Chicago -- Social conditions.
             Afro-Americans -- Social conditions -- 1975- -- Case studies.
             Poor -- Illinois -- Chicago.
             Poor -- United States -- Case studies.
             Chicago (Ill.) -- Social conditions.,.
             United States -- Social conditions -- 1980- -- Case studies.

2.
Subjects: Socially handicapped -- United States.
             Poor -- United States.

3.
Subjects: Socially handicapped -- United States.
             Poor -- United States.

Press RETURN to see the next screen.
-)

31

FIGURE 5

PROPOSED GLADIS COMMAND TREE

```
                  ┌────────PAU (Main/added entry – Personal name)
                  │           (Bibl tags: 100, 700, 796)
                  │           (Auth tags: 100, 190; 400, 490; 500, 590)
                  │
         ┌──AU──┤ ┌────────CAU (Main/added entry – Organization/Conf. name)
         │        │           (Bibl tags: 110, 111, 710, 711, 797, 798)
         │        │           (Auth tags: 110, 111, 191; 410, 411, 491; 510, 511,
         │        │                 591)
         │        │
         │        ┌────────BTI (Bibliographic (book) title)
         │        │           (Bibl tags: 212, 245, 246, 247, 740)
         │        │
         ├──TI──┤ ┌────────STI (Series added entry – Title)
         │        │           (Bibl tags: 490 0_, 830, 840, 899)
         │        │
         │        ┌────────UTI (Main/added/subject entry – Uniform title)
         │        │           (Bibl tags: 130, 630, 699, 730, $t (any tag))
         │        │           (Auth tags: 130, 193; 493; 593)
ALL──┤
         │        ┌────────PSE (Series added entry – Personal name/title)
         │        │           (Bibl tags: 800$t, 896$t)
         │        │           (Auth tags: 100$t, 190$t; 400$t, 490$t; 500$t, 590$t)
         │        │
         └──SE──┤ ┌────────CSE (Series added entry – Organization/Conf. name/title)
                  │           (Bibl tags: 810$t, 811$t, 897$t, 898$t)
                  │           (Auth tags: 110$t, 111$t, 191$t; 410$t, 411$t, 491$t;
                  │                 510$t, 511$t, 591$t)
```

|-------STI (Series added entry - Established title)
| (Bibl tags: 490 0, 830, 840, 899)
| (Auth tags: 130, 193; 430, 493; 530, 593)
|
|-------PSU (Subject entry - Personal name)
| (Bibl tags: 600, 696)
| (Auth tags: 100, 190; 400, 490; 500, 590)
|
|-------CSU (Subject entry - Organization/Conf. name)
| (Bibl tags: 610, 611, 697, 698)
| (Auth tags: 110, 111, 191; 410, 411, 491; 510, 511,
| 591)
|
|----SU---|-------TSU (Subject entry - Topical subject)
| (Bibl tags: 650, 690)
| (Auth tags: 150, 195; 450, 495; 550, 595)
|
|-------GSU (Subject entry - Geographic name)
| (Bibl tags: 651, 652, 691)
| (Auth tags: 151, 196; 451, 496; 591, 596)
|
|-------USU (Subject entry - Uniform title)
        (Bibl tags: 630, 699)
        (Auth tags: 130, 193; 430, 493; 530, 593)

lation and multiple window possibilities to immerse the user gradually into the system in an atmosphere of playful learning. In such ways, we will foster an imperceptible shift from improving the user to improving the system. We cannot expect that dramatic changes will occur rapidly. We are still very far from the day when anyone will be able to walk up to a terminal, to type in a natural language query, and to wait placidly for the books to fall out of the terminal like money from an automatic teller machine. In the meantime, catalogers can start creating more doors and windows into the system so that no one can fail to enter or to get a glimpse at what's inside. Systems people can then take over and provide the visitor within the gates with clearly marked paths and with Ariadne's thread through the labyrinth.

NOTES

1. Marcia J. Bates, "Optimal Use of Controlled Vocabularies in Online Searching," *Proceedings, Online 87*, Anaheim, California: October 1987.

2. Marcia J. Bates, "Subject Access in Online Catalogs: A Design Model," *Journal of the American Society for information Science*, 37 (November 1986): 357-376.

3. Lois Mai Chan, "The Library of Congress Classification as an Online Retrieval Tool," *Information Technology and Libraries*, 5 (March 1986): 181-192.

4. Pauline R. Cochrane, "Subject Access in the Online Catalog," *Research Libraries in OCLC*, 5 (January 1982) 1-7.

5. Mary Dykstra, "LC Subject Headings Disguised as a Thesaurus," *Library Journal*, 113 (March 1, 1988) 42-46.

6. Daniel Gross, "AI Online: The System is the Solution," *Information Today*, 5:8 (Sept. 1988): 9.

7. David Henige, "Library of Congress Subject Headings: Is Euthanasia the Answer?" *Cataloging & Classification Quarterly*, 8 (1 1987) 7-19.

8. Charles R. Hildreth, "Beyond Boolean: Designing the Next Generation of Online Catalogs," *Library Trends*, 35 (Spring 1987) 647-667.

9. Charles R. Hildreth, "Communicating with Online Catalogs and Other Retrieval Systems: The Need for a Standard Command Language," *Library Hi Tech*, 4 (Spring 86): 7-11.

10. Robert P. Holley, "Subject Cataloging in the USA," *International Cataloguing*, 14 (Oct/Dec 1985) 43-45.

11. Simone Klugman, "Conversations with MELVYL," *Database*, 5 (February 1982) 43-51.

12. Carol Mandel, "Enriching the Library Catalog Record for Subject Access," *Library Resources & Technical Services*, 29 (Jan/March 1985) 5-15.

13. Carol A. Mandel, *Subject Access in the Online Catalog*, (August 81) ERIC document. ED212286.

14. Karen Markey, *Subject Searching in Library Catalogs Before and After the Introduction of Online Catalogs*, (Dublin, Ohio: OCLC Online Computer Library Center, 1984)

15. Joseph R. Matthews, *Public Access to Online Catalogs*, 2nd. ed. (New York; Neal Schuman, 1985)

16. Jeff Pemberton, "Linear File," *Database*, 3 (March 1980): 4-5.

17. James Rice, "Serendipity and Holism, the Beauty of OPACS," *Library Journal*, 113 (February 15, 1988) 138-142.

18. Barbara Settel and Pauline Cochrane, "Augmenting Subject Descriptions for Books in Online Catalogs," *Database*, 5 (December 1982) 29-37.

19. Michael J. Simonds, "Database Limitations and Online Catalogs," *Library Journal*, 109 (February 15, 1984); 329-330.

Matching *LCSH* and User Vocabulary in the Library Catalog

Allyson Carlyle

SUMMARY. Central to subject searching is the match between user vocabulary and the headings from *Library of Congress Subject Headings* (*LCSH*) used in a library catalog. This paper evaluates previous matching studies, proposes a detailed list of matching categories, and tests *LCSH* in a study using these categories. Exact and partial match categories are defined for single *LCSH* and multiple *LCSH* matches to user expressions. One no-match category is included. Transaction logs from ORION, UCLA's online information system, were used to collect user expressions for a comparison of *LCSH* and user language. Results show that single *LCSH* headings match user expressions exactly about 47% of the time; that single subject heading matches, including exact matches, comprise 74% of the total; that partial matches, to both single and multiple headings, comprise about 21% of the total; and that no match occurs 5% of the time.

INTRODUCTION

Analysis of a user's success in searching the subject catalog is one of the first steps toward meeting the challenge of improving subject access. Basic factors in determining successful subject searching include: the subject of interest to a user; the expressions chosen by users to search for a subject; the subject vocabulary of a

---

Allyson Carlyle is a doctoral student at the Graduate School of Library and Information Science, University of California, Los Angeles, where this paper began as a specialization paper for the fulfillment of the requirements of the master's degree in library science. The author wishes to thank those who offered helpful editing advice, with special thanks to Elaine Svenonius for her guidance and support in writing this paper.

37

catalog; the access system of a catalog, either manual or online; and the contents and indexing policy of a catalog. Recently much attention has been given to the examination of the third element above — the subject vocabulary of the catalog. Most of this attention has focused on the *Library of Congress Subject Headings (LCSH)*.[1] *LCSH* is used in many American libraries with no indication of its replacement in the near future. Only a handful of studies, however, have been undertaken to determine just how well *LCSH* performs. If we are to use *LCSH*, and, indeed, if we are to criticize it, as many have, we must study its current performance.

An important way to evaluate *LCSH*'s performance is to see how closely it matches user expressions.[2] Matching studies should offer insights that will improve subject searching by pointing out directions for changes in *LCSH* and for improvements in online catalog retrieval algorithms. Learning more about the nature of user language at the catalog may also guide us in the development of intelligent computer interfaces for online catalogs. So far, the few completed matching studies have given little guidance about how such improvements might be accomplished. This paper examines previous matching studies while pointing out their problems and the problems of matching studies in general; it defines more detailed matching categories than those previously proposed; and, finally, it applies these new categories in a study of users' success in matching *LCSH* online.

DISCUSSION OF PREVIOUS STUDIES

We found only four matching studies which have defined matching categories and tested them at the catalog. Patricia B. Knapp investigated the match between user expressions and subject headings in the Chicago Teachers College and Woodrow Wilson Junior College libraries as well as the difference between expressions selected by users and their verbal accounts of what they were actually interested in.[3] R. Tagliacozzo and M. Kochen studied matching at three University of Michigan libraries and the Ann Arbor Public Library.[4] Marcia J. Bates examined subject searching in a laboratory setting. In this study she included a small sub-study for illustrative purposes, which matched user expressions and *LCSH*.[5] Finally,

Karen Markey collected user expressions from transaction logs of an online catalog and compared them to *LCSH*.[6]

Although these studies all examine subject headings to see how well they match user expressions, they vary so greatly that they are not satisfactorily comparable. One critical problem is a confused perception of the *purpose* of a matching study. Matching studies ideally enable us to see how the subject searching language of users matches the indexing language of the catalog. Their purpose is not, as some of the studies assume, to show us the number of headings retrieved by a user expression, or to what degree headings selected by users retrieve items of interest, or to what extent a user expression actually expresses the subject of interest.

The most serious example of confusion of purposes appears in the Knapp study. Knapp tallied expressions in three categories: expressions "identical with the terms used in the catalog"; expressions which "differed from those used in the catalog" and expressions which did not match any headings in the catalog. Some expressions tallied in the second category were identical to headings existing in the catalog but did not "match" what the user was actually looking for. For example, although the user expression "animals" was an exact match to a catalog heading, it was not tallied in the identical category because the user said he was looking for material on African animal life, a topic better expressed by the headings "Zoology—Africa" or "Vertebrates—Africa." Because Knapp tried to answer two questions at once, her results tell us only how often users entered the catalog with expressions that matched their true request *and* also matched catalog headings. We cannot compare the results of Knapp's study to those which looked at language as a distinct issue.

Another example of cross purposes is found in the Markey study. In her analysis of transaction log data, Markey attempted to categorize search expressions by both their success in matching *LCSH* and by the presence or absence of errors. Two separate tallies would have shown more clearly the two different characteristics of the search expressions: first, were errors present or not; and second, in those expressions in which no errors were present, did a match to an *LCSH* occur or not. The inclusion of categories for user errors in a matching tally puts *LCSH* to the unhappy test of matching spelling and other input errors. Fortunately, Markey's results are reported in separate categories such that readers can exclude user errors and refigure matching percentages.

The lack of a common operational definition of a subject search creates another obstacle to the comparison of matching studies. Markey's population of subject searches included user expressions gleaned from two types of online search commands: one that searches subject heading fields only and another that searches both subject heading fields and title fields. Although the purpose of the combination subject heading/title word command is enhanced subject searching, this command can be used for title searches as well as for subject searches. Markey's inclusion of the combination subject heading/title word search in her population of subject searches puts *LCSH* at a disadvantage because it does not contain titles. Again, because she reported results in separate categories, the title matching category may be removed and matches to *LCSH* alone recalculated. The confusion of issues in both the Knapp study and the Markey study reflect the complexity of the process of subject searching and indicate the need to separate individual questions for testing and research.

Matching itself is an elusive concept. We may agree that the LCSH "Computer graphics" matches exactly the user expression "computer graphics," but would we still agree if asked whether the user expression "radio history" matched exactly the LCSH "Radio — History?" Definitions of what constitutes a match have varied from study to study. Most studies have dealt with this problem by defining different degrees of matching and then by assigning matching categories based on these different degrees. Three types of categories are most commonly defined: exact match, partial match, and no match. However, what constitutes inclusion into any particular category is seldom clearly defined. For example, none of the studies examined in this paper stated a policy regarding punctuation except Bates, who disregarded it.[7] Markey did not state a policy, but it must have been different from Bates, since in her study the user expression "radio history," the example noted above, fell into a category called "whatever popped into the searcher's mind."[8]

Another major limitation in our ability to compare results of matching studies exists because not all the studies matched user expressions to Library of Congress headings alone. When Knapp and Tagliacozzo and Kochen matched subject headings to user expressions, they used headings found in the catalogs of particular libraries and made no attempt to separate LCSH's from other headings which may have been present in these catalogs. Catalogs of particular libraries often contain headings from sources other than *LCSH*, such as *MeSH*, individual thesauri, and local cataloging. And, of course, every catalog has a different selection of LCSH's. These two studies, therefore, cannot measure *LCSH*'s performance entirely accurately; nor should they be compared to other studies testing *LCSH* alone.

The environments tested and the methods of data collection also varied in the matching studies. Two studies, Knapp, and Tagliacozzo and Kochen, were conducted in the traditional card catalog using questionnaires. Bates conducted her study in a laboratory setting using a card catalog. Markey's study tested *LCSH* in an online catalog using transaction log analysis. It could be said that this variety of search environments is healthy and gives us a clearer picture of subject searching in general. However, searching in the online catalog and searching in the card catalog may involve considerably more than a change in venue. Evidence of this is the discovery of increased persistence in subject searching in the online catalog.[9] In any case, can we say with certainty that we are studying the same phenomenon?

A final problem with matching studies is their intrinsic limitation because some types of matching can be operationally defined only within the context of a particular catalog. An example of this is proximity matching, in which the proximity of a heading to the point at which a user enters the catalog determines whether or not a match occurs. For example, a user expression may differ from an LCSH only by the presence of a suffix in the first word. This difference would create an obstacle to the user in some catalogs but not in others. As an example, imagine that a user enters a card catalog with the term "behavioral therapy" and does not find an exact match. If no headings (or cards) appear in alphabetic sequence between "Behavior therapy" (the most closely matching LCSH) and the point at which "behavioral therapy" would file in that catalog, then the user would presumably find "Behavior therapy" and be satisfied. If, however, headings such as "Behavioral assessment" and "Behavioral embryology" existed in the catalog, the user might *not* find the heading "Behavior therapy" because it is too far from her entry point into the catalog.

The success of proximity matching in online systems with keyword searching of subject headings also varies. In one catalog where a subject search expression retrieves only three headings, the user might immediately perceive a match: while in another catalog where the same search retrieves 500 headings, the user might either give up or move on to another search statement in hopes of retrieving a more manageable list of headings. Proximity matching, then, may depend on the structure of *LCSH*, on which and how many LCSH's exist in a particular catalog, and on how many records are cataloged under each LCSH.

Proximity matching is an essential part of subject searching in most catalogs, both online and manual. Often a user's success in subject searching depends upon it. When, in a matching study, we remove considerations of individual catalogs to concentrate on *LCSH* itself, we ignore this very real aspect of subject searching in library catalogs.

As this discussion has shown, the body of data collected from matching studies is far from adequate to provide guidance for changing *LCSH* and for improving online catalog interfaces. Needed is a list of categories sufficiently detailed to pinpoint differences between the language of *LCSH* and user language. Such a list was developed for the study which follows. The categories in this list are based on the degrees of similarity and difference between user expressions and *LCSH* and were developed by examining user expressions selected from transaction logs from the UCLA Library's online information system, ORION.

MATCHING STUDY

Categories

As has been shown above, the way in which an LCSH may match a user expression varies. The categories defined below attempt to operationalize these. Although the categories defined in this study would apply to most library catalogs, some apply only to online systems with keyword searching. The categories were defined with a keyword searching system in mind because keyword searching is becoming a "standard" feature in online catalogs.[10]

Degree of similarity between languages, such as a user's language and the language of *LCSH*, may be shown by differences in vocabulary, syntax, and semantics. Although the ordering of categories is semantic insofar as expressions falling into the first categories are likely to be closer in meaning than those falling in the later categories, the ordering is not truly semantically based. Differences in vocabulary and syntax form the basis for the categories and for the most part these differences do reflect semantic differences. There are exceptions: an idiom, for example, may consist of the same vocabulary and have the same syntactic structure as an English expression and yet have an entirely different meaning.

At times it is difficult to tell if a match occurs because the meaning of a user expression is not always ascertainable. Sometimes the context provided by neighboring expressions on a transaction log proffers clues to meaning, and sometimes it does not. Also, it is debatable how much context from a transaction log ought to be used, particularly from systems which do not indicate when one user leaves and another begins. How often is a researcher justified in deciding the meaning of a user expression gathered from a transaction log? Is it possible to operationalize this process? Unless users are questioned immediately after a search, a certain amount of judgment on the part of the researcher is inevitable. Logistical constraints prevented this study from including matching that takes user's meanings into account. If semantic matching were included, both new categories and possibly separate tallies would be necessary.

Matching categories are defined below, and examples given. The categories are not mutually exclusive. In order to make them so, each user expression was tallied in the first category into which it fell. Thus, the order of the categories is crucial and was chosen in an attempt to reflect the degree of similarity that might be expected between a user expression and an LCSH. Further subdivision of the categories is given in the results tally in Table 1. Expressions

TABLE 1

SINGLE HEADING MATCHES	Number	Percent
A1. Exact Match	69	43
A2. Exact, Punctuation Variation	7	4
Exact Match Subtotal	76	47%
A3. Exact, Word Order Variation	2	1
A4. Exact Substantive Word	5	3
A5. Spelling Variation	0	—
A6. Singular/Plural Variation	10	6
A7. Suffix Variation	4	2*
A8. Abbreviation Variation	0	—
A9. Date or Numerical Variation	0	—
Variation Match Subtotal	21	13%*
A10. Partial	16	10
A11. Combined Partial	6	4
Single Heading Subtotal	119	74%

MULTIPLE HEADING MATCHES		
B1. Exact Match	7	4
B1a. Two-heading match	(7)	
B1b. Three + heading match	(0)	
B2. Singular/Plural Variation	3	2
B3. Suffix Variation	0	—
B4. Spelling Variation	0	—
B5. Abbreviation Variation	1	1
B6. Date or Numerical Variation	0	—
B7. Partial	23	14
Multiple Heading Subtotal	34	21%

C. NO MATCH	8	5%
	----	----
TOTAL	161	100%

* Disparity in subtotal due to rounding error.

marked with an "'*'" in the examples below are actual user expressions collected in this study.

Single Heading Matches

Categories of exact matchings (A1-A4 below) allow us to see how similar user vocabulary and syntax are to *LSCH*'s vocabulary and syntax.

A1. *Exact Match*
　　　—LCSH matches user expression (including subdivision) exactly, including punctuation
　　　Example: **User** "economic history—periodicals"*
　　　　　　　 LSCH "Economic history—Periodicals"

　　　Capitalization of letters is disregarded in all categories. User expressions in examples appear in lower case, regardless of how they actually appeared in transaction logs.

A2. *Exact Match, Punctuation Variation*
　　　—LCSH matches user expression (including subdivision) exactly, but punctuation is disregarded
　　　Example: **User** "drama explication"*
　　　　　　　 LSCH "Drama—Explication"

　　　Punctuation is disregarded in all the categories following this one.

A3. *Exact Match, Word Order Variation*
　　　—LCSH contains the same words as user expression, but not in the same order
　　　Example: **User** "medieval cities and towns"*
　　　　　　　 LSCH "Cities and towns, Medieval"

A4. *Exact Substantive Word Match*
　　　—LCSH consists of the same substantive words which are in a user expression; word order may differ
　　　Example: **User** "history of the frontier thesis"*
　　　　　　　 LSCH "Frontier thesis—History"[11]

Articles, common prepositions, and conjunctions will be disregarded in all categories following this one. See list of non-substantive, or "stop" words in Appendix 1.

Spelling, singular/plural, suffix, abbreviation, and date or numerical variation categories (A5-A9) show how often truncation or word stemming algorithms might be helpful in an online system.

A5. *Spelling Variant Variation*
   — LCSH includes a spelling variant or variants of a word or words in a user expression
   Example: **User**   "water colour"
                         "water color"
                LSCH "Watercolor"

Two types of variation are included in this category, one word/two word variation and spelling of a single word. These two variations could be separated into two categories.

A6. *Singular/Plural Variation*
   — LCSH differs from user expression in that one contains a word or words that are plural (ending in "s" or "es") and the other contains a word or words that are singular
   Example: **User**   "x ray"*
                LSCH "X-rays"

The only singular/plural variations allowed in this category are those in which "s" or "es" is the only difference between words. Another category could be added for the singular/plural variation of the "mice"/"mouse" variety.

A7. *Suffix Variation*
   — LCSH differs from user expression in that one or more of the words of the LCSH have a different suffix from a word or words in the user expression (See Appendix 2 for variations allowed in this category.)
   Example: **User**   "computer programming"*
                LCSH "Computer programs"

This example shows how a close match may not be the best semantic match. "Programming (Electronic computers)" is an LCSH that is probably closer in meaning to the user expression "computer programming" and yet, because of the presence of "electronic," is not the closest match.

A8. *Abbreviation Variation*
  —User expression contains abbreviation of a word in an *LSCH* or vice versa
  Example: **User** "mba"
  LSCH "Master of business administration"

A9. *Date or Numerical Variation*
  —LCSH contains a date that differs from a date in user expression *or* LCSH does not include a date that user asks for; or a difference such as "20"/"twenty" occurs
  Example: **User** "20th century"
  LSCH "Twentieth century"

  If a user expression has no date, but an LCSH does, it is tallied in the partial match (A10) category below.

A10. *Partial Match*
  —LCSH consists of the same substantive words which are in a user expression, but LCSH includes one or more additional substantive words
  Example: **User** "diffusion copper"*
  LSCH "Copper—Diffusion rate"

  If a user expression contained a word or words not in a single LCSH, the expression would be tallied in a multiple heading match category or the no match category.

A11. *Combined Partial Match*
  —LCSH is a partial match to a user expression and exhibits an additional variation, such as singular/plural, as well
  Example: **User** "organ donor"*
  LSCH "Donation of organs, tissues, etc."

Combined types of matches are not enumerated here. All is included as an illustration of this type of match.

Multiple Heading Matches

Multiple heading categories indicate how often a user's conceptual needs are such that one LCSH alone is not sufficient to meet them. They also give us an idea of how often a capability that allows retrieval of multiple subject headings from a single search would be useful in an online system.

B1. *Exact Multiple Heading Match*
—user expression consists of the same substantive words that are in two or more LCSH's
Example: **User**   "crystallography geometry"*
          LSCH "Crystallography"
                   "Geometry"

An exact word matching category parallel to category A1 was not included for multiple heading matches because punctuation considerations are not applicable.

B2. *Multiple Heading Match with Spelling Variation*
—one or more LCSH's include a spelling variant or variants of a word or words in a user expression
Example: **User**   "watercolour brush"
          LSCH "Watercolor"
                   "Brush"

This example illustrates how multiple heading matches occasionally retrieve false drops. At first glance, it looks like an acceptable semantic match, but **LSCH**'s "Brush" is of the "shrub and brush" variety. The user's "brush" is, of course, most likely a paintbrush.

B3. *Multiple Heading Match with Singular/Plural Variation*
—multiple LCSH's differ from user expression in that one or more contains a word or words that are plural (ending in "s" or "es") and the other contains a word or words that are singular

Example: **User** "joint prosthesis"*
        LSCH "Joints"
              "Prosthesis"

B4. *Multiple Heading Match with Suffix Variation*
— multiple LCSH's differ from user expression in that one or more words in the LCSH(s) have a different suffix from a word or words in the user expression
Example: **User** "books typesetting computerization"
        LSCH "Books"
              "Computerized typesetting"

B5. *Multiple Heading Match with Abbreviation Variation*
— user expression contains an abbreviation of a word or phrase in an LCSH or vice versa
Example: **User** "engineering and mba"*
        LSCH "Engineering"
              "Master of Business Administration"

B6. *Multiple Heading Match with Date or Numerical Variation*
— LCSH contains a date that differs from a date in user expression or LCSH does not include a date that a user asks for; or a difference such as "20"/"twenty" occurs
Example: **User** "computers and privacy 1980s"
        LSCH "Computers"
              "Privacy"

B7. *Partial Multiple Heading Match*
— multiple LCSH's consist of the same substantive words that are in the user expression, but the LCSH(s) contain more words; in addition, one heading may contain any of the variations listed in categories A5 to A9
Examples: **User** "culture composition"*
         LSCH "Culture"
         "_____ — Composition"

         User "scene simulation"*
         LSCH "Scene painting"
              "Computer simulation"

Because the Library of Congress limits use of the subdivision "Composition" to headings which are "natural substances of unfixed composition, including soils, plants, animals, farm-products, etc., for the results of the chemical analysis of these substances," the heading "Culture — Composition" is not a valid LCSH, and the user expression "culture composition" falls into a multiple heading match category.

The user expression "scene simulation" illustrates why it is impossible, short of asking individual users, to discover exactly what is meant by words used in catalog searching. What does "scene simulation" mean? Since the context in the transaction log did not clarify the content of this user expression, it must be understood as is. Is the "scene" in this expression the same "scene" that is in the LCSH "Scene painting?"[12] And, is the simulation this user is interested in computer simulation, simulation games, or any of the other senses of simulation used in *LSCH*?

User Expression Not Matching LCSH

C. *Use of Language Not in LCSH*
  —*LCSH* does not contain word or words which are in user expression
  Examples: **User** *"apartheid"**[13]
            "employment *opportunities* overseas"*
            "mortgage rate *deregulation*"*
            "55 *mph* speed limit"*
            "*petit* mal epilepsy"*
            "women *elderly*"*
            "*movie* encyclopedia"*
            "*freaks*"*

METHODOLOGY

One hundred seventy-one user expressions were collected using transaction logs dated October 3 to November 5, 1984 from the

University of California, Los Angeles (UCLA) Library's online information system, ORION. A systematic sample collected user expressions from every tenth subject search statement. The ORION system has two different keyword search commands: the "find" command, with "ti" (title), "na" (name) and "nt" (name and title) indexes; and the "browse" command, with an "su" (subject) index. A search statement was defined as any statement entered by a user and followed by the "enter" command key. A subject search statement was defined as any statement that began with an identifiable subject command (browse subject, bro su, b su, fsu, su). A user expression was defined as that part of a search statement following a search command.[14]

Certain user expressions following allowed subject commands were not used in the study: expressions consisting wholly or partially of proper names, including all forms of geographic names; expressions which included limiting commands (allowed on ORION in name and title searches only and indicated at the end of a search statement with a "/"); and expressions which included truncation features (indicated on ORION by a "#," "*" or "?"). Name and geographical name searches were excluded because of the complications foreseen with the consultation of name authority headings. User expressions containing any of the following were not counted: misspellings; words not in *Webster's Third New International Dictionary*;[15] incorrectly entered searches (e.g., moviesamerican); and all immediately identifiable obscenities, questions and comments.[16]

After search statements were collected, they were searched in ORION using the browse subject command. Each user expression was searched first in its entirety to see if it fell into a single heading match category.[17] Failing such a match, it was searched in the hard copy *LSCH* (10th edition) to see if it matched LCSH's not included in ORION. If a user expression did not fall into a single heading exact match category, it was searched one word at a time using the browse subject command to identify multiple heading matches. If any words were not matched, they were also searched in the hard copy **LSCH** for matches to headings not in ORION. Truncation features were used to identify singular/plural and suffix differences. A user expression matching an LCSH in any way was tallied in the first appropriate category into which it fell. When a user expression contained a word that appeared in **LSCH** as a "floating" subdivision, the *Subdivision Guide* was consulted, and placement into an appropriate category was made allowing for use of the subdivision as instructed by the *Guide*. For example, the user expression "history of the frontier thesis" was considered to be an exact substantive word match to the LCSH "Frontier thesis" with the free floating subdivision "History" attached.[18]

RESULTS AND ANALYSIS

Table 1 lists the number and percentage of expressions in each category. Subtotals for various categories are also listed. Table 2 lists comparable results from previous matching studies. Although

TABLE 2

Markey (Refigured)[20]

Type of Match		Number	Percent
1.	Exact match of LCSH	154	25
2.	Exact match of x-ref	44	7
3.	Close variant of LCSH or x-ref	50	8
4.	Multiple heading matches	68	11
8.	Whatever popped into the searcher's mind	310	50
	Total	626	101%*

Bates[21]

Type of Match		Number
1.	Exact matches	35
2.	Partial matches	60
3.	Non-matches	5
	Total	100%

Tagliacozzo and Kochen[22]

Type of Match		% at General Library	% at Combined Libraries
1.	Exact matches	67	57
2.	Partial matches	16	18
3.	Non-matches	17	25
	Total	100%	100%

* Not 100% due to rounding error.

the methodological diversity of these studies renders comparison unreliable, I will, in analyzing the results of this study, attempt to identify some of the differences among the studies, including how their methodologies might have influenced the results.[19]

Single Heading Matches

The percentage of exact matches in this study (47%, categories A1 and A2) is lower than the percentage of exact matches reported in Tagliacozzo and Kochen (57%) and higher than Bates (35%) or Markey (25%). Bates pointed out several reasons for the disparity between her results and Tagliacozzo and Kochen's that may be applicable to this study as well. The most important one may be that Tagliacozzo and Kochen's sample user expressions contained a relatively high percentage of personal names, and their criteria for exact match for names were not stringent. Their exact matching figures may have been inflated for this reason.[23] Varying environments in the studies, laboratory vs. on-site interview, card vs. on-line catalog, may also have been factors. Bates pointed out that her low exact matching score may have been partially accounted for by the fact that her study dealt with assigned searches that may have been "narrower and more specific than is the case in the average real catalog search situation."[24] In addition, her study was limited to the subject areas of psychology and economics. Tagliacozzo and Kochen's high exact matching figure (57%) is also partly explained by the fact that they included exact matches to cross references in their exact match category.[25] This does not, however, help explain why Bates, who also included cross references in her exact match category, had a lower number of exact matches than this study.

Markey's exact match results, lowest of all the studies, may be explained by two factors. First, one of her categories, "Whatever popped into the searchers mind," was not operationally defined. It is likely, based on her examples, that some of the expressions tallied in this category would have been tallied in an exact match category (A1-A2) in this study.[26] Second, because of the commands included in her sample (one of them is a combination title/subject search command), some expressions tallied in less-than-exact matching categories could have actually been titles; and these may have contributed to a lower matching percentage in the *LCSH* category.

The percentage of matches in the singular/plural category seems unsurprising at 6%. If the results of this category are added to those in the suffix variation category, the results (8%) are equal to those in Markey's close variant category. Low percentages in the singular/plural and suffix categories may validate the decision of some online catalog designers to not provide automatic truncation in their online systems. Of course, in view of relatively low exact matching rates, an increase of eight or nine percent may be a desirable one.

After exact matches, the largest category of single heading matches is the partial match category (10%). An informal and incomplete count shows that one fourth of the expressions falling into this category were exact matches to cross references. Some user expressions falling into this category would have been exact matches if the Library of Congress had not, either deliberately or inadvertently, omitted levels of a subject hierarchy. For example, the user expression "migration" is a broader term for both "Migration, Internal" and "Emigration and immigration" but is not in *LCSH*. In these cases, users must look under more than one LCSH to see all the materials indexed under what they may consider to be one subject.[27] The cry that *LCSH* is not specific enough is often heard, but the data tallied in the partial match category suggest the contrary. We know that users sometimes go to the catalog at levels broader than their actual needs. Ironically, given omissions of broad terms in *LCSH* subject hierarchies, users may, if they are using systems with keyword access to subject headings, have a better chance of finding what they want. It may not be inaccurate to say that when users retrieve headings that are partial matches, many of the subject headings retrieved are narrower, since they may be modified by additional words or subdivisions. Certainly this study, since it offers no semantic analysis, has no evidence to support this hypothesis; but it would be an interesting one to pursue.

In other partial matches, the effect of additional words in the LCSH's is less clear. For example, the user expression "dominance" partially matches the LCSH "Dominance (Psychology)." If asked, would the user say that this was a more precise description of the subject he was looking for, a part of the subject he was looking for, or a different subject altogether? Only semantic analysis with user input could answer this question.

Bates, in a paper proposing an approach to subject searching not seen in current online catalogs, suggests displaying subject hierarchies as a part of an effort to guide users to narrower or broader headings that might be of interest. Such a design would help highlight omissions in LCSH's hierarchies and allow users to suggest changes to *LCSH*.[28]

The sample used in the present study contained few differences with respect to abbreviations, spelling, and use of dates. Only one user expression contained a date, and it matched the date in the LCSH exactly.

Overall, 74% of the user expressions fell into single heading match categories. *LCSH*'s precoordination of terms, then, may be said to have coincided with user's requests about 74% of the time. However, since *LCSH* only matched user vocabulary exactly about 47% of the time, users could have been helped by some sort of stemming or matching algorithm 30% of the time in systems that allow keyword searching of single subject headings. This kind of help is already available in some online catalogs, NLM's CITE, for example.[29] Use of stemming or matching algorithms which would raise matching success to 70% or more suggest that *LCSH* may not be in need of such drastic revision as has been suggested.

Multiple Heading Matches

The largest percentage of multiple heading matches, 14%, fell into the partial match category. The criticism that *LCSH* headings are not specific enough may be validated by expressions falling into multiple heading match categories. The user expressions "artist loft," "hypovolemic shock," and "court dancing" are all examples of user expressions falling into the multiple heading partial match category that are more specific than available LCSH's.[30] Again, the judgement that *LCSH* does not contain specific enough headings must be substantiated by further research.

If a measure of currency is found by counting the number of user expressions containing words not in *LCSH*, then the criticism that *LCSH* is not current enough may be challenged. Only 5% of user expressions contained words not found in *LCSH*.[31] We may ask if such words have characteristics that cause their exclusion from *LCSH*. Semantic analysis could help discover these characteristics and thus provide guidance on forming headings or cross references using these types of terms.

IMPLICATIONS

One might hope that a comparison of these studies would reveal differences regarding matching in the online catalog versus the card catalog. Unfortunately, anything but a trend can be seen: in the card catalog, 57% (Tagliacozzo and Kochen) and 35% (Bates) exact matches; in the online catalog, 47% (this study) and 25% (Markey). In addition to methodological differences in the studies, it is necessary to consider the many variables affecting each of the tested catalogs' design and content. Perhaps these variables, such as size and nature of collection, and policies regarding arrangement or form of headings, have a greater impact on matching in the catalog than we suspect. Only further research will provide an answer.

More comprehensive comparison with other studies is not possible, or, at least, not advisable. Only Tagliacozzo and Kochen reported their results in categories similar to the ones used here, and they did not follow these criteria exclusively. Bates used the Tagliacozzo and Kochen categories; but, as discussed earlier, did so on such a small sample of her total data that even the comparisons made already may be unreliable. Knapp's results cannot be considered for comparison because she tallied not according to where users actually looked in the catalog, but according to where they *should* have looked considering responses to questioning about the object of their searches. Also some user expressions tallied in this study as exact matches (e.g., "directories") would have been tallied by Knapp in her "more general" category; that is, as an expression that did not fit the actual search topic as explained later by the user. Markey's results, even after refiguring, are not suitable for comparison because of the ambiguous "whatever popped into the user's mind" category, which comprised 50% of the results. Future matching studies should keep in mind such differences and include unambiguous categories which allow refiguring of results for comparability.

DISCUSSION

As this study was done in an uncontrolled environment, many independent variables may have influenced the nature of the sample user expressions. These variables spring from two sources: first, the environment of the UCLA Library, and second, the features of the ORION system.

Because user expressions were taken from transaction logs at the UCLA Library, a large university research library, they may be representative only of users who frequent such libraries. They may also be representative of users who have had higher than usual exposure to *LCSH*. *LCSH* has a high profile at UCLA as shown by its presence near ORION terminals, its mention in error messages on ORION, and its exposure in a variety of bibliographic instruction programs.

Because *LCSH* has long been regarded as a librarian's tool and not a general reference tool, it might be asked whether the "best" test of matching *LCSH* and user vocabulary is a setting in which users are likely to have had some exposure to *LCSH*. Testing where users have and have not had exposure to *LCSH* might shed some light on whether knowledge of *LCSH* improves matching success or not, and perhaps validate the growing belief that *LCSH* ought to be available and understandable to catalog users.[32]

Variables directly related to ORION and UCLA cataloging policy include a change in ORION's subject searching command prior to the collection of transaction log data and the inclusion of MeSH headings in catalog records from UCLA's Biomedical Library.

Experience with keyword searching is also a variable that may affect the order and choice of words used in catalog searching. For example, it seems unlikely that in an interview a user would, in response to being queried about the subject of a search or about the words used to search the catalog, reply "unemployed psychological," which is one of the user expressions collected in this sample. Also, does the use of *LCSH* in a keyword environment "teach" users to make requests with few and general words instead of many and specific words because longer, more specific requests so often retrieve zero hits? Other investigations could measure the extent of the interaction of a specific type of online system and an indexing or classificatory language, in this case, *LCSH*. One pertinent question to ask in this context is whether keyword access would be more likely to provide higher matching percentages with *LCSH* than a search key or truncation matching system. The answers to such questions would have an impact on how the results of this and other matching studies should be evaluated.

The effect on user expressions of the variables discussed above is unclear. To achieve greater understanding of *LCSH* and its role in subject searching, more studies are necessary in which such variables are isolated and varied. Knowledge of the effect of the variables could help librarians make decisions regarding how much emphasis to place on teaching users about *LCSH*, whether or not to include terms from other thesauri in a single catalog, and what features of online catalogs provide the highest levels of matching.

In addition to the variables discussed above which limit generalizability of this study's results are factors unique to its methodology. A study like this demands keyword access with a sophisticated truncation feature to search all *LCSH* headings and cross references. Unfortunately, such access was not available locally when this study was done. The exclusion of cross references meant that some user expressions which would have fit into exact cross reference match categories were instead tallied in single heading partial and multiple heading categories. The availability of *LCSH* on CD-ROM with its varied searching features should help ensure that future studies overcome these limitations.

CONCLUSION

The development of in-depth matching categories and execution of this study is a small gain, by building on the work of others, in the effort toward analyzing the language of catalog users and uncovering the means by which online systems may help produce successful subject searching at the catalog. Further work is called for at every level of inquiry. Matching categories must be refined and expanded to include cross references and the types of matching which occur in systems that do not feature keyword matching. Research in the area of systems design must be undertaken to discover to what extent the structure and content of a catalog interface affect the structure and content of user expressions. For example, would significant differences in matching percentages appear in transaction logs from another type of system? If differences occurred, what would the nature of these differences be? A clearer picture of how users succeed in using *LCSH* and an idea of what type of system yields the highest percentage of matches should be the product of such investigations.

A deeper level of analysis of *LCSH* and user language must take place at the semantic level. Much has been said already in this paper about the specific areas in which this kind of analysis must take place. In general, semantic analyses will broaden our understanding of the connection between what users say and what they mean, and how well *LCSH* headings are constructed to match user expressions on the semantic level. Do users really get what they ask for? How can the language of the catalog, *LCSH*, be developed to give them more?

Questions such as these could also be asked of thesauri other than *LCSH*. How do PRECIS and MeSH compare to *LCSH*? Thus far, tests of different indexing languages have shown mixed results. Experimentation could also attempt to discover whether a particular type of online system is more successful in matching user language with one indexing language than with another. More must also be learned about the impact of the use of multiple thesauri in a single catalog. This topic has been addressed by Carol Mandel, who has demonstrated the serious problems which may occur in catalogs with multiple thesauri.[33]

Subject searching is a process dependent upon a host of variables. The extent to which a user expression matches an LCSH may be the most critical factor in obtaining a successful subject search in today's online catalogs. *LCSH*'s performance level in a keyword system, with an exact matching rate of approximately 50%, demands improvement. In-depth analysis of the relationship between user language and *LCSH*, coupled with research on the role of online systems in the process of subject searching, should provide input necessary to make intelligent decisions toward improving user success in subject searching.

NOTES

1. *"LCSH"* refers to *LCSH* (10th edition) as a whole; "LCSH" or "LC-SH's" refer to the individual subject headings.

2. *LCSH* may be evaluated with respect to other criteria, for example, internal consistency, understandability of notes, and currency of terminology.

3. Knapp, Patricia B. 1944. "The Subject Catalog in the College Library," *Library Quarterly*, 14: 214-228.

4. Tagliacozzo, R. and M. Kochen. 1970. "Information-Seeking Behavior of Catalog Users," *Information Storage and Retrieval*, 6: 363-381.

5. Bates, Marcia J. 1972. *Factors Affecting Subject Catalog Search Success.* Ph.D. Dissertation. University of California, Berkeley, and Bates, Marcia J. 1977. "System Meets User: Problems in Matching Subject Search Terms," *Information Processing and Management*, 13: 367-375.

6. Markey, Karen. 1984. *Subject Searching in Library Catalogs.* Dublin, Ohio: OCLC. Chapter 4.

7. Bates, 1972, pp. 85,89.

8. Markey, p. 72. The exact LCSH is "Radio — History."

9. Markey, p. 65.

10. The categories do not apply as aptly to systems featuring truncation, although categories could be created which would illustrate matching success in these settings. Tagliacozzo and Kochen developed partial-match categories assuming truncation in a manual environment. (See their study, pp. 371-372.)

11. See discussion in "Methodology" section regarding assignment of free floating subdivisions in this study.

12. The word "scene" in *LCSH* appears only in the context of scene painting.

13. These examples include all the sample user expressions that fell in this category that were gathered for this study. "Apartheid" was a cross reference in the 10th edition of *LCSH*; it has subsequently been made an authorized heading. "Movie" and "elderly" occur in *LCSH* only in cross references. "Petit" occurs in *LCSH* only in a geographic heading.

14. Some of the subject statements contained commands that could not be used on ORION, e.g., "su." User expressions following these commands were included because they were felt to be identifiable as subject search statements.

15. This may have discounted words so new or esoteric that they have not yet reached dictionary status, for example, the expression "uprootment."

16. See complete specifications in Appendix 3.

17. The ORION subject authority file contains subject headings taken from bibliographic records. Because some non-LC headings may have been present in these records, whenever a user expression matched a heading in the subject au-

thority file that had fewer than five postings, it was checked in *LCSH* to see if it was an official heading.

18. Matching with *LCSH* cross references was not done in this study mainly because time was not available to search manually for the large number of user expressions which would have required it (cross references are not yet included in ORION). Since cross references are used in most libraries, they should ideally be included in a study of *LCSH* terminology.

19. The only major matching study not included here is the Knapp study, not discussed because tallying was not done with the same assumptions as the other studies. See discussion in the introduction to this paper.

20. Markey, p. 66. This tally has been refigured by excluding the following categories: 5. Spelling errors, 6. Known-item access point, 7. Entry error.

21. Bates, 1972, p. 127.

22. Tagliacozzo and Kochen, p. 373. Combined libraries includes the General Undergraduate, and Medical Libraries at the University of Michigan, and the Ann Arbor Public Library. The total percentage in this category was derived from the figures published in Tagliacozzo and Kochen. Bates preferred to compare her figures to the General Library results only, while in this paper comparisons will be made to the results of the combined libraries.

23. Bates refigured only a small number of her sample user expressions according to the categories defined by Tagliacozzo and Kochen. Percentages based on this refiguring are those presented here. Unfortunately, the number of search statements she refigured was relatively small.

24. Bates, 1972, p. 132.

25. Bates, 1972, p. 126.

26. The user expression "radio history" matching the LCSH "Radio—History" is an example of this.

27. In fact, if see also references were not included in a catalog, a user could retrieve the heading 'Migration, Internal" from a search on "migration" and never realize that other materials under that subject are cataloged under "Emigration and immigration."

28. Bates, Marcia. 1986. "Subject Access in Online Catalogs: A Design Model." *Journal of the American Society for Information Science.* 37: 357-376.

29. For an explanation of how computer matching algorithms might work, see Lawrence, Gary S. 1985. "System Features for Subject Access in the Online Catalog." *Library Resources & Technical Services,* 29: 16-33.

30. It could be, of course, that no books have appeared on these topics.

31. Of course,, new concepts may be formed by combinations of words already in *LCSH*.

32. Bates (1977, pp. 368-372) has shown that knowledge of *LCSH* heading formation policies may indeed have an influence on matching. The belief that *LCSH* ought to be available to catalog users, presumably to improve matching success, has undoubtedly fostered format changes in the new edition of *LCSH* which drop the "xx," "sa," and "x" in favor of more commonly used thesaurus terms.

33. Mandel, Carol. 1987. "New Directions in Subject Authority-Control," presented at the RTSD CCS SAC/LITA/ACRL BIS/PLA program "Subject Authorities in the Online Environment," ALA Annual Conference, June 29, 1987.

BIBLIOGRAPHY

Bates, Marcia J. 1971. *Factors Affecting Subject Catalog Search Success*. Ph.D. dissertation. University of California, Berkeley.
———1986. "Subject Access in Online Catalogs: A Design Model." *Journal of the American Society for Information Science*. 37: 357-376.
———1977. "System Meets User: Problems in Matching Subject Search Terms." *Information Processing and Management*. 13: 367-375.
Knapp, Patricia B. 1944. "The Subject Catalog in the College Library." *Library Quarterly*. 14: 214-228.
Lawrence, Gary S. 1985. "System Features for Subject Access in the Online Catalog." *Library Resources & Technical Services*. 29: 16-33.
Mandel, Carol. 1987. "New Directions in Subject Authority-Control." presented at RTSD CCS SAC/LITA/ACRL BIS/PLA program, "Subject Authorities in the Online Environment." ALA Annual Conference, June 29, 1987.
Markey, Karen. 1984. *Subject Searching in Library Catalogs*. Dublin, Ohio: OCLC.
Tagliacozzo, R. and M. Kochen. 1970. "Information-Seeking Behavior of Catalog Users." *Information Storage and Retrieval*. 6: 363-381.

APPENDIX 1:   STOP WORDS

a	and	for	of	the
an	by	in	on	to

APPENDIX 2:   SUFFIXES ACCEPTED FOR SUFFIX DIFFERENCES
              (CATEGORIES A7 and B3)

"-ical"   as in psychology--psychological
"-ing"   as in programs--programming
"-al"   as in architecture--architectural
"-ular"   as in cells--cellular
"-ism"   as in alcohol--alcoholism
"-ial"   as in presidents--presidential
"-ication" as in diverse--diversification

APPENDIX 3:   USER EXPRESSION EXCLUSION CRITERIA

User expressions were excluded from the study which:

--consisted of or included proper names, including all forms of
  geographic names (e.g., German language) or identifiable parts
  of these names (e.g., united history colonial [presumably
  United States colonial history])
--included limit or truncation commands
--consisted of or included unidentifiable words, initialisms
  (that is, were not abbreviations found in LCSH or Webster's
  Third New International Dictionary), spelling errors, input
  errors or apparent user errors caused by some misunderstandings
  of the system (e.g., bsu Library of Congress Subject Headings)
--consisted of two parts (e.g., fsu women and su battered)
--were character for character the same user expression
  previously included in the sample and appearing in a log taken
  from the same terminal on the same day
--were identifiable titles, e.g., Bible, Communist Manifesto

Other Rules:

--count only "su" expressions in count from 1 to 10
--count "bsu women bsu women" as one search for "bsu women"

Cataloging Catalysis:
Toward a New Chemistry of Conscience, Communication and Conduct in the Online Catalog

Paul R. Murdock

SUMMARY. This paper explores the potentialities of an empowered public services/technical services interface as a liberating and exhilarating vehicle for change, improvement, understanding, and access in the online subject catalog.

We catalogers have a problem. You public services people share it. It isn't our legendary work loads. It isn't your legendary ringing telephone. It isn't our frustration with production quotas. It isn't your frustration with our backlogs. It isn't our perception of how you perceive us. It isn't your perception of how we perceive you. It isn't our ability to formulate and apply a complex edifice of descriptive cataloging rules, nor your ability to understand them. It isn't our mild paranoia over the notion that some of our professional authorities think we're an endangered species.[1] It isn't your paranoia that if this is true you might have to take up cataloging.

These are real problems, but not THE PROBLEM. In this online age so filled with promise and frustration, we share another problem. This one concerns our insufficient understanding of and impotent response to an online malaise: "cataloging catalysis." Webster Nine says "catalysis" is "an action or reaction between two or more persons or forces precipitated by a separate agent and especially by one that is *essentially unaltered by the reaction*."[2]

I'm a cataloger. Among other things, I assign subject headings to

Paul R. Murdock is Head, Cataloging Unit, Technical Services, Jefferson County (Colorado) Public Library, 10200 W. 20th Ave., Lakewood, CO 80215.

bibliographic records – certainly an action. Public services staff use and react to those headings. This is precipitated by their need to use a tool – a separate agent, the online catalog – to find out something. Unfortunately, in the presence of so many failed subject searches, the impotent invisibility of the cataloger/public services staff interface leaves the agent, the online public catalog of whatever kind and whatever description, *essentially unaltered by the reaction.* When the subject search fails or achieves frustratingly marginal success, the online public catalog is powerless. The subject terminology that might reveal its glorious contents remains unaltered, unenhanced, unimproved. Fail to match *your* term with *our* term and presto! What a result! An ubiquitous, often unreported, commonly accepted – indeed widely tolerated – FAILED subject search in the online catalog. It's an epidemic. It's the black plague of contemporary bibliographic life.

We catalogers are clearly uneasy because we know this happens. Generally, we have no mechanism to remedy the problem. You public services people are really uneasy. You experience, live, and feel this problem nearly every work day. Generally, you have no mechanism to remedy the problem. The public patron? That situation should keep everyone awake at night.

The online public catalog with its subject content, a key to the catalog's very heart and soul, remains immutable, unimproved, unintelligible, and inaccessible. The cataloger/public services staff interface, OUR interface, a potentially empowering and liberating vehicle for change, improvement, understanding, and access is not irretrievably lost. It may be irretrievably dead. We catalogers need to aggressively assume the lead in recognizing the urgent need to design a mechanism to forcefully and effectively interface the subject catalog with the people who try to use it. But we need to do this WITH public services staff.

Professionally, I am deeply concerned about developing a new cataloging chemistry for and with the people we claim to support. Such a chemistry will enhance the crucial cataloger/public services interface and will be designed to actively promote successful online searching by all patrons of the online public catalog. This chemistry involves our professional conscience, our communication skills, and ultimately, our conduct; for I believe that subject cataloging *is* the exercise of professional conscience. It *is* a complex form of interpersonal communication. It *does* demand a new code of conduct.

Simply stated, the question is: If we believe, as we say we do, that technical services exists not for professional self-aggrandizement but to act as agents for public services and to support their needs, how might catalogers and public services staff most effectively, most economically, and most humanely interface to promote and enhance subject access in the online catalog? I hasten to add this caveat: I am not concerned here with the universe of public services/technical services relations. I am only concerned with the online catalog and specifically with subject access to its contents. And since I manage the cataloging operation of a large suburban library in the Denver area,[3] I have particularly focused on how my colleagues in other public libraries in this area handle public services input to the subject analysis function within their cataloging units. What kind of cooperation occurs between catalogers and front line public services staff to continually improve, indeed to actively promote, successful subject searching by all users of their online public catalogs? Is there a need for sensitive new perceptions of what we're doing, why, and how? Is it time to ask some basic questions?

In the face of overwhelming evidence of monumental problems and of outright failures in subject searching in the online public catalog[4], we might want to join forces with our front line colleagues to define and to implement strategies to banish these failures and frustrations because currently we're not doing a good enough job.

To answer these and other questions, I composed a brief questionnaire to survey colleagues along the Colorado Rocky Mountains Front Range—real catalogers, performing real cataloging, for real people. The results of this admittedly modest survey have left me with a cataloging melancholia. We catalogers indeed have THE PROBLEM: cataloging catalysis. Also, we probably have a crisis in cataloging as conscience; we might have a crisis in cataloging as communication; we undoubtedly have a crisis in cataloging as conduct.

I submitted my questionnaire of fifteen questions to the heads of cataloging or their counterparts at seventeen public libraries, small, medium, and large. Seventy-six percent (13/17) of the questionnaires were returned. The results are fascinating. A small survey by library research standards, it was not especially scientific in its construction and conduct. But that's all right. I was after ideas, opinions, and activities.

OVERVIEW OF QUESTIONS AND RESPONSES

1. Does your library have a mechanism to solicit, encourage, permit or facilitate input from public services staff to cataloging staff on any and all matters pertaining to subject searches and vocabulary in the online catalog?

  YES 45.5%
  NO 54.5%

2. If so, what is it? Is it formal or informal? Describe in detail.

  FORMAL 20%
  INFORMAL 80%

3. If not, do you think this would be a good idea and would you work to see such a mechanism developed?

  YES 33.3%
  NO 16.6%
  NO OPINION 50.1%

4. Does your library encourage public services staff to suggest improvements, enhancements, and upgrades to the subject catalog and its vocabulary?

  YES 72.7%
  NO 27.3%

5. If not, why not?

6. When a public services staff member perceives the need for enhanced, upgraded, or improved subject access, is that need communicated to cataloging staff?

  YES 90%
  NO 10%

7. How do they accomplish this?

> (Ranked by frequency of mention)
> MEMOS/NOTES 6
> VERBAL COMMUNICATION
> (FACE TO FACE, PHONE, ETC.)...............6
> COMMITTEE DISCUSSION 2
> ELECTRONIC MAIL.........................2
> SPECIAL FORMS 2
> CONFERENCE BETWEEN DEPARTMENT
> HEADS 1
> PERSONAL VISIT TO TECHNICAL
> SERVICES 1

8. Are cataloging staff able to follow through with implementation of the suggestion?

> YES.....................................45.6%
> SOMETIMES............................27.2%
> ONLY WITHIN PARAMETERS
> OF ONLINE PUBLIC
> CATALOGS, *LCSH*, ETC.: 27.2%

9. Are cataloging staff able to respond to the request if not able for any reason to achieve implementation?

> YES:....................................100%

10. How do they accomplish this?

> VERBAL COMMUNICATION
> (FACE TO FACE, PHONE, ETC.)..............10
> NOTES/MEMOS 6
> SUPERVISORY CHANNELS..................2
> ELECTRONIC MAIL.........................2

11. In your opinion and experience, what might catalogers and public services staff do to improve the public services/catalog-

ing staff interface in order that both groups might enhance and promote successful subject searches by all catalog users?

(Ranked by frequency of mention)
PUBLIC SERVICES/TECHNICAL
SERVICES MEETINGS........................4
BETTER REPORTING MECHANISMS 3
IMPROVED FORMAL COMMUNICATION 3
PROVIDE SUBJECTS FOR ALL RECORDS
IN ONLINE PUBLIC CATALOG................2
PUT CATALOGERS AT ONLINE PUBLIC
CATALOG 2
JOB SHARING..............................2
NO OPINION 2
PUT CATALOGERS ON REFERENCE
DESK......................................1
REORGANIZE TO ELIMINATE
FUNCTIONAL BARRIERS.....................1
INCREASED AWARENESS
OF PUBLIC SERVICES PROBLEMS 1
TEACH PUBLIC SERVICES PERSONNEL
TO BETTER USE ONLINE
PUBLIC CATALOG 1
NO IMPROVEMENT IS NEEDED...............1
PROVIDE COMPLAINT FORMS
AT ONLINE PUBLIC CATALOG 1
CONDUCT RANDOM SURVEYS
TO MONITOR SEARCH
SUCCESS RATES 1
TAKE TIME TO COMMUNICATE..............1

12. What are the greatest obstacles preventing cataloger/public services staff cooperation in enhancing and promoting successful online subject searches by all catalog users?

(Ranked by frequency of mention)
INSUFFICIENT TIME........................7
LCSH 4

INEFFECTIVE COMMUNICATION 3
ONLINE PUBLIC CATALOG
SOFTWARE/HARDWARE LIMITATIONS 2
NO MECHANISM TO FACILITATE
REPORTING OF PROBLEMS 2
NO COMMON USAGE VOCABULARY 1
LACK OF PERSONAL CONTACT 1
INADEQUATE STAFFING. 1
FORGETTING PROBLEMS 1
LIBRARY FUNCTIONAL BARRIERS 1
UNWILLINGNESS OF PUBLIC
SERVICES TO PROVIDE FEEDBACK. 1

13. Is it your experience that public services staff believes or does not believe that cataloging staff truly works to ensure successful subject retrieval by all catalog users?

BELIEVES. 28%
SEEM TO BELIEVE. 28%
IT'S QUESTIONABLE THEY BELIEVE. 37%
DON'T KNOW 7%

14. Have you ever speculated if patrons might benefit from a cataloging/public services staff "Code of Cooperation and Constructive Communication for Interface" designed to ensure successful subject retrieval by all catalog users?

YES 20%
NO 80%

15. Do you have additional suggestions, comments, opinions or observations you might share with me concerning these or related matters?

The *Overview of Questions and Responses* should interest you. Nearly three-quarters of the reporting libraries believe they promote public services input to the catalogers' subject analysis. But over one-half have no formal mechanism to accomplish this. It appears that the "promoters" promote chiefly informally. That's okay, but is it effective? Read on.

Of the twenty-seven percent with no reporting mechanism between public services and technical services, one-third favor development of such a mechanism. Regrettably, perhaps unconscionably, one-half of my colleagues possess no opinion on the matter.

We appear to favor the CONCEPT that public services should suggest upgrades and improvements to the subject catalog and its vocabulary, but less than one-half of us ever actually implement the enhancements. We do, however, in unanimous fashion, respond to public services as to why we can't provide what we've asked them to tell us they need.

It will come as no surprise that barely one-quarter of catalogers believe that *they* are perceived by public services staff as effective promoters of successful subject searching by all online public catalog users.

There are lots of reasons for this perception. Insufficient time and ineffective communications are the chief culprits. And as it just about always is, we believe that treading the trail to the conference room will solve some problems, will raise some consciousness, and will improve our communications.

If you're a cataloger, you might possibly recognize some of the other barriers; and you might agree with some of the suggestions for their removal. For instance, while we have noticeably insufficient time for effective interface with our public services colleagues, we have quite sufficient time to continue assigning headings which we know don't work. We love our professional conferences and workshops—we even MAKE time for them—but we can't make time to communicate meaningfully and effectively with colleagues in the same library.

We recognize software and hardware limitations in the online public catalog we rushed to create, but we tend to shift responsibility for its improved usage to those least able to master it. We're painfully aware of the deficiencies of *LCSH*, but that doesn't stop us from clinging to this deficient standard.[5]

We know that most subject searchers approach the catalog with common word vocabulary—often the English-type language that they use successfully in the *Yellow Pages* or *L.L. Bean Catalog* — but find, evidently, that catalog librarians don't think, speak, write, or catalog in anything related to common English.

We lament the lack of personal contact with public services peers yet hope we can increase our awareness of their problems without raising their awareness of ours. We're always understaffed but sometimes forget that so too are they. We lament the absence of mechanisms to report problems but concede we've not tried very hard to create them.

We believe we're confronted with functional barriers in the job-specific tasks we perform. We conclude then that reorganization of our library hierarchy would eliminate the barriers and with them the problems. Sometimes, we even forget the problems, perhaps because deep down we really believe no improvement is needed or perhaps ever achievable.

We also believe that if we can just get a subject heading or two on all records representing our nonfiction collection (including literature?) we'll improve access to THE COLLECTION. We need to ponder how that achievement is going to improve access to our fiction collection where Library of Congress policy forbids the use of subject headings for almost everything.

Some of us feel, too, that cataloger types stationed at the online public catalogs might help users find the headings that we ourselves spend endless hours ferreting out in the RED BOOKS. If a cataloger has a direct-indirect-topical-form-period-subdivision-then-comma-and-dash-closed-parens-period-hang-up, do you really want to be the one chosen to explain *that* to a frantic user at the online public catalog? Can you?

And of course, some of us believe that reference desk duty, since reference work is a bibliographic gum-shoe sort of activity, would well equip us to track down and apprehend that elusive subject heading. Now really! Do we as a profession honestly believe that entering the catalog through something as elegantly modest as a subject heading should require the skills and perseverance of a Colombo? Reference work *is* complex, demanding, and challenging. Using the subject vocabulary in our catalogs shouldn't be.

Finally, we believe that if only our online public catalog software would accommodate cross-references, we could successfully lead users through the nearly impenetrable thicket of "see's," "see from's," "see also's," "see also from's," "search under's," "see under's," "BT's," "NT's," "RT's," "UF's" and carefully crafted "public notes," "history notes," and "scope notes." I think the software issue is moot. Too many of us long ago stopped trying to manage this sort of catalog maintenance. It is no surprise to me that so many patrons prefer browsing our collections. Searching our online catalogs has become a litany of frustrations and a plague of failures.

A CRISIS IN CATALOGING AS CONSCIENCE?

Most of us, maybe all of us, will not enjoy career spans of sufficient duration to see in our day-to-day cataloging the subject changes we so desperately crave from the Library of Congress. That's not cynical. It's how it really is and how it has been for a very long time. For example, consider Jerrold Orne's statement:

> Let's pour out the stuff without this time consuming predilection for cross references, see from's, see also's and even finally see me's. . . . This obsession of the cataloger with providing the poor ignorant public with see also's to everything related is an elaborate conceit. . . . We cannot possibly make all the connections, just as we can't know everything, and we should do one thing at a time. We should and will index as much material as possible, using recognizable terms, terms which can usually be found in the material itself, and leave the connections to posterity.[6]

Although I wasn't around in 1948 when that was written, it appears the problem of "recognizable terms" was and indeed remains with us forty-one years later. Change is of a glacial pace at LC. Why do we think we have time to wait it out?

Sanford Berman has noted:

> Frankly, it would be irresponsible to advocate destruction of LCSH, even though proposed substitutes might be theoretically purer and intellectually more appealing, because: 1) Most new systems — like Precis — would not mesh into existing

files; 2) Split files are anathema to maximum catalog use; 3) Substitute schemes would still be no more effective than the people who apply them; 4) All types of American libraries have an incalculable investment in an existing scheme like LCSH.[7]

Now let's be candid. *We* are the people applying the schemes, and we know we're not always doing so effectively. Earlier I alluded to my belief that intelligible, findable, and usable subject cataloging *is* the exercise of professional conscience. Since we've not imparted these qualities to our subject cataloging, cataloging catalysis may provoke us to examine the reasons for our torpor. Perhaps we need fewer studies of catalog use and more studies of online catalogers.

Eugene Frosio, Principal Subject Cataloger, Library of Congress, expressed some sympathy for subject catalogers and subject catalog users when he modestly observed:

> The various LC subject heading strings of today were not devised for online operations. They are in fact artifacts of another era, the card catalog era, when "main entry" catalogs were the best that we could do. . . . But the conventions governing the creation of the strings are inflexible, arbitrary and often downright illogical. . . . I have actually had librarians recently say to me that they could not possibly construct one of our strings themselves and get the place right: it all appears to be mumbo jumbo. . . . They are right, I feel.[8]

Why, in the face of unassailable evidence that what we're doing often hinders rather than helps, do we continue our retreat to islands of ineffectiveness? It should bother us mightily that despite our unprecedented achievements in cooperation, our much heralded codes, our realization of national, international, in fact "universal" standards, we've still left an unconscionable number of our online public catalog users (not to mention catalogers) gasping for breath when using our subject catalogs.

Conscience demands that we ask, question, challenge—intellectually, psychologically, and professionally—why we knowingly assign headings, neglect maintenance work, devise bizarre routines and procedures, all of which regularly antagonize ourselves and our users. If we conclude that the economic constraints Berman mentions are so sweepingly powerful as to be immutable, we must ceaselessly convey that fact to online public catalog patrons and do so with purpose, pride, and resolve. Otherwise, we need to find a better way. When you consult *LCSH* for authoritative terms, also consult your conscience a la Frosio. Because, if you have difficulty in your search, don't you think it likely that so too will a colleague or patron?

If we must articulate a new theory of subject cataloging or cataloging in general by abandoning our cherished Cutterisms and Haykinisms, we can and should do so.[9] Immediately.

We need to think and act less like catalogers and more like communicators with something important to say. We must perceive and perform subject cataloging more as coalition cataloging, as COALITION BUILDING with public services staff. When our tools can't or won't do the job, can or will the people who use them do any better? The best tools to empower catalogers are in the hands of the people challenging, questioning, using, and reacting to our product.

A CRISIS IN CATALOGING AS COMMUNICATION?

Subject cataloging is a highly coded complex of interpersonal communication filled to the brim with overtones of transformational linguistics. We've made our machines master digital representations of this grammar, but we've been less successful in achieving mastery by human users. Machines communicate with machines. People with machines. Machines with people. But catalogers with our public services counterparts? Or they with us? This communication has proven elusive at worst, informal at best. Since we've not achieved it, cataloging catalysis may again provoke it. Effective human communication has been and might continue to be subsumed by our fascination with the grandeur of our electronic interfaces. We've found it more comfortable to commune with our machines and their files than with our counterparts and their facts.

We've simply got to talk less and listen more to the people who need us most. Then we can successfully practice interactive subject cataloging with all users of our product. Successful subject searching, in fact, the ultimate success of any subject heading in fulfilling its destiny, may not hinge as much as we think on the tissue of its vocabulary or syntax. It might depend much, much more on how catalogers communicate subject cataloging to the people who must use our headings.

A CRISIS IN CATALOGING AS CONDUCT?

We catalogers cannot be complete in conscience and confident in communication until we change our conduct. We need to demonstrate our belief that conscience and communication are as important as codes and standards. We need to transform our conduct. How we achieve, enhance, and promote subject access will depend on how and if we choose to interface with our public services counterparts. Since we've rarely achieved this, cataloging catalysis may once again provoke it. As Josefa B. Abrera states:

> It is an observable fact that retrieval elements in a system are not always compatible with user terminology. Conversely, users are not always conversant with retrieval vocabulary in the system — a condition that often presents a serious problem in requests for subject information. . . . It's of particular importance that a better cross reference structure is built into the system to facilitate alternative paths of searching. This calls for the establishment of a feedback loop to the indexing process that allows for inclusion of the user's vocabulary in the list used for indexing materials thus developing a system control oriented to an operating system.[10]

The flash point for interface, interaction, and subject utility occurs when the catalog user tries to access what we've put there. The fact that the online public catalog as agent usually remains unaltered by frequently futile interaction is not an invariable physical law. We've got to show public services this changed truth by asking, interacting, hearing, and implementing. Exactly how we individually or institutionally do that is not as important as conceding that it must be done. We're smart, resourceful, and creative. And we desperately need feedback loops.

TOWARD A NEW CHEMISTRY
IN THE ONLINE CATALOG

Catalogers and public services people, we won't be complete in our conscience, confident in our communication, changed in our conduct, until we commune more with each other. We can create a new chemistry. *"Pro Bono Publico"* cataloging will supplant *"Pro Forma"* cataloging. We need to synthesize four ingredients to do this: electronics, formal principles, formal mechanisms, and human resources. We can then begin to answer THE QUESTION: How can catalogers and public services staff most effectively, most economically, and most humanely interface to promote and enhance subject access in the online catalog?

We're pretty well fixed for the electronics. We have the formal principles. Do we need a formal mechanism, a sort of "Code of Cooperative and Constructive Communication for Interface" between public services and technical services? It might help us stop continually losing our way. It could challenge us to creatively employ human resources for communicative, interactive, coalition cataloging.

Find out how your colleagues in public services—*your* patrons and *their* patrons—are searching your subject catalog. Ask whomever you need to ask. If you must proceed through formal library hierarchies of communication—your head of technical services and public services—do so. It might slow you down, but it won't stop you. They want the same things you do.

If you use *LCSH* with gritted teeth, make time to supplement it heavily with references from the Hennepin County Library Export Authority List or one of the many other available authority lists based on common sense. Try not to use interminable and convoluted "see also's." Use vernacular "see's." Do whatever you need to do to place your users where they need to be in your subject files. Most patrons and certainly your public service colleagues really don't have the time to play subject heading password games.

Here at Jefferson County (Colorado) Public Library, I feel fortunate because I'm part of a group of people that is beginning to meet the challenge of THE QUESTION. Three years ago our library administration created the Public Services/Technical Services Interface Roundtable made up of representatives from key public and technical services positions throughout the system. This roundtable is encouraged — in fact empowered-to dissect and to analyze, to recommend and to report, on virtually any aspect of the public services/technical services interface. We examine things like automated acquisitions, materials ordering, matters pertaining to the use, content, and design of our online public catalog, channels of communication, mechanisms to ACTIVELY PROMOTE SUBJECT ACCESS in the online catalog, and many, many other issues, concerns, problems, ideas, and challenges. The potentialities of an empowered interface as a liberating and exhilarating vehicle for change, improvement, understanding, and access is being realized. And it's exciting.

Yes, this takes time from our "real jobs." But we believe and our administration endorses the notion that "real jobs" in the information services are, by definition and by demand, multidimensional. Our mechanism works. If you are an academic, public, special or private librarian, if you are involved in public, technical or interlibrary loan services, if your library or professional services are small, medium or large, I urge you to create and use a similar roundtable mechanism.

In the unlikely event that you're criticized for promoting vehicles for access, rejoice in knowing you'll not be condemned for inaction. If your conscience complains about "catalogers cataloging for catalogers," renew and refresh it with interactive, coalition cataloging. Agitate *for* cooperation and *against* one dimensionalism in your and your colleagues' jobs. Be bold in your examination of alternatives and timid in your embrace of tradition. Seek or create substantive lines of communication, thereby promoting the interrelatedness of our cause and the interdependency of our actions. Confidence in your communications will transform your conduct. Transform your conduct, and you'll transform your subject cataloging. Discover *your* feedback loop, and you'll discard your frustrations. Mechanisms to help you balance what you are currently doing with what you could be doing will empower you to do what you should be doing better, with both skill and meaning.

The best catalogs and the most successful subject access paths within them — the ones fortified with cataloging catalysis — are the products of many minds, many points of view, many varieties of activity, many kinds of experience, many hours of listening, and of course, many hours of doing.

You have the data. Now for the deed.

REFERENCES

1. Robert P. Holley. "The Future of Catalogers and Cataloging." *The Journal of Academic Librarianship* 7 (May 1981): 90.

Several other probing discussions of the future of catalogers, cataloging and technical services generally are contained in: *Beyond "1984": The Future of Library Technical Services*, Ed. by Peter Gellatly (New York: The Haworth Press, 1983). Of special interest are contributions by Grams p. 19; Gorman p. 65; Parsons p. 105; Preston p. 129.

2. *Webster's Ninth New Collegiate Dictionary*. (Springfield, Mass.: Merriam-Webster Inc., 1988), s.v. "catalysis."

3. Jefferson County (Colorado) Public Library provides library service to a county population of approximately 430,000 residents. The system includes 9 branch libraries and a bookmobile, and is building two new branches. Annual circulation is about 1.4 million. JCPL is a leading suburban system along the Colorado Rocky Mountains Front Range, the 13 populous counties of Colorado located near the eastern edge of the Rocky Mountains.

4. Karen Markey. *Subject Searching in Library Catalogs Before and After the Introduction of Online Catalogs*. OCLC Library, Information, and Computer Science Series, No. 4. (Dublin, Ohio: OCLC Online Computer Library Center, Inc.: 1984), 65-73.

5. Pauline A. Cochrane. *Improving LCSH for Use in Online Catalogs: Exercises for Self-Help with a Selection of Background Readings* (Littleton, Colo.: Libraries Unlimited, Inc.: 1986), 4.

Cochrane's landmark work should be an indispensable part of every cataloging department's reference collection.

It is an illuminating, compelling and perceptive collection of criticisms, suggested improvements and self-help exercises for enhancing online LCSH use.

6. Quoted in Cochrane, *Improving LCSH*, 45.

7. Sanford Berman. "Proposal for Reforms to Improve Subject Searching." *American Libraries* 15 (April 1984): 254.

8. Quoted in Cochrane, *Improving LCSH*, 54.

9. Shelia S. Intner. "Dialectic Retrievalism, or, Looking Closely at the Objects of the Catalog." *Technicalities* 8 (February 1988); 7-9. See also: Intner. "Solutions for Dialectic Retrievalism." *Technicalities* 8 (June 1988): 12-14.

10. Josefa B. Abrera. "Bibliographic Structure Possibility Set: A Quantitative Approach for Identifying Users' Bibliographic Information Needs." *Library Resources & Technical Services* 26 (January/March 1982): 28.

PRECIS in the Online Catalog

Mary Dykstra

Derek Austin's PRECIS (PREserved Context Index System) was expressly designed and developed for the computer generation of printed indexes. In the early 1970s when their design and development took place, online catalogs were not a factor to be considered because they did not yet exist.

Despite its original purpose, however, PRECIS has been used in online catalogs with very impressive results. Furthermore, the classification and indexing concepts, which Derek Austin used to create a state-of-the-art indexing system for the technological environment of those years, still hold enormous potential for the improvement of subject access in the online catalogs of today and tomorrow.

It is important first of all to acknowledge that subject access in the online catalogs of the 1980s is not as good as it must be. Given this acknowledgement, it then becomes important to analyze how PRECIS currently works online and how the theories which underlie PRECIS can be utilized to improve subject access to document content in an increasingly more sophisticated technological environment.

What do we know about subject access in today's online catalogs, most of which are OPACs (Online Public Access Catalogs)? In the first place, we know that user expectations are high. The statistics, which reveal that approximately eighty-five percent of users' online searches are subject searches, speak for themselves. Users who long ago gave up trying to find helpful information in manual subject catalogs now expect that the magic of technology will make all the difference. Suddenly, they expect that they will be

Mary Dykstra is Director, Dalhousie University School of Library and Information Studies, Halifax, Nova Scotia B3H 4H8 Canada.

able to sit down at a keyboard, ask what libraries have on specific subjects, and then the invisible magician in the black box in front of them will give them the answers they could never get in the card catalog or at the microfiche reader. It is evident that these expectations for subject access are fed by users' experiences with computer systems in other contexts. Automatic banking machines provide many previously unavailable services. Automatic supermarket checkouts can now produce discount coupons which are actually useful since they are based upon the system's knowledge of the kinds of items shoppers buy. Within this environment of improved services from computerized systems, why should the newly automated systems in libraries be any different?

The fact is that the library situation is different. This is so because, instead of redefining their service functions in the light of what technology can do, libraries have for the most part simply transferred manual systems and procedures to machines. What has not occurred is an analysis of the ramifications of the technology itself upon library functions. Such an analysis would have resulted in a much clearer idea of how these functions can be performed differently—and much more effectively—by capitalizing upon the possibilities and opportunities inherent in the present technological environment.

In the second place, we know that today's OPACs are not much different *conceptually* from the manual catalogs they replace. Despite the obvious differences in physical appearance (which users notice of course and have expectations about), online catalogs are still actually card catalogs. As the saying goes, they are "card catalogs on wheels."

Specifically, the databases of today's OPACs consist of records still organized around the concept of "main entry," which was relevant for card catalogs but is superfluous online. The points of access offered in today's OPACs are still author, title, and subject, despite the fact that many other useful data elements are now as readily accessible. As for the means of providing subject access, Library of Congress Subject Headings are still used as they have been for so long in manual catalogs. It is well known that these headings reflect the rules of Charles Cutter—rules developed as early as 1876 in an environment in which card catalogs were just beginning to flourish. The emphasis in libraries in Cutter's time was very much upon the physical book as an item to be described and made accessible; serial publications were negligible; and cross references were placed in the card catalogs of libraries primarily as devices to bring about the moral enlightenment and perfection of the reader through a process of self-education.

Along with the advances in technology throughout the 20th century, there have in fact been advances in the theories and techniques of subject retrieval. These include the development of pre-coordinate and post-coordinate indexing systems, the more than two decades of research which saw the evolvement of analytico-synthetic classification with its computer applications, and the international standardization of thesaurus design and construction. Curiously however, and almost without exception, the subject retrieval possibilities of today's OPACs in North America reflect few if any of these advances.

The subject retrieval advances listed above are actually very much inter-related. Analytico-synthetic classification cannot be seen apart from the development of pre-coordinate and post-coordinate indexing systems. Nor could the present standards for thesauri have been developed without both the theory of analytico-synthetic classification and the practical development of pre-coordinate and post-coordinate systems of indexing. There is in fact a subject indexing system available today which reflects and embodies *all* of these advances; that system is PRECIS.

Standard descriptions of PRECIS and how it works have appeared in several publications.[1] What requires emphasis here, in the context of its embodiment of 20th century subject retrieval advances and of how and why it works online, is the contention that PRECIS is in fact a "dual system."[2] Furthermore, it is a dual system in three interrelated ways; the first two become the rationale for the third. The three dualities are:

1. PRECIS consists of two parts, a syntactic part and a thesaural part.
2. PRECIS is both a pre-coordinate and a post-coordinate system.
3. PRECIS is a system both for the production of printed indexes and for online retrieval.

PRECIS has other versatilities. For example, it can be used both for document retrieval systems and for information or data retrieval systems. It has been applied to many different types of media including films, filmstrips, video, stock shots, maps, and realia such as puppets and other theatrical materials. It has been applied in systems at various levels of specificity. Not least important, it has been used in several languages—the UTLAS Inc. software, for example, produces indexes in both English and French, either interfiled or in separate alphabetical sequences. However, this article concentrates upon the three dualities mentioned above.

SYNTACTIC AND THESAURAL

Ferdinand de Saussure, considered the father of modern linguistics, has called the two aspects of language the syntagmatic and the associative. All speech involves the merger of these two aspects— we choose specific words to say from a vast storehouse of words and their associates, and we string these chosen words in a certain linear order. Or do we first design the order and then choose the words? Presumably we perform these two tasks simultaneously, which together with several other factors makes the speaking or writing of a language so extremely complex. Both the vocabulary and the syntax in which the vocabulary is placed serve to fund the message with the meaning one hopes to convey. In other words, a message does not just consist of signs or slices of sound which signify concepts; but also and perhaps primarily it consists of *relationships between signs*. Or, to put it in yet another way, the linearity which we impose upon the sounds we use to signify the concepts we mean is an integral and highly significant part of message conveyance.

Linguists after Saussure refer to these two aspects of language as the syntagmatic and the paradigmatic. John Hutchins also uses these terms in his book, *Languages of Indexing and Classification*.[3] It is significant to note that both the syntagmatic and the paradigmatic aspects consist of *relationships between terms* (i.e., between the signs): the relationships on the syntagmatic side are syntactic or grammatical, and those on the paradigmatic side are thesaural.

Note now that PRECIS, as an *indexing* language, consists of exactly the same dual set of relationships. (See Figure 1.) The side of

PRECIS which consists of the rules and algorithms for placing terms together in a string to describe the contents of a specific document is called the syntactic side. The rules and algorithms for placing each of those terms, which have been used in a string, within its own structural *a priori* context of synonyms, broader terms, narrower terms, and associative terms is called the thesaural side.

SYNTACTICAL & THESAURAL RELATIONSHIPS

Subject: The pollution of rivers in Ontario

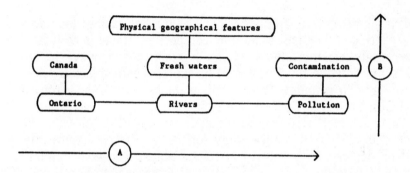

A — Syntactical relationships: *a posteriori* or document-specific relationships between concepts

B — Thesaural relationships: *a priori* relationships which are independent of the treatment of a concept in any particular document

---

The syntactic side of PRECIS is the one for which the system is perhaps best known. Various syntactic operators and codes are assigned to terms to form a string, and this string is then computer manipulated (on the basis of the instructions embedded in the operators and codes) to produce the actual index entries. An example of how a fully coded PRECIS string would appear in a MARC record is as follows:

$z01030$d United States
$z11030$a libraries
$z21030$a management

On the basis of the instructions embedded in the codes, the computer would produce the following entries for the subject index, which would of course then be interfiled in alphabetical order with the other entries:

UNITED STATES
   Libraries. Management

LIBRARIES. United States
   Management

MANAGEMENT. Libraries. United States

It is significant to note in these entries that, as each of the terms in the string is "shunted" into the lead position, there is no loss of contextual meaning in the entry. Each index entry conveys the entire subject, while the terms used to express that subject are *preserved in their original context*. This is the essence of the acronym PRECIS: Preserved Context Index System.

There is much more to the syntactic side of PRECIS since the several operators and codes allow for many different expressions and refinements of grammatical relationships. The goal of these refinements is the creation of a printed index which is optimally readable and easy to use.

The rules which govern the thesaural side of PRECIS, on the other hand, are not significantly different from those for general thesaurus construction. Indeed, the PRECIS machine-held thesauri which exist at the British Library, at UTLAS Inc. in Canada, and elsewhere have been carefully built up according to the international standard *Guidelines for the Establishment and Development of Monolingual Thesauri*.[4] Perhaps the only point to be stressed in connection with the thesaural side of PRECIS is that it consists not of an actual vocabulary or list of terms, even though such authority files do exist and may be used as guides. Rather, it consists of rules for the *generation* of such a list. PRECIS is a set of *working procedures*, translated into algorithms and computer programmes, for the generation of subject indexes. The syntactic part of the system consists of rule-based software for the generation of the index entries themselves. The thesaural part consists of rule-based software for the generation of the references which support the terminology used in the construction of the index entries, thereby providing the index user with preferred, alternative, or related points of subject access.

PRE-COORDINATE AND POST-COORDINATE

PRECIS is of course a pre-coordinate system—the act of string-writing is quite clearly and simply an act of pre-coordination. Each index entry expresses the entire subject of a document; the syntactic side of the system provides the indexer with the grammatical rules whereby this can be accomplished. PRECIS, a direct product of the work of the Classification Research Group in England, is an analytico-synthetic system. In other words, each index entry generated by the computer is the result of the analysis and the synthesis by an indexer of all the terms or descriptors which comprise and are utilized in the expression of a particular subject.

This last sentence merits very careful scrutiny; for within it are several clues that PRECIS, while being a pre-coordinate system, does in fact also incorporate several features of a post-coordinate one.

Implicit, first of all, is the fact that the computer does *not* manipulate already congealed phrases. Rather, it works piece by piece with the individual terms or descriptors as they appear in those phrases. Secondly, the individual terms or descriptors which form the "building blocks" of particular syntactic arrangements are themselves determined on the basis of analysis. And thirdly, the individual terms thus generated by the system are as amenable to thesaurus construction as is the vocabulary of any post-coordinate system.

We have already established the fact that PRECIS consists of two sides, the syntactic and the thesaural; these sides are two distinct yet related sets of *relationships between terms*. So far the emphasis has been upon the *relationships* component of that phrase. Equally significant in the phrase "relationships between terms," however, is the word "terms." PRECIS is a system of relationships, but it is *terms* which are being related.

Terms denote single *concepts*. They differ from subject headings, which of course denote *subjects*. While some subject headings happen to consist of single or compound terms, many more incorporate several terms in a variety of unanalyzed constructions.

The ramifications of PRECIS being a system of terms, not a system of headings, are significant.

First of all, terms, being simpler, are easier to manage and control. Since the time of Charles Cutter there have been attempts to analyze the various grammatical constructions of subject headings, the most comprehensive of these being David Haykin's *Subject Headings: A Practical Guide*[5] and more recently Lois Chan's *Library of Congress Subject Headings: Principles and Application.*[6] Yet even these works offer no workable set of rules. Indeed Lois Chan makes it clear from the beginning that her book has no such ambition.

Chan has every right to be cautious because subject headings, being as complex, composite, and congealed as they are, are also extremely "unruly." Vickery was quite right when he referred to Cutter's rule of inversion, for example, as "no rule at all."[7] The chief reason for this unruliness is Cutter's legacy to us of placing subject headings into something called "subject cataloging," rather than classification. Any subject indexing system at once becomes more "structurable" when it is considered as a system of classification, and this is one major difference between thesauri and lists of subject headings.

By applying consistently the rules of analytico-synthetic classification, PRECIS provides clear definitions of what terms are, whether these are single terms or compound terms. Once this kind of rigorous analysis has taken place, the synthesis aspect (or what can be done with these terms to form various syntactic constructions) can be just as clearly spelled out. Certainly this is the case in the PRECIS indexing language.

In other words, by applying a framework of analytico-synthetic classification to various multi-word expressions—a framework which is supported and complemented by that of linguistic analysis—workable rules for the *control* of terms have emerged in PRECIS. Besides offering control, the rules also offer all of the *accessibility* of a post-coordinate system. And maximum *flexibility* is ensured, in that one can go on to further specify or modify if necessary any of the fully analyzed basic terms. For example, by separating the expression "Teacher education" into its constituent concepts "Teachers" and "Education," the way is left entirely open for handling a document which is about "the continuing education of science teachers."

Because of this framework of analytico-synthetic classification in which analysis is carried out to the level of terms which represent single concepts, a true thesaurus is possible with PRECIS. It should go without saying that a thesaurus cannot be constructed from anything other than terms which represent single concepts. Any attempt to create a thesaurus of headings, rather than terms, both violates existing national and international standards and is doomed to failure from the start. Thesauri provide the referential structure and support for post-coordinate systems — systems of keywords, descriptors, or whatever else the individual terms may be called. PRECIS, although it is a pre-coordinate system, nevertheless has as its basic units terms which represent single concepts. Therefore the PRECIS vocabulary is as amenable to thesaurus construction as is the vocabulary of post-coordinate systems.

So far we have considered that PRECIS, although it is an alphabetical subject indexing system, has evolved from the work of the Classification Research Group and as such has as its framework the principles of analytico-synthetic classification. In other words, PRECIS incorporates rules for both the analysis and the synthesis of concepts. Its analytic units are terms. From a different perspective, PRECIS can be seen as an indexing language with features which closely parallel those of a natural language. Most importantly in this respect, PRECIS has both a syntactic and a thesaural side. With a syntactic side, PRECIS is of course pre-coordinate. However, because its basic analytic units are terms and because in the thesaural side these terms form the building blocks of a machine-held thesaurus, PRECIS also displays several features of post-coordinate systems.

It is primarily because of its post-coordinate features that PRECIS has responded so well to the online environment.

One of the most important ramifications of online technology has been the obliteration of the traditional distinction between input and output, or between indexing and searching. Many graphic representations of information systems exist today in which the traditional indexing function is shown as identical to the traditional reference function, except that the former involves data pertinent to documents and the latter involves data pertinent to questions. The same system vocabulary functions as both the indexing language and the language of searching. This has of course always been the case, even in manual systems; but it has not become clear until now when both functions are performed on the same invisible database in the "black box."

Most subject searching in online systems is of course post-coordinate; coordination is achieved by means of the searcher's use of the Boolean operators AND, OR, and NOT. Such coordination is called "developing a search strategy," although as noted earlier the application of similar syntactic procedures involved in pre-coordination is called "indexing."

Because the building blocks of PRECIS are terms, the system is as adaptable to online searching as is any post-coordinate system. One simply devises a search strategy using the Boolean operators. However, since hits in online systems using PRECIS are achieved not on separately listed keyboards but on the terms as they appear in pre-coordinate strings, a major difference occurs in retrieval. Instead of proceeding directly to the titles recalled as a result of a particular query, the searcher can first be informed of all of the various syntactic arrangements in which the query terms occur in the database and of the number of titles associated with each.

Consider, for example, a search on the truncated terms "Teacher" AND "Student" AND "Assessment." Using PRECIS, this particular search might yield the following entries:

> Student teachers. Assessment
> Students. Assessment by teachers
> Teachers. Assessment by students
> United States. Students. Interpersonal relationships with teachers. Assessment
> Universities, Students and teachers. Assessment by administrators

Beside each entry would be an indication of the number of documents in the database relevant to each subject.

Presumably not all subjects retrieved will be equally relevant to the searcher. Therefore an advantage of a post-coordinate search on a pre-coordinate index is that it eliminates irrelevant retrieval or "garbage." What the use of PRECIS in online systems provides is an intermediate step, in which the searcher is able to screen the various term configurations retrieved *before* an actual display or printout of titles. Or, if this step were considered unnecessary in a particular system, one could proceed immediately to a title display or printout which would provide as additional information the PRE-CIS entry for each title, as a kind of "mini-abstract." In either type of system, increased relevance is achieved with no loss of recall.

Once individual terms in PRECIS strings are retrieved, there is of course no need for the computer to go through all the shunting procedures to place these terms in the lead position as would be required for access in a printed index.

For example, we have seen that in order to provide access to all key terms in the string "Sz01030$d United States $z11030Sa libraries $z21030$a management," the following index entries are required in a printed index:

UNITED STATES
Libraries. Management

LIBRARIES. United States
Management

MANAGEMENT. Libraries. United States

Online, however, each term in the string can be retrieved simply by a computer scan of the original coded string. All that is required afterwards for the user's benefit is simply the generation of the entry:

United States. Libraries. Management

This fact, together with the increasing emphasis upon online systems over systems where printed indexes are required, has led the British Library to propose a rather drastic reduction in software for the syntactic side of PRECIS. The National Film Board of Canada, whose national automated system for Canadian audiovisual materials uses PRECIS for subject access, is presently proposing the development of microcomputer software for PRECIS which similarly would modify those parts of the syntactic side which have to do with the shunting or permutation of entries. Since most of the perceived complexity of the PRECIS system had to do with all of the operators and codes required for the elegant permutations necessary in order to provide all the access points required in a printed index, the net effect of concentrating upon the use of PRECIS online is that it becomes a much simpler system.

How does PRECIS online work? Because PRECIS data is an integral part of MARC records, PRECIS subject access is an integral part of the online systems so far developed on the basis of these records. For example, the online system developed by the National Film Board of Canada offers the following "selection criteria," or access points for searching:

1-PRECIS SUBJECT INDEX	8-COLOR / B & W	15-AVAILABILITY
2-TITLE	9-RUNNING TIME	16-CREDITS
3-SERIES/PROGRAM TITLE	10-DATE OF PRODUCTION	17-CAST
4-TITLE CODE	11-PRODUCER	18-BROAD CATEGORY INDEX
5-DESCRIPTION	12-DIRECTOR	19-OTHER
6-LANGUAGE	13-PRODUCING BODY	
7-ORIGINAL FORMAT	14-DISTRIBUTOR	

In formulating a search on this system, one simply combines selection criteria (or elements within selection criteria) in Boolean combinations. A typical search is for a *film* (criterion 7), AND on the subject of *Lake* OR *river* AND *pollution* (criterion 1), AND produced *after 1985* (criterion 10), AND *between twenty and thirty minutes long* (criterion 9). All of the data pertaining to these selection criteria are retrieved directly from the appropriately tagged elements in the MARC records.

The National Film Board's online system has been operational across Canada since 1982. It has recently become available commercially through QL Systems Ltd. The online system is actually just a component of a larger system, which generates a variety of outputs from the UTLAS-held database. The outputs of the total system include an assortment of both comprehensive and selective printed catalogues, including the national filmography *Film and Video Canadiana*.

Several years of experience (both in England and in Canada) have made it clear that PRECIS online works both effectively and efficiently, taking advantage of the technology presently available. Even more, the use of PRECIS so far in online retrieval has revealed avenues for further investigation and research. Nearly all of these avenues spring directly from the dualities of the system which have been described. For example, the duality of PRECIS as a system with a syntactic and a thesaural side has led to research on two fronts: the ramifications of the close affinity of PRECIS with abstracting (a skill as yet under-utilized for online systems) and the possibility of using PRECIS as a model for the computer analysis of text. The duality of PRECIS as both a pre-coordinate and a post-coordinate system has opened the way for an investigation into the possibility of replacing or enhancing a standard Boolean search with a search based upon the grammatical or syntactic role of a particular term — a search, for example on the term "Teacher" *as agent* AND the term "Student" *as object*. Any or all of these research and development activities could lead to even more powerful subject retrieval capabilities.

In the longer term, the development of these more powerful and effective subject retrieval capabilities, based upon what PRECIS has to offer, would most logically pave the way for major multidisciplinary research in complex semantic information processing and the development of expert systems for textual analysis and retrieval. For what remains of PRECIS, stripped of the operators required to produce printed indexes, is a rigorously defined set of rules for the structural analysis and synthesis of terms, both as they relate to each other grammatically and in their categorical or thesaural relationships. Given certain elementary rules, it has become fairly routine by now for a computer to parse a sentence. What remains extremely difficult, however, is to fathom the structural or logical relationships between the words in that sentence to determine what it *means*. If there is a future role for any subject indexing system in our increasingly automated environment, one based upon the rules of analytico-synthetic classification would seem to hold by far the most promise.

NOTES

1. See for example the author's *PRECIS: A Primer*. Revised reprint, in agreement with the British Library. (Metuchen, N.J.: Scarecrow Press, 1987)

2. This concept was introduced by the author in a paper entitled "PRECIS as a Dual System," delivered at the Symposium on Subject Analysis, Durham, North Carolina, March 29-30, 1985.

3. W. J. Hutchins, *Languages of Indexing and Classification: A Linguistic Study of Structures and Functions* (Stevenage, Harts.: Peter Peregrinus, 1975).

4. International Standards Organization, *Guidelines for the Establishment and Development of Monolingual Thesauri*. 2nd. ed. (ISO 2788-1986 OE) Geneva: 1986).

5. David Judson Haykin, *Subject Headings: A Practical Guide* (Washington, D.C.: U.S. Government Printing Office, 1951).

6. Lois Mai Chan, *Library of Congress Subject Headings: Principles and Application*. 2nd ed. (Littleton, Colo.: Libraries Unlimited, 1986).

7. B. C. Vickery, "Classificatory Principles in Natural Language Indexing Systems", in *Classification in the 1970s: A Second Look*. Revised ed., edited by Arthur Maltby. (London: Bingley, 1976), p. 119-141.

The Role of Classification
in Online Systems

Nancy J. Williamson

INTRODUCTION

Indexing languages, and consequently retrieval languages, are the tools of access to documents and to data stored in information systems. Indexing languages belong to one of two basic types—natural language or controlled vocabulary. Natural language can be described as the language of discourse and the language of written text, from which the terminology used in retrieval is derived. Controlled vocabularies are derived from natural language; but the terminology is selected, structured, and controlled (often by subjective means). Terms or concepts from such vocabularies are intended to be assigned to represent documents or text, to be used to plan search strategies, and to aid users in browsing and retrieving the contents of databases.

Among the several types of controlled vocabularies are classification systems, while other controlled vocabularies, for example thesauri, contain various kinds of classificatory structure.

CLASSIFICATION IN THE ONLINE CONTEXT

The term "classification" describes a broad spectrum of methods by which thoughts, facts, objects and, indeed, our very lives are organized. It is a term which means different things in different contexts. In the field of science, the term generally connotes taxonomy, whereas in the information community it is most frequently

Nancy J. Williamson is Professor, Faculty of Library and Information Science, University of Toronto, 140 St. George St., Toronto M5S 1A1 Canada.

equated with book classification systems such as the Dewey Decimal, the Library of Congress, and Universal Decimal classifications. Unfortunately, in the library and information science context, classification in general is often understood only in its traditional role "as an approach to the arrangement of materials"[1] or as the means of ordering shelf lists, bibliographies and classified catalogues. In reality, classification is much more than this. In conjunction with computerized information systems, the terms "classification," "categorization" and "classificatory structure" are not limited to hierarchical classification but rather describe a whole spectrum of devices and operations which establish various kinds of relationships among terms, concepts, documents, or data, based on characteristics which they have in common.

For obvious reasons, very little use is made of traditional book classification in online bibliographic databases and full-text retrieval systems. In most cases, classification data are not readily available because the contents of databases are frequently not co-extensive with the contents of particular physical collections. Therefore, there is no need to classify for purposes of shelf browsing or shelf retrieval. However, this does not mean that some kind of classificatory structure is not needed. Useful order is still important to retrieval. Bibliographic and textual systems must be capable of guiding users to documents or to facts relevant to their needs, whether the search is for known items, for precise topical subjects, or whether users wish to browse new subjects and new ideas or to clarify ill-defined information problems.

In small databases a very simple approach may be all that is required; but, as databases become larger, the need to provide some kind of structure or framework to accomplish various kinds of retrieval requirements becomes increasingly essential. However, the instrument need not be one of the well known book classifications. Indeed, there are other kinds of categorization and classificatory structure which might better serve computerized information systems. "Non-traditional classification systems are needed . . . "[2]

Up until now the role of classification in online bibliographic and full-text databases has received little serious consideration as an important factor in database design. This can be regarded as a mixed blessing. On the one hand, such databases have not been hampered by the use of classificatory structures which are unsuitable for online retrieval; while on the other, the importance of such structures in some form has been largely ignored by most database designers. Ease of use in manipulating a system has been all important. The same concern has not been shown for ease in browsing its contents. Boolean search techniques, frequently supplemented by truncation, wild cards, and proximity search mechanisms, are generally regarded as the major, and often the only, necessary "power" behind database retrieval. Indeed most intermediaries and vendors would react positively to the idea that traditional library classification systems are not necessary and not used in online retrieval systems. However, it is becoming increasingly apparent that *some kind* of classificatory structure is essential in most databases. Recent evidence indicates that all is not well in the retrieval of documents and text from very large online systems. Structured aids for searching large full-text databases appear to be assuming increasing importance, while there is growing recognition that Boolean operators[3,4] need to be supplemented and complemented by other kinds of search aids, and structures.

There is much evidence to suggest that, at the present time, information professionals do not have sufficient understanding of classificatory structures to speak with authority to systems designers and vendors about how such structures could be used to improve retrieval performance. Research data are too insufficient and unreliable[5] either to support or refute some of the myths and assumptions which presently exist. Fortunately there is concern for these problems, and serious investigation has already begun.[6]

Because of the erroneous perception that classification *per se* equates with book classification, it is frequently assumed that classificatory devices and methods must be unintelligible, cumbersome to use, and static in nature. Terms such as "classification," "structure," and "controlled vocabulary" tend, often unnecessarily, to conjure up, in the minds of vendors, subscribers, and database users, visions of complex, inflexible, archaic mechanisms. In this context, simplicity is easily confused with ease of use when such is not necessarily the case. It can certainly be argued that "ease of use" contributes to effective retrieval, but this is only of the factors involved. Moreover, ease of use is not necessarily achieved through "simple" database design. Nor does it need to be. The technology now exists to design systems in which classificatory structures can be used to advantage, while their complexity is largely hidden from users.

A second assumption is that classificatory structure is expensive to create, use, and maintain. Some intermediaries find the use of a thesaurus cumbersome and time consuming; and there is some evidence that browsing is discouraged where it increases connect-time and therefore the cost of searching. Moreover, some experts have suggested that both the human intermediary and search aids such as thesauri could cease to be cost-effective in the future.[7] But the thesaurus as it is now known is probably not the thesaurus of the future. What should the thesaurus of the future be like? Or, what kinds of structures should replace the thesaurus as we know it? Some answers are needed.

Cost-effectiveness is often confused with rapid retrieval—a somewhat simplistic approach to economic problems. Cheaper is not necessarily better; and cost-effectiveness of online systems is a complex measure of many variables, not just one. The size and nature of the database, speed of retrieval, ease of use, ease, and cost of maintenance and updating, and, above all, quality of retrieval are among the factors which must be considered. It is equally important to determine the point in the storage and retrieval operation at which costs are incurred. Faulty design and ineffective access to a system have the potential to transfer costs saved in design to the retrieval process where the costs, both financial and intellectual, may be incurred not once but many times over. This is not a new idea. It was true of the card catalogue and traditional reference service. The difference is that the cost of computer time is visible in terms of dollars and cents, whereas manual systems tended to be viewed in terms of human effort.

Online databases, particularly bibliographic databases, are no longer "new" inventions; but they have not developed and evolved with changes in the technologies. To a large extent, their design is based on knowledge of the manual systems from which they evolved, coupled with computer manipulation. This state of affairs has been attributed to a number of factors—lack of innovation, faulty research,[8] insufficient cumulative research, and contentment with the status quo. While these criticisms are not new, they were all reaffirmed at a recent Conference on Database Users involving information scientists, information professionals, and members of the database industry. During the discussions it was pointed out that on the one hand "the database industry . . . has been slow to make real innovations,"[9] while on the other "users are content because they do not know what else is possible."[10] Vendors tend to design databases along traditional lines because this is the kind of database they have come to know and understand. It is also a product which they are assured is commercially marketable and promises the least financial risk. By the same token, subscribers and users are not in a position to make educated value judgments because they have no alternative types of systems for making comparisons. This is not surprising, given the inconclusive research upon which to make decisions on substantive changes in database design. Databases vary widely, and there are few standards. Moreover, there is little substantive and productive discussion among database vendors, information professionals, and researchers. Each group has its own goals and priorities, which frequently do not coincide.

In this context and in the interests of future database design, it is essential that the full potential of classification as a tool for computerized information storage and retrieval systems be explored. What structures are presently in place? How are they used? Are they effective? Are they suitable for the use for which they were designed? How could they be improved? Do they make the best use of the technologies available? These are but a few of the questions which need to be addressed.

BIBLIOGRAPHIC DATABASES
AND CLASSIFICATORY STRUCTURE

If the retrieval effectiveness of bibliographic databases is to be optimized, the direct access to citations through Boolean search must be supplemented and complemented by search mechanisms which permit and encourage systematic browsing of these systems. Classification or classificatory structure of some kind will support this function in retrieval. Research is needed to determine the kinds of structures which will be effective and under what conditions they will work best. An obvious place to begin an investigation of this kind is to examine the role of the thesaurus in online searching. Fortunately, some research in this area has already begun.[11]

Thesauri are classificatory in nature and were originally designed for use in computerized retrieval. An examination of a spectrum of types of thesauri shows that they vary greatly in their content, organization, and methods of display. Some could be described as simple term or synonym lists, while many embody much more complex structures as aids to the indexer in assigning descriptors and in assisting search editors and users to conduct searches. Elements of classification can be seen in the broader term/narrower term relationships of the traditional thesaurus displays, which, if properly developed, are hierarchical in nature. A different approach to hierarchical display can be found in the hierarchical indexes included in the supplementary displays of some thesauri. Rotated displays of the KWIC and KWOC variety can also be regarded as classificatory structures because they group or cluster various occurrences of the same term in different conceptual contexts. More sophisticated approaches to classificatory structure include the application of the principles of facet analysis to produce an overview of a discipline through facet categories (e.g., *Unesco: IBE Education Thesaurus*). In other systems, such as *Thesaurofacet* and its more modern counterpart the *ROOT Thesaurus*, are found fully developed faceted classification systems completely integrated with alphabetical thesauri. Less common, but with extremely interesting potential for online display, are the graphic displays in form of arrowgraphs (e.g., *EURATOM Thesaurus*) and terminographs or box charts (e.g., *EUDISED Thesaurus*). No less important are the tree structures used in MeSH, which are indeed classificatory structures.

In spite of the sophistication of some thesauri and their association with computerized systems, there is considerable evidence to suggest that the thesaurus as a tool has not truly entered the computer age. Many current thesauri look much like the thesauri of the late 1960s and are indeed used much in the same way.

In a recent survey, 140 thesauri in 35 broad subject areas and 5 languages, randomly selected from *The Thesaurus Guide*[12] were examined. Approximately 61% of the lists were available in printed form only, while 32.8% were in both machine-readable and printed form. Only one thesaurus professed to be online. These thesauri were seen as indexing tools in 80% of the cases, as manual retrieval tools 47.8% of the time, and for use in online retrieval in 65.7% of the systems for which they were used. In the cases where it was stated that a thesaurus was used in mechanized retrieval, 54.3% of the thesauri fell into the "printed form only" category. As a result, only 42, or 30% of the sample of 140 lists, could possibly have been available online. These are not encouraging figures. While they are based on secondary data, a more recent guide to *Thesauri Used in Online Databases*[13] supports the observation that in the majority of cases thesauri are used as adjuncts to online systems rather than as fully integrated tools within the system. If, as expected, more and more bibliographic and information retrieval will be carried out online in the future, the situation just described is surely not the wave of the future. Evidence suggests that very little is known about how and under what circumstances thesauri are actually used with online systems or whether they *are* used at all. A small survey of experienced search editors, who search the ERIC database, regularly suggests that the *Thesaurus of ERIC Descriptors* is consulted infrequently, whereas discussions with those who search MEDLINE constantly indicate that they consult the MeSH tree structures frequently. Is this what actually happens? If so, why? Does the nature of the subject area determine the use and non-use of thesauri with online systems? Possibly, but this is probably only one of several factors. Carol Tenopir's study[14] indicates that "it depends" on at least four variables — the nature of the database, the vocabulary and the indexing policies which dictate its application, the topic being searched, and the requestor.

If a thesaurus is used, is it preferable to use it in printed form or online? Some searchers will say that they prefer the paper version because they can "see more" or because they are more familiar with the paper version. Unfortunately, as the foregoing statistics suggest, the fact that most thesauri are in printed form provides many indexers and searchers with very little basis on which to make comparisons.

Not only is it important to investigate the use of thesauri, it is essential to explore ways and means of making this tool or its functions a more integral part of retrieval systems. A logical step into the future should be the eventual replacement of printed thesauri with online tools which are fully integrated with the bibliographic systems which they support. However, it will be important to avoid simply converting existing thesauri into machine-readable form. To be effective, thesauri and thesaurus-like structures should be designed specifically for online use by incorporating appropriate sophisticated methods of manipulation and display while maintaining ease of maintenance and use. In this context, research on possible innovations in thesaurus design is needed; and the standards for thesaurus construction should be re-examined to see whether they will still accommodate the online requirements.

Finally, research on other approaches should look beyond the thesaurus as a search aid in retrieval. For example, what can expert systems and artificial intelligence[15] do for bibliographic retrieval, especially since there is a strong relationship between artificial intelligence and classification.[16]

FULL-TEXT DATABASES AND CLASSIFICATION

An examination of the state-of-the-art in full-text databases reveals a situation similar to that of bibliographic systems.[17] Such databases may be fact databases or full-text document databases. Both are growing rapidly in number and in size. Although it should not be assumed that full-text databases are the same as bibliographic systems, many of the document databases have been developed and maintained by vendors of bibliographic systems. Consequently, Boolean search methods are common to both, with full-text databases largely dependent on free text searching. As such databases have grown in size, there has been increasing evidence that searchers are having difficulties with retrieval[18]. Some experts[19] have made strong pleas for some kind of vocabulary control. It is also suggested that the most effective retrieval from full-text databases will come from the use of a combination of natural language and controlled vocabulary. There appears to be a need for subject access at more than one level — at the document level through controlled vocabulary, and at the text level through natural language. Full-text databases are also candidates for artificial intelligence and hypertext[20] as well as other approaches to structuring which are being explored.

CONCLUSION

With recent advances in technology, an enormous potential exists for further development in the retrieval mechanisms used in online bibliographic and textual databases. Research is already intensifying. There is a role for classification in online retrieval such that classification and classificatory structure can operate in concert with other means of access to improve bibliographic and information retrieval in the future.

NOTES

1. Herbert S. White, "Oh, Why (and Oh What) Do We Classify?" *Library Journal* 113 (June 15, 1988): 42.

2. Harold Borko, "The Role of Classification in Online Retrieval Systems and Automated Libraries." *Universal Classification: Subject Analysis and Ordering Systems*, editor, Ingetraut Dahlberg (Frankfurt: Indeks Verlag, 1982); v. 1, p. 235.

3. Charles Hildreth, "To Boolean or Not to Boolean", *Information Technology and Libraries* 2 (September 1983): 235-237.

4. Joseph M.A. Cavanaugh, "Bye, Bye Boole: the Case for Associative Adaptive Retrieval Systems." *National Online Meeting: Proceedings 1987*, compiled by Martha E. Williams and Thomas H. Hogan. (Medford, NJ: Learned Information, 1987). pp. 67-70.

5. Raya Fidel, "What is Missing in Research About Online Searching Behavior?" *The Canadian Journal for Information Science* 12 (3/4 1987); 54-61.

6. Marcia J. Bates, "How to Use Controlled Vocabularies More Effectively in Online Searching", *Online* 12 (November 1988); 45-56.

7. Jeffrey Katzer, "User Studies, Information Science and Communication", *The Canadian Journal of Information Science* 12 (3/4, 1987): 22.

8. Raya Fidel, *Ibid.*, 54-55.

9. Charles T. Meadow, "Remarks from the Conference Chair: (First Toronto Conference on Database Users)" *The Canadian Journal of Information Science* 12 (3/4 1987): 3.

10. *Ibid.*

11. Marcia J. Bates, *Ibid.*

12. *Thesaurus Guide: Analytical Directory of Selected Vocabularies for Information Retrieval.* (Amsterdam; Office of Official Publications of the European Community, 1985).

13. Lois Mai Chan and Richard Pollard, *Thesauri Used in Online Databases: An Analytical Guide* (New York: Greenwood Press, 1988), p. 268.

14. Carol Tenopir, "Searching by Controlled Vocabulary or Free Text?" *Library Journal* 112 (November 15, 1987): 58.

15. Irene L. Travis, "Applications of Artificial Intelligence to Bibliographic Classification", paper presented at the conference on "Classification Theory in the Computer Age" at Albany, NY, November 18-19, 1988. (To be published in the Proceedings).

16. Norbert Meder, "Artificial Intelligence as a Tool of Classification, or: The Network of Language Games as Cognitive Paradigms", *International Classification*, 12 (3, 1985): 128-132.

17. Carol Tenopir, "Full-Text Databases", *Annual Review of Information Science and Technology*, Martha E. Williams, editor (New York: Knowledge Industry Publications), pp. 215-246.

18. Susan H. Veccia, "Full-Text Dilemmas for Searchers and Systems: The Washington Post Online", *Database* 14 (April 1988): 13-42.

19. Pauline Duckitt, "The Value of Controlled Indexing Systems in Online Full Text Databases". In: *Proceedings of the 5th International Online Information Meeting, 1981 December* (London: Learned Information, 1981), pp. 447-453.

20. Karen E. Smith, "Hypertext — Linking to the Future", *Online* 32 (March 1988): 32-40.

The Online Catalog:
Dictionary, Classified, or Both?

Elaine Broadbent

SUMMARY. The main purpose of the study was to determine if the online catalog can function both as a dictionary and classified catalog without requiring additional time or intellectual effort on the part of the cataloger. A total of 1842 MARC bibliographic records listed in the 370-379 classified section of *American Book Publishing Record* were studied. These records displayed 2735 subject headings. Of these, 1491 (55%) had a Library of Congress classification number linked to them. An alphabetical and classified index was created using primary subjects and their related classification numbers. While such an index could be a useful browsing device if integrated into an online catalog, creating a *bona fide* classified catalog would require assigning classification numbers to the secondary subject headings.

INTRODUCTION

"This is 1957, and it is time to bury Cutter."[1] These words, written by Scheerer more than thirty years ago, have been echoed by many other frustrated librarians since then. They are aware that, although the library catalog (whatever its form) is good at retrieving known-items, the subject catalog has performed less satisfactorily. In fact, the online catalog has made the shortcomings of the subject catalog more evident. Perhaps it is not too much to say that the advent of the ubiquitous computer has forced librarians to reexam-

---

Elaine Broadbent was Head of the Original Cataloging Section, Cataloging Division, Marriott Library, University of Utah before her retirement. Correspondence may be sent to 3526 Fowler Road, Odgen, UT 84403.

105

ine the subject catalog: what it is, what it should include, and what is its function. Among the broad range of suggested remedies are adopting PRECIS or some other form of chain indexing in place of conventional subject headings, sophisticated key word searching, full text searching, uncontrolled subject vocabulary, and an increased number of subject headings per record.[2]

The suggestion, however, which has received the most attention began with Pauline A. Cochrane's "Subject Access Project" in 1978.[3] She proposed enhancing the cataloging record with additional subject rich information. Many researchers believe this route shows the most promise. The Dewey Decimal Classification Online Project studied the effectiveness of enhancing the bibliographic record with information from the Dewey Decimal schedules including both classification numbers and the relative index.[4] This study made special use of several MARC fields. The most important innovation was the creation of a "Schedules DDC class number" which allowed subject rich information to be added automatically to bibliographic records from the DDC schedules and relative index.[5] However, as Mandel notes:

> Before we pursue any of these suggestions for augmenting records, it is essential that we step back and ask ourselves precisely what we really want from a database of expanded MARC records. It was noted earlier that record creation is, in the long run, the most expensive component of our subject access system. . . . If the subject work, including LC and Dewey classification, on each title costs $15, we are looking at an ongoing annual cost of $2.4 million dollars at L.C. alone.[6]

But she concludes: "Should we enhance the MARC record to improve subject access? We won't know until we try."[7] Thus, researchers realize that it is impractical either to discard years of bibliographic data and millions of MARC records to begin anew or to provide extensive enhancements to these records. Any such record enhancement would also increase current cataloging costs.

The study described below makes use of Library of Congress subject headings and Library of Congress classification numbers as displayed on current MARC bibliographic records. In other words, the study will attempt to determine if online catalogs can become more efficient subject retrieval tools, even though the MARC cataloging records continue to contain the same number of traditional Library of Congress subject headings and Library of Congress classification numbers. The author thus advocates evolution, not revolution. This is not to say that in the future Library of Congress subject headings could not and should not evolve into a more exact indexing language nor that the Library of Congress classification cannot be made more suitable for the online environment. Change is inevitable. For example, the recent adoption by Library of Congress of thesauri type terms "USE," "UF," "BT," "NT," "RT" is a definite improvement over the old "sa," "xx" and "x" reference structure by making more explicit the hierarchical relations. Library of Congress also plans to reduce the number of "orphan" headings—those headings without cross-references.[8]

Before describing this study's aim, several points remain to be considered. First, in spite of the current close examination of the subject catalog, most librarians still think of the classified catalog and the dictionary catalog in terms of "either/or" as if they were mutually exclusive, even though many online catalogs already provide call number access—something previously unavailable to patrons since the shelflist traditionally was not a public access file. As stated in the report of a conference on classification in the online catalog: "The online catalog obviates the need to choose among alphabetical, classed or some form of alphabetico-classed catalogs; all can exist within the same tool when the records and indexes are structured thoughtfully."[9] Secondly, call number access in online catalogs is presently not very effective. Cochrane and Markey point out "the major drawback to call or classification number searching in all existing online catalogs: the searcher must know the subject matter represented by a particular call or class number to effectively use such number searching."[10] Markey and Demeyer state that patrons enter a classification number into the catalog like a "shot in the dark" because they do not know the meaning of the classification number until the online catalog displays the retrieved items or list of topics.[11] Cochrane and Markey also note that transaction log analysis indicates that patrons use call or classification number searching the least frequently of all available access points since they account for less than 10% of searches.[12] This study proposes an obvious reason: the catalog user has no available index to the classification system!

PURPOSE OF THE STUDY

This experiment will attempt to answer the following specific questions: (1) Can the online catalog function both as the traditional dictionary catalog with a verbal or alphabetical approach to subjects and also as a classified catalog with a systematic approach to subjects by arranging the bibliographic records in the catalog by notation from a standard classification scheme? (2) Can this be done without requiring any more time or intellectual effort on the part of the cataloger? (3) Can this he done within the present bibliographical framework of Library of Congress subject headings and the Library of Congress classification system?

Why has this study chosen the Library of Congress classification and Library of Congress subject headings? Williamson, describing her research project on the Library of Congress classification in the online catalog, states:

> The Library of Congress Classification (LCC) has been chosen for this particular study for several reasons . . . LCC is among the most widely used general classification systems in the world. As such it can be described as a "standard" system. Its development and use by a major national institution engaged in the wide distribution of MARC records ensures its evolution and perpetuity.[13]

For much the same reason, this study has also chosen the Library of Congress classification. However, the choice was not made without much thought. As Wellisch has written:

If . . . the classification scheme used [in the classified catalog] is L.C., failure is almost certainly assured, because that classification scheme was never designed to serve as a notational device for a classified catalog, and its very structure makes it highly unsuitable for such a purpose.[14]

However, as Chan states:

On the other hand, there is an advantage in LCC's size and enumerative nature: it offers very specific numbers for certain categories of subject. For example, in literature, unique call numbers are provided for individual authors and in some cases even for individual works. Geographic aspects of many subjects are pinpointed to the city level (and in some cases, even to districts, e.g., maps and atlases). Such specificity could be very beneficial in online retrieval.[15]

The experiment will also test the feasibility of using conventional Library of Congress subject headings to index the Library of Congress classification scheme. On the use of Library of Congress subject headings as an index to LCC. Chan states:

But under current conditions, not much can be expected from depending on LCSH as an LCC index-substitute. Only a small proportion of LC subject headings carry class numbers, and even these are not routinely updated in the case of changed numbers. How useful LCSH/LCC links could be were the connections more nearly complete, and if they were fully maintained, is a question that deserves attention.[16]

METHODOLOGY

During the planning stage of the project to find a strategy for creating a verbal index to the Library of Congress classification, the following works were examined as possibilities: two lists of subject headings and their associated Library of Congress classification numbers (James G. Williams, Martha L. Manheimer, and Jay E. Daily, ed., *Classified Library of Congress Subject Headings*, 2nd ed. New York: Dekker, 1982; and *Subject Authorities: A Guide to Subject Cataloging*, New York: Bowker, 1981) and two combined indexes to the Library of Congress classification (J. McRee Elrod, Judy Inouye, and Ann C. Turner, ed., *An Index to the Library of Congress Classification* . . . Ottawa: Canadian Library Association, 1974; and Nancy B. Olson, *Combined Indexes to the Library of Congress Schedules*, Washington: U.S. Historical Documents Institute, 1974, 15 vols.). None of these works were used in this study because a definite decision was made early in the project to evaluate the feasibility of using Library of Congress subject headings as an index to the Library of Congress classification system so that the indexes per se to the classification system were not within its scope. The Williams index is not linked to any bibliographic records and includes only those subject headings with classification numbers.

Instead this study turned to another source. The "Subject Guide" in *ABPR* was used for the years 1984-1985 and for the months January to June 1986. *Subject Authorities* is a cumulation of the list of subject headings and their associated Library of Congress classification numbers from *American Book Publishing Record (ABPR)*; it was the "Subject Guide" for the years 1973-1981.

The study adopted the following procedure: from the classified section of *ABPR*, the bibliographic records listed under the Dewey classification for education — 370 to 379 — for the time period noted above were selected as the "database" of the theoretical catalog. These bibliographic records in *ABPR* are full MARC records and include the Library of Congress call numbers. Each subject heading — primary and secondary — listed on these catalog records was recorded on a 3 x 5 card. If it was the first or primary subject heading, the classification number on the record was also noted. The study also tabulated the number of times each subject heading was used.

The next step was to check those secondary subject headings against the *ABPR* "Subject Guide" of primary subjects. In this way a classification number was assigned to some subject headings even though not used as primary subjects in the 370s. For example, BASIC (Computer Program Language) is given the number QA76.73.B3 in the Library of Congress classification; and classes variously in 001.64, 005.133, 620, etc. in Dewey when used as a primary subject. For works dealing with computers and education, it was used as a secondary subject. Also, not all titles classified in the Dewey 370's were correspondingly classified in the Library of Congress L (Education) schedule. For example, J. Krishnamurti's book *Things of the Mind* had the Dewey number 370.1 but the Library of Congress number BD331.K66. In other words, the classification numbers linked with the subject headings in this group of MARC records were not exclusively in the L (Education) LCC classification schedule.

The following points should be noted about the Bowker "Subject Guide" index. First, the Library of Congress classification number linked with a subject heading is truncated. If the classification number includes a decimal or a double Cutter, the complete classification number is not given in the index—only the portion to the decimal or to the first Cutter. Secondly, as stated in the preface to *ABPR*: "The Subject Guide . . . is arranged alphabetically by traced primary subjects, personal names used as subject, and uniform titles." In a few instances, a second subject heading may also correspond to the classification number but not be listed in the "Subject Guide" even though, according to the Library of Congress Subject Heading Manual: "In case two headings are required to represent the complete class number, these two headings should be listed as Tracings 1 and 2."[17]

After the subject headings were recorded for the two and a half year time period, two indexes were created: (1) An index of classified subject headings from the classification numbers linked with the subject headings on the MARC bibliographic records; (2) An alphabetical list of subject headings containing the classification number or numbers linked with the given heading. These indexes, described in more detail below, were produced on a Macintosh personal computer with Microsoft Works software.

FINDINGS

For the time period 1984-85 and January-June 1986, 1842 MARC cataloging records were listed in the classified section of the

ABPR Portion under Dewey 370-379 (Education). The breakdown by time period is as follows:

	1984	751
	1985	769
January	1986	46
February	1986	41
March	1986	42
April	1986	60
May	1986	49
June	1986	84

The 1842 bibliographical records contained 2735 subject headings, an average of 1.48 headings per record. This average correlates quite closely with previous findings. For example, O'Neill and Aluri found an average of 1.4 subject headings in a sample of 33,455 catalog records in the OCLC database. However, 18.6%, mostly in the Literature (P) classifications, had no subject heading assigned. They found that records classified in the L (Education) schedule had an average of 1.575 subject headings per record.[18] Markey and Demeyer report that their two experimental catalogs averaged 1.41 and 1.46 subject headings per bibliographic record. By disregarding records with no subject headings, the average increased to 1.8 subject headings per record.[19]

Table 1 shows the pattern of use of the 2735 subject headings selected for this study. To explain this table more fully, the 203 subject headings, whose primary classification designation does not fall within the 370-379 section of the *ABPR* classified bibliography, had 307 uses as secondary subjects within the 370-379 section. No attempt was made to record their use in other sections of the bibliography. In addition, 62 of the 1306 headings with no linked call number in the bibliographic records had an 053 field (the field for the Library of Congress classification number) in the subject authority record; but these subject headings and their related numbers were not used in producing the index. However, if these cases are added to the 1429 headings which have linked classification numbers, a total of 1491, 55%, have a classification number or numbers linked to them. In comparison, about 30% of authority records in the Library of Congress subject authority file have an 053 field.

In order to determine the effect of including additional years in the "database," the next step was to check a stratified random sample of 130 headings, 10% of the 1306 headings used as secondary headings, against the 1980-1984 cumulation of *ABPR*. Only 14, 11%, were used as primary subjects prior to 1984. By interpolation, if the cataloging in the database had extended back to 1980, 143 additional subject headings would have had classification numbers attached to them.

The use of form subdivisions may be another influencing factor in the number of headings with or without corresponding classification numbers. For example, in 1986 the Library of Congress discontinued the use of the subdivisions "Addresses, essays, lectures" and "Yearbooks." In practically all cases, the classification number linked to headings with and without these subdivisions was the same. With the elimination of these form subdivisions, the number of headings without corresponding classification numbers should decrease because the subject heading itself without the form division may have a classification number linked to it.

What can be said about those subject headings in Table 1 which had no classification number linked with them? First, these secondary subjects are much less frequently used than the primary subjects. Primary subjects are used an average of more than two times while secondary subjects are used little more than once. Most are unique headings. Also, of the 116 subject headings in the 130 heading random sample without a linked classification number, 94% were topical headings, 2% geographical headings, and 6% names. This sample may be too small to be statistically significant. For example, Khosh-khui's statistical analysis of the relationship between subject headings and classification numbers on MARC records found that 75% of the subject headings were topical, 13% geographical and 12% names.[20]

The alphabetical and classified indexes (Appendixes A and B) were derived from those subject headings used as primary subjects and from their linked classification numbers. However, whenever a primary subject heading was connected with more than one classification number, it was repeated in the classified index under each

TABLE 1: Number of Subject Headings and Times Used

Pattern of use	Number	Number of Uses
Used as primary subject in 370–379 section of ABPR	1226	2592
Used as primary subject but not in 370-379 section of ABPR	203	307
Used as secondary heading with no linked classification number	1306	1469
TOTAL	2735	4368

number; and these subject headings include multiple classification numbers in the alphabetical index. As stated previously, headings not used as primary subjects were not included in the indexes, even though 62 of them had an 053 field in the subject authority record. Whenever a subject heading in the indexes had such a linked classification number, it was noted in brackets to the right of the heading. Also, the alphabetical index includes no cross-references. This is different from a subject catalog which depends upon cross-references to guide the user to the authorized heading and also to broader, narrower, and related terms. It is also different from the verbal index to the classified catalog. The index to the classification system in a traditional classified catalog does not include cross-references but repeats under each synonym or alternative term the appropriate classification number.

COMMENTS

This study did not have the resources to integrate these indexes into an operational or experimental online catalog. But such an index could be generated automatically from the MARC bibliographic record and thus would require no extra effort on the part of the cataloger; nor would extra fields need to be added to the bibliographic record. In fact, during the course of his research, Khoshkhui created classified lists, arranged both by Dewey and LCC, and alphabetical lists of subject headings from MARC tapes. He states:

> Using the method described in this study, one may generate an index for either LCC or DDC and create a specific alphabetical listing of LC Subject Headings and their equivalent LCC or DDC notations. The effectiveness of such classified lists for both library users and library professionals can be studied.[21]

Also, the present author believes that such indexes would be useful browsing tools. Consider the following scenario, described so vividly by Markey:

Classification has been visible to library users as a device for
shelf arrangement of library materials. Typically, patrons record a call number from the library catalog, search for the
book bearing the recorded number, then browse the book-
shelves for other books similar to the one just found.[22]

Let us analyze for a moment the activity of these hypothetical patrons: are they not, first, attempting to use the catalog itself (often
via a known-item search—a known book on the subject—and/or
subject headings) as an index to the classification scheme and, secondly, using the library shelves as a surrogate for the shelflist?
But would these indexes make the catalog a true classified catalog? The answer is an emphatic no! Not unless all subject headings
were assigned a corresponding classification number. As Wellisch
so bluntly states: "A shelflist does not a classified catalog make."[23]
Thus, in order to make the catalog a true classified catalog, those
1306 secondary subject headings which lacked a classification number linked to them in the bibliographic or authority records would
require an assigned classification number. One of the purposes of
this study was to determine whether the online catalog could function as both a dictionary catalog and a classified catalog without any
further intellectual effort or time on the part of the cataloger. Has
this been demonstrated? The answer again would have to be "no"
because of the need to assign classification numbers to some secondary headings. But all of this is highly speculative. As Holley
states:

> The main stumbling block to using classification in American
> online catalogs is the fact that the online shelf list essentially
> remains a one entry catalog. In many cases, secondary subject
> aspects cannot be indicated through classification, though they
> are brought out by multiple subject headings. Comprehensive
> subject access is not possible through classification, unless
> American libraries redecide in favor of the classified catalog in
> addition to the dictionary catalog. Given the current scarcity of
> resources, I doubt that the providers of cataloging data (princi-
> pally the Library of Congress) will be persuaded to provide
> multiple classification numbers.[24]

Would it be worth the effort? We can only say with Mandel: "We won't know until we try."[25] The conferees at a conference on classification in the online catalog agreed: "While few libraries are clamoring for the added workloads of assigning multiple classification numbers and training patrons to use them, the area is ripe for pilot projects involving specialized collections and applications."[26]

NOTES

1. George Scheerer, "The Subject Catalog Examined," Library Quarterly 27 (July 1957): 198.

2. Most of these are listed in Pauline A. Cochrane, "Modern Subject Access in the Online Age," *American Libraries* 15, no. 5 (May 1984): 338. For a discussion of chain indexing as a list of subject headings and as an index to the Library of Congress classification see John Phillip Immroth, *Analysis of Vocabulary Control in Library of Congress Classification and Subject Headings* (Littleton, Colo.: Libraries Unlimited, 1971).

3. Pauline Atherton, *Books are for Use: Final Report of the Subject Access Project to the Council on Library Resources* (Syracuse, N.Y.: Syracuse University School of Information Studies, 1978.)

4. Karen Markey and Anh N. Demeyer, *Final Report to the Council on Library Resources: Dewey Decimal Classification Online Project"* (Dublin, Ohio, OCLC, 1986)

5. Ibid., p. xxvii.

6. Carol A. Mandel, "Enriching the Library Catalog Records for Subject Access," *Library Resources and Technical Services* 29, no. 1 (Jan./Mar. 1985): 7.

7. Ibid., p. 15.

8. Pauline A. Cochrane, "Modern Subject Access in the Online Age." *American Libraries* 15, no. 5 (May 1984): 337.

9. Carol A. Mandel, *Classification Schedules as Subject Enhancement in Online Catalogs: a Review of a Conference sponsored by Forest Press, the OCLC Online Computer Center, and the Council on Library Resources* (Washington: Council on Library Resources, 1986), p. 11.

10. Pauline A. Cochrane and Karen Markey, "Preparing for the Use of Classification in Online Cataloging Systems and in Online Catalogs," *Information Technology and Libraries* 4, no. 2 (June 1985): 98.

11. Markey and Demeyer, *Final Report*, p. xxxvii.

12. Cochrane and Markey, "Preparing for the Use of Classification," p. 8.

13. Nancy J. Williamson, "The Library of Congress Classification: Problems and Prospects in Online Retrieval," *International Cataloguing* 15, no. 4 (October/Dec. 1986); 46.

14. Hans H. Wellisch, "Letter," *Library resources and Technical Services* 24, no. 4 (Fall 1980): 382.

15. Lois Mai Chan, "Library of Congress Classification as an Online Retrieval Tool: Potentials and Limitations," *Information Technology and Libraries* 5, no. 3 (September 1986); 182.

16. Ibid., p. 186.

17. Library of Congress. Subject Cataloging Division. *Subject Cataloging Manual: Subject Headings*: (Washington: 1985), H 80.

18. Edward T. O'Neill and Rao Aluri "Library of Congress Subject Heading Patterns in OCLC Monographic Records," *Library Resources and Technical Services* 25, no. 1 (Jan.-Mar. 1981): 63-80.

19. Markey and Demeyer, *Final Report*, p. 301.

20. Abolghasem Khosh-khui, "Statistical Analysis of the Association Between Library of Congress Subject Headings and Their Corresponding Class Notations in Main Classes of LCC and DDC" (Ph.D. diss., Indiana University, 1985), p. 128-129.

21. Ibid., p. 234.

22. Karen Markey, "Subject-Searching Experiences and Needs of Online Catalog Users: Implications for Library Classification," *Library Resources and Technical Services* 29, no. 1 (Jan./March 1985): 42-43.

23. Wellisch, "Letter", p. 382.

24. Robert P. Holley, "Classification in the Online Catalog," *Advances in Library Automation and Networking* 1 (1987): 78-79.

25. Mandel, "Enriching the Library Catalog Records," p. 15.

26. Mandel, *Classification Schedules as Subject Enhancement in Online Catalogs*, p. 12.

APPENDIX A:
LIBRARY INDEX LISTING (SORTED BY SUBJECT)

LC5251	ADULT EDUCATION – UNITED STATES
LC5251	ADULT EDUCATION – UNITED STATES – ADDRESSES, ESSAYS, LECTURES
LC5251	ADULT EDUCATION – UNITED STATES – FINANCE
LC5251	ADULT EDUCATION – UNITED STATES – HISTORY
LC5251	ADULT EDUCATION – UNITED STATES – PLANNING
LG718.S643	ADVANCED SCHOOL FOR GIRLS (SOUTH AUSTRALIA)
LC2771	AFRO-AMERICAN CHILDREN – EDUCATION
LC2803.C5	AFRO-AMERICAN CHILDREN – EDUCATION – ILLINOIS – CHICAGO – HISTORY
LC2781.7	AFRO-AMERICAN STUDENT MOVEMENTS
LC2781	AFRO-AMERICAN UNIVERSITIES AND COLLEGES – ADDRESSES, ESSAYS, LECTURES
LC2801	AFRO-AMERICAN WOMEN – EDUCATION (HIGHER) – HISTORY – SOURCES
E185.7	AFRO-AMERICANS – BIOGRAPHY
E185.97	AFRO-AMERICANS – BIOGRAPHY
LC2801	AFRO-AMERICANS – EDUCATION (HIGHER) – UNITED STATES – CASE STUDIES
LC2781	AFRO-AMERICANS – EDUCATION (HIGHER) – (LC2781)
LC2801	AFRO-AMERICANS – EDUCATION (LC2701-2853)
LC2801	AFRO-AMERICANS – EDUCATION – HISTORY – 19TH CENTURY
LC2801	AFRO-AMERICANS – EDUCATION – HSITORY – 20TH CENTURY
LC2803.N5	AFRO-AMERICANS – EDUCATION – NEW YORK (N.Y.)
LC2801	FRO-AMERICANS – EDUCATION – STATISTICS
LC2801	AFRO-AMERICANS – EDUCATION – UNITES STATES – HISTORY
LC5457	AGED – EDUCATION
LB2353.48	AMERICAN COLLEGE TESTING PROGRAM
LB2353.48	AMERICAN COLLEGE TESTING PROGRAM – STUDY GUIDES
LD131.A8	AMERICAN UNIVERSITY (WASINGTON D.C.) – CURRICULA
LA2383.162	AMRIK, SINGH, 1920-
B808.5	ANALYSIS (PHILOSOPHY) (B808.5)
BF39	ANALYSIS OF VARIANCE (QA276)
QA279	ANALYSIS OF VARIANCE (QA276)
QA76.8.A66	APPLE COMPUTER – PROGRAMMING
QA76.8.A66	APPLE II (COMPUTER) – PROGRAMMING
QA135.5	ARITHMETIC – STUDY AND TEACHING (ELEMENTARY)
LD245	ARKANSAS STATE UNIVERSITY – HISTORY
LB1591	ART – STUDY AND TEACHING (ELEMENTARY)
N350	ART – STUDY AND TEACHING (ELEMENTARY)
N362	ART – STUDY AND TEACHING (ELEMENTARY) – UNITED STATES
NX304	ART – STUDY AND TEACHING (ELEMENTARY) – UNITED STATES
LB1140.5.A7	ART – STUDY AND TEACHING (PRESCHOOL)
N361	ART – STUDY AND TEACHING (PRIMARY) – UNITED STATES
RJ496.57	ARTICULATION DISORDERS IN CHILDREN (RJ496.57)
NX303	ARTS – STUDY AND TEACHING – UNITED STATES
LG414.A843	ATHLONE EARLY LEARNING CENTER – HISTORY
BF321	ATTENTION (LB1065)

BF323.C5	ATTITUDE CHANGE
LB1043	AUDIO-VISUAL EDUCATION (LB104.3-1044.9)
LB1043	AUDIO-VISUAL MATERIALS
LC3501.A3	AUSTRALIAN ABORIGINES – EDUCATION – CASE STUDIES
LC4181	AUTISTIC CHILDREN – EDUCATION – UNITED STATES – CONGRESSES
HF5548.5.B3	BASIC (COMPUTER PROGRAM LANGUAGE) (QA76.73.B3)
QA76.73.B3	BASIC(COMPUTER PROGRAM LANGUAGE) (QA76.73.B3)
LC1035.2	BASIC EDUCATION – CURRICULA
LC1035.6	BASIC EDUCATION – UNITED STATES – CONGRESSES
LC1035.6	BASIC EDUCATION – UNITED STATES – CURRICULA
LC1035.6	BASIC EDUCATION – UNITED STATES – CURRICULA – ADDRESSES, ESSAYS, LECTURES
BF637.B4	BEHAVIOR MODIFICATION (BF637.B4)
BF199	BEHAVIORISM (PSYCHOLOGY) (BF199)
LD131.A817	BERENDZEN, RICHARD
LA306.B48	BEVERLY HIGH SCHOOL – HISTORY – 19TH CENTURY
Z1037	BIBLIOGRAPHY – BEST BOOKS – CHILDREN'S LITERATURE (Z1035)
LB2193.N393	BIGELOW, KARL W. (KARL WORTH) – ADDRESSES, ESSAYS, LECTURES
P115	BILIGUALISM (LB1131)
LA2375.G72	BIRLEY, ROBERT, SIR, 1903
LB1139.C7	BLOCK BUILDING/EDUCATION – (LB1139.C7)
GV902.5	BOWLING – JUVENILE LITERATURE
QP385	BRAIN – LOCALIZATION OF FUNCTIONS (QP385)
QP385	BRAIN – LOCALIZATION OF FUNCTIONS – ADDRESSES, ESSAYS, LECTURES
LB1043.58	BULLETIN BOARDS – HANDBOOKS, MANUALS, ETC.
LC214.523.N37	BUSING FOR SCHOOL INTEGRATION – TENNESSEE – NASHVILLE – HISTORY
LB3060.33.C34	CALIFORNIA BASIC EDUCATION SKILLS TESTS – STUDY GUIDES

APPENDIX B:
LIBRARY INDEX LISTING (SORTED BY INDEX)

AG105	HANDBOOKS, VADE-MECUMS, ETC. (AG103-191)
AG106	HANDBOOKS, VADE-MECUMS, ETC. (AG103-191)
AS6	SEMINARS-HANDBOOKS, MANUALS, ETC.
AZ221	LEARNING AND SCHOLARSHIP
AZ346	LEARNING AND SCHOLARSHIP
B105	THOUGHT AND THINKING (BF455)
B105.C45	CHILDREN AND PHILOSOPHY (B105.C45)
B1618	KNOWLEDGE, THEORY OF (BD150-241)
B1649	KNOWLEDGE, THEORY OF (BD150-241)
B171	PHILOSOPHY, ANCIENT (B108-708)
B188	PHILOSOPHY, ANCIENT (B108-708)
B2581	KNOWLEDGE, THEORY OF (BD150-241)
B2778	KNOWLEDGE, THEORY OF (BD150-241)
B2824	KNOWLEDGE, THEORY OF (BD150-241)
B3329	KNOWLEDGE, THEORY OF (BD150-241)
B491	PHILOSOPHY, MEDIEVAL (B720-785)
B505	PHILOSOPHY, ANCIENT (B108-708)
B5134	THOUGHT AND THINKING – ADDRESSES, ESSAYS, LECTURES
B721	PHILOSOPHY, MEDIEVAL (B720-785)
B808.5	ANALYSIS (PHILOSOPHY) (B808.5)
B829.5	PHNOMENOLOGY (B829.5)
BD161	KNOWLEDGE, THEORY OF (BD150-241)
BD161	KNOWLEDGE, THEORY OF – COLLECTED WORKS
BD162	KNOWLEDGE, THEORY OF (BD150-241)
BD331	ONTOLOGY (BD300-444)
BF176	ITEM RESPONSE THEORY
BF176	PSYCHOLOGICAL TESTS (BF176)
BF199	BEHAVIORISM (PSYCHOLOGY) (BF199)
BF1999	SPIRITUAL LIFE (BV4485-4596) (BX2349-2373)
BF295	MOTOR LEARNING
BF311	COGNITION (BF311)
BF321	ATTENTION (LB1065)
BF323.C5	ATTITUDE CHANGE
BF323.E8	EXPECTATION (PSYCHOLOGY)
BF371	MEMORY (BF370-385) (LB1063)
BF39	ANALYSIS OF VARIANCE (QA276)
BF39	EXPERIMENTAL DESIGN
BF39	PSYCHOMETRICS (BF39)
BF408	CREATIVE ABILITY (BF408)
BF411	CREATIVE ABILITY (BF408)
BF431	INTELLIGENCE TESTS (BF431.5)

BF432.5.W42	WECHSLER INTELLIGENCE SCALE FOR CHILDREN (BF432.5.W42)
BF441	PROBLEM SOLVING – STUDY AND TEACHING
BF455	PSYCHOLINGUISTICS (P37)
BF455	THOUGHT AND THINKING (BF455)
BF455	THOUGHT AND THINKING – STUDY AND TEACHING
BF561	EMOTIONS – JUVENILLE LITERATURE
BF575.S75	STRESS(PSYCHOLOGY) (BF575.S75)
BF637	LEADERSHIP (APPLIED PSYCH: BF637.L4) (CHILD PSYCH: BF723.L4) (MILITARY SCIENCE: UB210) (SOCIOLOGY: HM141)
BF637.B4	BEHAVIOR MODIFICATION (BF637.B4)
BF637.L4	LEADERSHIP (APPLIED PSYCH: BF637.L4) (CHILD PSYCH: BF723.L4) (MILITARY SCIENCE: UB210) (SOCIOLOGY: HM141)
BF637.S8	SUCCESS (BJ1611.1618) (BF637.S8)
BF697	SELF PERCEPTION – PROBLEMS, EXERCISES, ETC.
BF717	PLAY
BF721	CHILD PSYCHOLOGY
BF722	PSYCHOLOGICAL TESTS FOR CHILDREN (RJ503.5) (BF722)
BF723.C5	COGNITION IN CHILDREN (BF723.C5)
BF723.M56	ACHIEVEMENT MOTIVATION IN CHILDREN (BF723.M56)
BF723.M6	MOTOR ABILITY IN CHILDREN (BF723.M6)
BF76.5	PSYCHOLOGY – RESEARCH
BF76.6.S56	SINGLE SUBJECT RESEARCH
BJ1031	VALUES – ADDRESSES, ESSAYS, LECTURES
BJ1243	CHRISTIAN ETHICS – ADDRESSES, ESSAYS, LECTURES
BJ1251	CHRISTIAN ETHICS – ADDRESSES, ESSAYS, LECTURES
BJ1611	SUCCESS (BJ1611.1618) (BF637.S8)
BL1900	LEADERSHIP (APPLIED PSYCH: BF637.L4) (CHILD PSYCH: BF723.L4) (MILITARY SCIENCE: UB210) (SOCIOLOGY: HM141)
BL42.5.U5	RELIGIOUS EDUCATION – UNITED STATES
BL624	SPIRITUAL LIFE (BV4485-4596) (BX2349 – 2373)
BM103	JEWISH RELIGIOUS SCHOOLS – UNITED STATES – ADDRESSES, ESSAYS, LECTURES (377.96)
BP189	SUFISM (BP189)
BP2555	SPIRITUAL LIFE (BV4485-4596)(BX2349 – 2373)
BP605	SPIRITUAL LIFE (BV4485-4596) (BX2349-2373)
BP610	SPIRITUAL LIFE (BV4485-4596) (BX2349-2373)
BR516	CHURCH AND STATE – UNITED STATES
BS1830	SPITIRUAL LIFE (BV4485-4596) (BX2349-2373)
BS391	SPIRITUAL LIFE (BV4485-4596) (BX2349-2373)
BT590	SPIRITUAL LIFE (BV4485-4596) (BX2349-2373)
BV1464	CHRISTIAN EDUCATION – PHILOSOPHY
BV1467	CHRISTIAN EDUCATION – UNITED STATES
BV1470.3.H66	HONG WOO JUN, 1927-
BV1471.2	CHRISTIAN EDUCATION
BV4501	SPIRITUAL LIFE (BV4485-4596) (BX2349-2373)
BX6191	SEVENTH-DAY ADVENTISTS – UNITED STATES – BIOGRAPHY
DA125.A1	RACISM-GREAT BRITAIN
DD253	NATIONAL SOCIALISM (DD253)

DD256	NATIONAL SOCIALISM (DD253)
DS422.C3	CASTE – INDIA
E158	UNITED STATES – DESCRIPTION AND TRAVEL – 1981 – GUIDEBOOKS
E165	UNITED STATES – DESCRIPTION AND TRAVEL – 1981 – GUIDEBOOKS
E184	UNITED STATES – RACE RELATIONS (E184-185.98)
E184.A1	UNITED STATES – RACE RELATIONS (E184-185.98)
E185	UNITED STATES – RACE RELATIONS (E194-185.98)
E185.7	AFRO-AMERICANS – BIBLIOGRAPHY
E185.97	AFRO-AMERICANS – BIOGRAPHY
E185.97.W4	WASHINGTON, BOOKER T. 1856-1915
E270.A1	UNITED STATES – HISTORY – REVOLUTION, 1775-1783 – EDUCATION AND THE REVOLUTION
E449	SLAVERY – UNITED STATES – ANTI-SLAVERY MOVEMENTS
F334.T96	TUSKEGEE INSTITUTE (ALA.)
F73.9.A1	DIVER FAMILY
GN345	ETHNOLOGY – METHODOLOGY

Implementing NOTIS
Keyword/Boolean Searching:
A Case Study

Randy J. Olsen
John O. Christensen
Kal A. Larsen
Kayla Willey

INTRODUCTION

In his 1970 landmark work, Alvin Toffler described a condition he termed "future shock" that occurs when an individual experiences "too much change in too short a period of time."[1] Manifestations of future shock were described as stress and bewilderment. Decrying the uncontrolled rate of change in our world today, Toffler singled out technology as the engine of that change and knowledge as its fuel.[2]

As a cure for future shock, Toffler called not for a halt to change but for its control through innovative social planning and management of technology. He challenged tomorrow's educational system to prepare students to adapt more readily to a rapidly changing world. From his perspective, instead of being required to memorize facts, students should be taught ways to manipulate information in response to their evolving environment.

If Toffler's analysis is correct, then libraries should plan an increasingly central role in the education system of the future. As the institution charged to collect, store, organize, and provide access to

Randy J. Olsen is Assistant University Librarian for Collection Development; John O. Christensen is General Science Librarian; Kal A. Larsen is Systems Analyst; and Kayla Willey is Computer Applications Librarian at the Harold B. Lee Library, Brigham Young University, Provo, UT 84602.

125

information, libraries are a crucial resource for students forced to sift through burgeoning amounts of data for knowledge relevant to their individual pursuits.

However, precisely because libraries are the storehouse for knowledge, Toffler's volatile fuel for change, they may themselves become victims of future shock. As they struggle to manage a deluge of new knowledge, they will constantly pursue the latest technologies for information storage, transfer, and retrieval. This pursuit could deteriorate into cycles of desperate response to waves of technological innovation. The result—future shock for libraries and librarians alike.

While we do not believe this scenario represents the inescapable fate of libraries, we do see signs of future shock in our profession today. Witness alone the swallowing up of reference services by CD-ROM products, the ongoing search by the Research Libraries Group and OCLC for software equal to their databases, and the number of articles on stress in library literature. Closer to home, it appears to us at Brigham Young University (BYU) that we have been exposed to, if not infected by, future shock as we moved into the realm of the integrated library system.

To illustrate our point, we will describe BYU's implementation of NOTIS keyword software and analyze a survey of student response to keyword searching. Because BYU was one of the first libraries to acquire the NOTIS software, our experience should provide useful information for other institutions interested in adding keyword searching capabilities. But beyond this, we hope this article will encourage library decision makers to consider more carefully why, when, and how they adopt new technology. For, as noted by Toffler, if we are to avoid future shock we must control the rate of change in our libraries.

BACKGROUND OF BYU'S ACQUISITION
OF KEYWORD SEARCHING

In 1984, after an exhaustive search for an integrated library system (ILS), BYU selected NOTIS, then marketed by Northwestern University. The decision was based primarily on the quality of the online catalog but also on vendor plans for future software development. In the purchase negotiations, BYU insisted that a schedule for software developments be appended to the contract and that a keyword search module be listed among the required enhancements.

BYU considered keyword searching an essential element of an effective online catalog. With expanded indexing capabilities, with the lack of dependency on controlled vocabulary, and with the use of boolean logic, keyword searching appeared to overcome many of the criticisms of online catalogs.[3] Experience with keyword searching on RLIN and on Dialog databases reinforced this perception.

BYU continued pressure on NOTIS Systems Inc. to supply keyword searching with the result that early in 1987 BYU was invited to serve as a beta test site for a pre-release version of the new software. The invitation was enthusiastically accepted, but because of BYU's three years worth of experience in implementing NOTIS releases, there was also a perceptible atmosphere of caution in some areas of the library. More than one librarian expressed feelings such as "Why can't we wait until we've got the rest of the system down pat before we add something new?"

Partially in response to these concerns, there was a conscious effort to anticipate problems that might arise during implementation of the new software. Automation staff investigated CPU requirements while public service librarians planned for advanced training of reference personnel. No systematic keyword searching training for patrons was established, however, because none was available from the vendor and because none had been developed or considered necessary for the basic online catalog.

From November through December 1987, the new keyword searching module was loaded and tested.[4] Training for library staff calmed initial misgivings about adding new ILS software. In January 1988, keyword searching was opened to the public with little fanfare for reasons that will be explained later. At the point of implementation, expectations for the new software were high.

SOFTWARE AND HARDWARE IMPLEMENTATION

Our local system hardware is an IBM 4341, a midsize computer compared to those now operating NOTIS software. Purchased in August 1984, the IBM was expected to provide adequate CPU capacity for at least five years. At the time of its purchase, however, our systems analyst observed that the useful life of the computer could not be accurately projected, since it would depend on the nature of the demands placed on the hardware. He cautioned that, without careful control, the computer's capacity could easily be exhausted much earlier.

Most of the terminals for the NOTIS ILS were dedicated to technical services functions, but more than 50 terminals were provided for public use. A campus network provided access from faculty offices and student housing; dial-up ports were installed for off-campus users.

Before keyword software was installed, the NOTIS online catalog, circulation, and acquisition modules had been successfully implemented. The acquisitions module had been enhanced to provide superior accounting functions; several other "patches" had been applied to customize NOTIS features. While the number of "patches" had complicated loading of NOTIS releases, the ILS was functioning smoothly with crisp response time in all areas.

Advance information about the keyword searching module warned automation staff that an additional disk drive would be required to index BYU's 650,000 records. Early software concerns centered on developing four new help screens for patrons, on establishing a stop word list, and on determining which MARC fields to index. After an initial conservative stance, we decided to maximize search capabilities by adopting the brief stop word list provided by NOTIS Inc. and by indexing every field in the MARC record. These preparations for keyword searching taxed neither the library's financial nor staff resources, since an adequate budget was available and a governing committee had already been established for the ILS.

In preparation for public use of the new software, we ran a test to determine the effect of keyword searching on system performance. Pre-designed keyword searches, varying from simple to complex, were entered while measuring CPU consumption and terminal response time. BYU increased the number of individuals simultaneously performing the searches from ten to fifteen, twenty and finally twenty-five. At the level of only twenty people, our system had already reached well over 80 percent of its CPU capacity; and intense input/output activity occurred. Response time of up to five minutes was recorded for complex searches. Adding more searchers did not seem to materially affect CPU usage but further degraded response time.[5]

Results of the performance test were disappointing, since it had been our intention to offer keyword searching on every public terminal. Given the system's response, however, it was obvious that no more than twenty keyword searching terminals could be operated during typical system load. Overall system response was considered acceptable only as long as circulation transactions and author, title, and subject searches could be completed in three seconds or less. More than twenty keyword searching terminals would make that standard unattainable. After some debate, thirteen keyword searching terminals were allocated for public access and seven for technical services.

The limitation placed on keyword searching almost immediately set in motion library planning to acquire a larger computer. The restriction on terminal access to keyword searching was viewed as a partial ILS failure. The failure was caused by the fact that software development outstripped hardware support; or, more accurately, software requirements exceeded library predictions for the future. It took only three and a half years to consume the computer's capacity and thereby to force the library to enter into another round of capital funding requests with the university.

We view the organizational stresses that accompanied this experience as evidence of future shock in our library. Service objectives failed to be realized because the rate of technological change in our ILS exceeded our ability to cope with it. All the ramifications of this experience are not yet clear, but at the very least funding now required for a new computer could have been devoted to achieving other library goals.

USER SURVEY

To further ensure that demand for keyword searching would not overburden our ILS, it was decided not to announce the new search capability to the university community. Nevertheless, keyword searching became at best a poorly kept secret among library users. The NOTIS search menu immediately reflected the keyword option, and librarians discreetly spread word of keyword searching availability through their bibliographic instruction lectures, keyword searching terminals had bright yellow stickers affixed to their monitors with the word "Keyword" in bold black type.

Even with such minimal publicity measures, within four months, an average of 360 keyword searches were performed daily. At that level of usage, the keyword software functioned successfully; and the other ILS modules continued to perform at acceptable levels. We lacked data, however, on user acceptance of and satisfaction with keyword searching. To investigate these questions, a user survey was developed to gather information in five areas: (1) user awareness of keyword searching, (2) student use of search modes, (3) student understanding of and preference for search modes, (4) user satisfaction with keyword searching compared to subject searching, and (5) the need for subject and keyword searching training.

The survey was administered to both students and faculty who sat at keyword searching terminals. One hundred ninety-one survey instruments were gathered over a two-week period through a stratified sampling of all keyword searching terminals, hours, and days of the week. Because only those who used keyword searching terminals were sampled, the target population of the survey was the keyword searching user rather than all users of the NOTIS online catalog.

The numbers of undergraduate and graduate students represented in the survey were roughly proportional to those populations at the university. However, as explained below, the few faculty responses did not yield information relevant to the objectives of the survey. Meaningful analysis of faculty response to keyword searching was therefore not possible.

User Awareness

Of those surveyed, 127 (66 percent) were aware of keyword searching (see Table 1). Questionnaires from this group supplied the data for analysis of user response to keyword software.

Of those who knew of keyword searching, the majority, 60 percent, had become aware of the option through the NOTIS screens. Another 27 percent had learned of keyword searching through bibliographic instruction. Very few, however, had been referred by reference librarians; this suggested that public service employees either were not yet comfortable with keyword searching as a research tool or discounted its value. However, it might also have

Table 1. Survey Response

Category	Aware of Keyword		Unaware of Keyword		Total
	Number	Percent	Number	Percent	
Freshmen	27	14%	10	5%	37
Sophomores	29	15%	12	6%	41
Juniors	29	15%	11	6%	40
Seniors	30	16%	20	10%	50
Graduate	11	6%	6	3%	17
Faculty	1	1%	5	3%	6
Totals	127	66%	64	34%	191

been that few individuals in our sample sought assistance from librarians.

Because only one of the six faculty surveyed was aware of the new software, the sample was considered too small to analyze faculty response to keyword searching. However, the low level of awareness suggested that faculty, with their more established and traditional research methods, may be the last group to become aware of innovations in online catalogs. If this is true, publicity campaigns and orientation efforts should target faculty audiences.

Keyword Utilization Compared to Other Search Modes

We asked respondents to estimate the percentage of author, title, and subject searches they performed before the introduction of keyword. As Table 2 shows, respondents heavily favored subject searching with an estimate that 62 percent of their searches fell into this category. These results paralleled the findings of several other catalog use studies, but indicated higher preference for subject access than had been found in other research.[6]

When asked to estimate the percentage distribution after adding keyword, respondents placed subject searching at 43 percent of their searches, keyword at 27 percent, author at 16 percent, and title at 14 percent. It must be remembered, however, that these estimates were provided only by users of keyword searching and therefore understate the actual use of author, title, and subject searching among the general population. Nevertheless, the results tend to val-

Table 2. Online Catalog Searching

Method of Searching	Prior to Keyword	After Addition of Keyword	Change in Percent of Total Searches
Author	19%	15%	4%
Title	18%	14%	4%
Subject	62%	43%	19%
Keyword	-	27%	-

idate BYU's initial assumption that keyword searching would become an essential element of the NOTIS online catalog. The survey also suggested that the greatest absolute shift in preference for search mode will occur between subject and keyword access.[7]

Student Understanding of and Preference for Search Modes

We hypothesized that user preference and satisfaction would be related to the user's ability to apply search methodologies effectively. For controlled vocabulary subject searching, we felt it was crucial that users be aware of and make use of the Library of Congress subject headings. When questioned about the Library of Congress guides, 74 of 128 (58 percent) indicated that they used the headings; 33 (26 percent) indicated they did not use them; and 17 (13 percent) stated that they did not know what Library of Congress subject headings were. In total, over 40 percent of those surveyed did not use Library of Congress subject headings when doing subject searches.

These findings agreed with earlier studies on patron use of Library of Congress subject headings.[8] Still, we found the results alarming, since subject searching was the most frequently used form of catalog inquiry by survey participants. From another perspective, however, the response suggested that alternative search methodologies should be provided for students who cannot use subject searching effectively. Keyword searching could be such an alternative.

To investigate how effectively respondents used keyword searching, we assumed that any student could enter a basic search but might have difficulty with NOTIS software's three specialized fea-

tures: (1) truncation, (2) boolean operators, and (3) field qualifiers.[9]
These special features are used to expand or to limit searches for
effective and efficient information retrieval. With many searches, if
special features are not employed, too few, too many, or extraneous
records will be retrieved.

When questioned about specialized features, 52 to 58 percent of
those surveyed used truncation, but the percentages who used boolean operators and field qualifiers were much smaller (see Table 3).
Far fewer survey participants used boolean operators and field qualifiers than made use of Library of Congress subject headings. This
finding cast doubt on whether keyword searching was in fact an
effective alternative to subject searching for many of those students.

We further explored whether keyword searching provided students with an effective alternative to subject searching by asking
survey participants if they were more or less likely to find relevant
library materials using keyword searching. Over 50 percent of those
surveyed felt that keyword searching offered superior retrieval capabilities, while another 28 percent felt that keyword and subject
searching offered about the same level of results (see Table 4). Only
about 19 percent of the respondents felt they were more likely to
retrieve library materials using subject searching.

In reality, of course, neither subject nor keyword searching is
more effective in retrieving relevant materials in all cases. For one
research question, the existence of appropriate Library of Congress
subject headings might dictate use of subject searching, while for
another inquiry it might be necessary to link keywords with boolean
operators to develop an effective search strategy. Nevertheless, response to the survey indicated that at least in the experience of

Table 3. Special Features on NOTIS Searching

Search Feature	Aware Of		Understand		Use	
	Number	%	Number	%	Number	%
Truncation	73	57%	74	58%	66	52%
Boolean Operators	41	32%	40	31%	31	24%
Field Qualifiers	35	28%	32	25%	25	20%
None	45	35%	43	34%	50	39%

Table 4. Likelihood of Finding Relevant Materials

With Keyword Searching

	No.	Percent
Much More Likely	18	15%
More Likely	50	41%
About the Same	36	29%
Less Likely	17	14%
Much Less Likely	1	1%

participants, keyword searching was as effective as or more effective than subject searching in meeting their needs.

Response Time and User Satisfaction

On the basis of our early performance, tests of keyword software, we assumed that user satisfaction with the new search mode would be related to response time. To confirm this assumption, we asked respondents to estimate the average response time for both keyword and subject searching and then to indicate whether they found those response times discouraging or encouraging. Table 5 reveals a somewhat surprising result.

Fifty-six percent of those surveyed estimated keyword response time to be 30 seconds or less. From our experience, actual response time was probably much slower for many of the participants. The students surveyed also indicated that keyword response time was either encouraging or of little or no consideration in their use of that search mode (see Table 6). We assumed that the unexpectedly positive evaluation of keyword response time reflected student satisfaction with search results. Participants were so pleased with the results of keyword searching that they were willing to overlook response time.

Survey participants accurately gauged the faster response time of subject searching and viewed it more positively than keyword. In general, however, it appeared that response time simply was not a factor or that it actually encouraged use of keyword searching as well as subject searching.

Next, we asked users how often they planned to use keyword searching in the future (see Table 7). The majority answered "frequently." The next highest response was "only when necessary."

Table 5. Response Time of Keyword Search

Time	Subject		Keyword	
	Number	Percent	Number	Percent
0-5 seconds	73	57%	12	5%
5-30 seconds	42	33%	63	51%
30 seconds to 1 minute	6	5%	19	15%
1-3 minutes	2	2%	8	7%
3 minutes or more	0	0%	0	0%
no opinion	4	3%	22	18%
no response	1	1%	4	3%

Table 6. Effect of Response Time on Use of Searching

Effect	Subject Searching		Keyword Searching	
	Number	Percent	Number	Percent
Very Discouraging	1	1%	0	0%
Discouraging	4	3%	14	11%
Of Little or No Consideration	59	46%	88	69%
Encouraging	46	36%	20	16%
Very Encouraging	17	13%	2	2%
No Response	1	1%	4	3%

Since keyword searching consumes machine resources, the best answer from the library's perspective would be "only when necessary." The selection of "frequently" was a source of concern and suggested that training should show students the instances when keyword searching is appropriate.

When questioned about how keyword searching affects their satisfaction with library services, respondents expressed overwhelmingly positive impressions of keyword searching (see Table 8). Sixty-seven percent of the users indicated that keyword searching had increased or greatly increased their satisfaction with the library services. No respondents indicated that keyword searching had negatively affected their satisfaction with library services.

Perceptions of Training Needs

Since at the time of the survey the major source of training available to most of the university community was through online help screens, we asked if respondents had used these screens. For both keyword and subject searching, a little less than 50 percent indicated that they had used the online instruction. This suggested that

Table 7. Planned Future Use of Keyword Searching

Future Use	Number	Percent
Not at all	2	2%
Only when necessary	44	35%
Frequently	66	52%
Almost every search	15	12%
No Response	1	1%

Table 8. Effect of Keyword Searching on Satisfaction

With Library Services

Effect of Keyword	Number	Percent
Greatly Decreased Satisfaction	0	0%
Decreased Satisfaction	0	0%
No Change in Satisfaction	40	31%
Increased Satisfaction	72	57%
Greatly Increased Satisfaction	13	10%
No Response	3	2%

either the NOTIS online catalog is so user friendly that many patrons require no instruction or that many users either cannot make or have not made use of the help screens.

The survey next questioned whether users felt that additional training should be provided for subject and keyword searching. The responses revealed a marked difference of opinion relative to the two search modes. Nearly 70 percent of those answering the survey felt that no additional training was needed for subject searching, while about the same percentage felt that training for keyword searching was necessary. These responses suggested that online help screens can provide adequate instruction for subject searching but not for keyword searching. They also may explain why so few respondents had used the special features, such as boolean operators, available on keyword searching.

We believe that student opinion of training needs may have been influenced by their previous searching experience. Most of the students surveyed would have had substantial experience with subject searching in both the card catalog and the online catalog. They might, therefore, have perceived that they needed no additional training, even if they could not perform effective searches. By contrast, at the time of the survey students would have had no more than three months experience with keyword software and would have been more predisposed to accept training for a new search methodology.

When the students surveyed were asked to rank their preferences for training methods, they overwhelmingly favored self-training methods over small-group methods or in-class instruction (see Table 9).

Survey Implications

We found the results of our survey disconcerting for three reasons. First, the objective of adding keyword searching to our online catalog was to improve collection access for our faculty and students. Keyword software was viewed as a sophisticated information retrieval tool that would assist in research at all levels in the university. The survey suggested, however, that faculty were largely unaware of keyword software and that students could use the new search mode only at its most elemental level. Therefore, our objective in acquiring keyword software was not fully realized.

Second, we had deliberately restricted use of keyword searching because of fears about CPU consumption and response time. But our survey indicated that student attitudes, at least, were not as strongly affected by response time as we had anticipated. We have placed stronger limitations on keyword searching than were necessary.

Third, we had expended a great deal of effort to improve NOTIS help screens on the assumption that they would be widely used and would provide adequate training for many users. The survey suggested that many students do not rely on help screens and that they need more training than we had anticipated. And although students

Table 9.   Training Methods Preferred

Method	Rank (1 = most preferred)				
	1	2	3	4	5
Small group sessions	13	10	19	25	24
Terminal help screens	56	18	13	11	5
Self instruction pamphlets	28	36	18	10	7
In-class lecture	7	7	10	25	40
Computer aided self-instruction	23	21	31	15	10

indicated that they preferred self-instructional training methods to more controlled learning environments like classroom lecture, self-instruction methods had not yet proven successful.

Despite this, keyword searching has been well received by students and has increased their satisfaction with the library. It appears that even if student use of keyword searching techniques is somewhat ineffective, keyword searching has provided an alternative to subject searching for many of the survey's participants. Many students indicated that they need additional training for keyword searching, so some are motivated to participate in whatever additional training the library eventually offers.

CONCLUSION

BYU's experience with keyword software is neither a total success nor a failure, but it does illustrate some of the problems libraries experience in managing technological change. By adopting keyword software at the earliest possible moment, BYU made available to its students and faculty the most advanced information retrieval technology. Because software demands exceeded hardware capabilities, however, access to the new research tool had to be restricted.

Librarians received excellent keyword searching training; this relieved their anxiety concerning the new search mode. Little instruction was developed for public users, however, by either the library or the software vendor. Availability of the new search methodology benefited students, but lack of training prevented them from taking advantage of its most powerful applications.

BYU will soon acquire a larger computer; and well designed keyword searching training will be developed for students and faculty. Use of keyword software will then begin to reach its potential, and the library will move closer to meeting Toffler's challenge for educational institutions. Keyword software will allow students and scholars to sift more effectively through mountains of accumulated knowledge. A cloud remains on this futuristic horizon: Will the library by that time be in the process of loading Medline or ERIC or some other database that will once again transform a powerful computer into an antique and leave bewildered library patrons in a state of future shock?

NOTES

1. Alvin Toffler. *Future Shock*. New York, Random House, 1970, p. 4.

2. Ibid, pp 29-30.

3. For discussion of problems with online public access catalogs see James R. Dwyer, "The Road to Access & the Road to Entropy," *Library Journal*, 112, no. 14 (Sept. 1, 1987): 131-36; Mary Noel Gouke and Sue Pease, "Title Searches in an Online Catalog and a Card Catalog: A Comparative Study of Patron Success in Two Libraries, *Journal of Academic Librarianship*, 8, no. 3 (July 1982): 137-43; Karen Markey, " Thus Spake the OPAC User," *Information Technology and Libraries*, 2, no. 4 (December 1984): 381-87; Carole Weiss Moore, "Under Reactions to Online Catalogs: An Exploratory Study," *College and Research Libraries*, 42, no. 4 (July 1981): 295-302; Chih Wang, "The Online Catalogue, Subject Access and User Reactions: A Review," *Library Review*, 34 (autumn 1985): 143-51.

4. The staff of NOTIS Inc. were extremely helpful in assisting BYU to lead and test its pre-release version of keyword/boolean software. Several software modifications were made during implementation to improve system performance. Nothing reported in this article concerning BYU's negative experiences with keyword searching should be construed as criticism of NOTIS Inc. or its products.

5. Hardware environment greatly affects response time and the necessity to limit keyword/boolean searching to only designated terminals. Notre Dame University and The National Geographic Society reported in Session 14 of the 1988 Notis Users Group meeting quicker average response times (10 seconds or under) than those generally experienced at Brigham Young University. One of the libraries reported that keyword/boolean searching was available on all terminals. When compared, Brigham Young University is operating on a smaller computer with a larger database than the other libraries. As reported in the *NOTIS User Profiles*, Notre Dame is using an IBM 4381 on an MVS operating system. Notre Dame reported a database of 785,000 records with 136 terminals. The National Geographic Society is using an IBM 3083 on an MVS operating system. They reported a database of 520,000 records with 150 terminals. Brigham Young University is using an IBM 4341/Group 2 computer on a VSE operating system. Brigham Young University has 1,000,000 records in the database and 250 terminals.

6. For other studies on frequency of access by author, title, and subject see Carolyn O. Frost, "Subject Searching in an Online Catalog, *Information Technology and Libraries*, 6 (March 1987): 60-63; Malcolm Getz, "Some Benefits of the Online Catalog," *College and Research Libraries*, 48, no. 3 (May 1987): 224-40; Neal K. Kaske, "The Variability and Intensity over Time of Subject Searching in an Online Public Access Catalog," *Information Technology and Libraries*, 7, no. 3 (Sept. 1988): 273-88; Carol Weiss Moore, "User Reactions to Online Catalogs: An Exploratory Study," *College and Research Libraries*, 42, no. 4 (July 1981): 295-316.

7. Statistics for actual use of the NOTIS system at BYU from April to August

1988 have placed actual subject searching at 44 percent, author searching at 25 percent, title searching at 26 percent, and keyword searching at 5 percent.

8. Reports of patron use of LC subject headings are found in Marcia Bates, "Factors Affecting Subject Catalog Search Success," *Journal of the American Society for Information Science*, 28, no. 3 (May 1977): 161-68; Carolyn O. Frost, "Searching in an Online Catalog," *Information Technology and Libraries*, 6 (March 1987): 60-63.

9. When incomplete search terms are entered in NOTIS author, title, or subject searching, the system defaults to truncation. In keyword searching, however, explicit rules and symbols must be used to truncate search terms.

Subject Access
in a Bilingual Online Catalogue

Paule Rolland-Thomas
Gérard Mercure

SUMMARY. Canadian library records, bilingual by statute, are created according to a common set of rules and standards. Subject access to the catalogue remains language dependent. Even searches by classification in some OPACs rely first on an alphabetical index as an entering key. Fully bilingual OPACs with authority control and reciprocal references in one file have yet to appear. Thus far the Canadian Workplace Automation Research Center has produced ISIR/SIRI with an online bilingual thesaurus. The National Library of Canada has developed within DOBIS a bilingual system providing automatic linkages between records and authority files. But true bilingual searching (a search in one language retrieving records in both languages) could be achieved by a built-in automatic translation module. Total accommodation of diacritical marks by terminal keyboards and display monitors is also a challenge to be met.

The literature on subject access in online catalogues is both voluminous and impressive. However, there is very little evidence of ongoing research and writing on subject access in bilingual catalogues save one article on multilingual catalogues.[1] We have therefore set out to investigate if such a catalogue is feasible online or otherwise within the unique Canadian library environment.

Canada is by federal law a bilingual country: English and French. This means that all services from the federal government must be

Paule Rolland-Thomas is Professor and Gérard Mercure is Associate Professor at the Ecole de bibliothéconomie et sciences de l'information, Université de Montréal, Montréal (Québec) Canada. The authors wish to acknowledge the gracious help of Ms. Monique Renaud, Chief, French Subject Analysis Division, National Library of Canada.

provided in both French and English all across the country. Services provided by provincial, territorial, or municipal governments conform to the tradition and legislation within their jurisdictions.

It must be stressed that, although French-speaking Canadians live in all provinces, they are mostly concentrated in the province of Québec, eastern Ontario, and in northern and eastern New Brunswick. In these provinces, some library and information services are provided entirely in French by public, school, academic, and special libraries. The government of Québec libraries, namely the Bibliothèque nationale du Québec, the library of the Assemblée législative (parliamentary library) and other government departemental libraries, "work in French." The users of these libraries expect to be served in French for all library functions whether it be the reference interview or the language used in the catalogue.

FRENCH, ENGLISH, AND BILINGUAL CATALOGUING

French language catalogues in Canada are constructed according to the French version of *AACR-II* (*Règles de catalogage angloaméricaines*, 2e edition),[2] use the Dewey or the *Library of Congress Classification*, and the *Répertoire de vedettes-matière*.[3] Tagging is done according to the Canadian MARC formats.[4] A French bibliographic record, regardless of the language of the item in hand, appears in many respects identical to an English library record except for the physical description area, for notes written by the cataloguer, and for subject headings. The choice and form of access points follow the provisions of *RCAA2*, and authorities are drawn accordingly.

English language cataloguing in Canada differs slightly from American practice. The *Library of Congress Subject Headings* are supplemented by *Canadian Subject Headings*[5] which, as stated by Barrie Burns, "reflect differences from the American list due to historical, social, and political patterns unique to the Canadian experience."[6]

Bilingual cataloguing is the speciality *par excellence* of the National Library of Canada. Burns has thoroughly described the policies and practices of Canada's national library whose mission is to serve Canadians in the two official languages of the country.

Hence, the cataloguing of French items is done in French; and the cataloguing of everything else is done in English. Bilingual items are treated in separate records.[7] Although Burn's paper was written a decade ago, very little has changed in terms of cataloguing tools, save for new editions.

CLASSIFICATION AS A SEARCH TOOL

A subject search whether using title words, subject headings, or classification is a most challenging and exacting undertaking, even in an unilingual online catalogue.

The use of the Dewey Decimal Classification for subject searches has been thoroughly investigated by Markey and Demeyer.[8] The conclusions drawn from the investigators state that the

> DDC enhances subject access to libraries' bibliographic re-
> cords. It also provides new and fruitful subject searching capa-
> bilities that are not possible through the alphabetical and key-
> word searching permitted by existing online catalogues. The
> DDC also enhances the display of subject-rich information in
> bibliographic records and in displays of the bookshelf areas
> where retrieved items in online searches are located.[9]

One has to take heed of the fact that access to the classification is done through the alphabetical index to the schedules; this index is quite obviously in English. A French index would access the classification in a French catalogue. This is one reason why we take exception with Paula Goossens when she writes that "a subject classification notation is composed of an alpha-numeric character string which is language independent. Thus the conclusion is straightforward: no language problems occur."[10] Moreover, Markey's conclusions cannot be generalized until more research is conducted with other classification schemes.

The ongoing research conducted by Nancy Williamson on Library of Congress Classification should yield interesting results.[11] It must be stressed that Library of Congress is not a minute classification in *sensu stricto*; hierarchies stop short and give way to an alphabetical order of names of places and things. These cutterized listings are devised in English. If such listings are entered in a French online catalogue where Library of Congress classification is used for subject searching, one can wonder if material dealing with "Spain" and "Espagne," with "silver" and "argent," will be classified and/or retrieved together. In our view, the French cataloger has two alternatives: either he/she preserves the integrity of Library of Congress call numbers by expanding the A-Z instructions in English or translates all alphabetical listings into French in order to avoid scattering subjects.

At first glance, classification notations would solve the problem of subject searches in a bilingual or multilingual online catalogue. But keys to the classification cannot be expressed by any other means than natural languages.

VERBAL SUBJECT ACCESS

The Répertoire de vedettes-matière is a French translation of *Library of Congress Subject Headings* by librarians at the Université Laval (Québec city) in 1962. Since then, the National Library of Canada, the Bibliothèque nationale du Québec, and the libraries of the Université de Montréal have joined together to expand and update the list. The last volume of the *Répertoire* lists Library of Congress headings along with their French equivalents and French headings with the Library of Congress equivalents. Many of the headings, however, do not match on a one-to-one basis; e.g., COLLEGE TEACHING yields two different French subject headings: ENSEIGNEMENT COLLEGIAL and ENSEIGNEMENT UNIVERSITAIRE; WOMEN – EMPLOYMENT equals TRAVAILLEUSES and FEMME – TRAVAIL.

Input into the DOBIS database truly reflects the bilingual concern of the National Library of Canada as illustrated in the following subject analysis reports for *Canadiana*, Canada's national bibliography (cf. Figures 1, 1A, 2, 2A).

But it is beyond the scope of this paper to untangle the subtleties of pairing subject headings in two different languages.

Since personal, corporate, and geographical names as well as uniform titles qualify as *bona fide* subjects, a few remarks are appropriate concerning accepted forms for such names and titles when using *RCAA2*.

Concerning all authorized translations, *AACR-II* rule 0.12 states "that users of the rules who do not use English as their working language will replace the specified preference for English by a preference for their working language." Furthermore, rule 0.13 allows translations of the code to use other transliteration tables than those adopted by most English speaking countries, namely the American Library Association/Library of Congress romanization tables. Consequently, *RCAA2* examples are written conforming to ISO (International Standards Organization) tables.

The differences on account of preferred language are evident in Part II of the code. In many cases, applying *RCAA2* will yield forms of headings different than those derived from *AACR-II*. The following examples illustrate this point: *RCAA2*, rule 22.383: the authorized form is "Pape Jean XXIII," not "Pope John XXIII"; geographical names are rendered in French when applying *RCAA2* rule 23.2 A; thus "Autriche" not "Austria."

In many instances, corporate names yield opposite results: the authorized form resulting from the application of *AACR-II* rule 24.3 A is "Canadian Committee on Cataloguing"; the French name for this corporate body, "Comité canadien de catalogage" is a *see from* reference. The application of *RCAA2* rule 24.3 A would yield the following: the authorized form is "Comité canadien de catalogage"; "Canadian Committee on Cataloguing" is a *see from* reference. One can easily acknowledge how English and French authority files differ (cf. Figures 3, 3A, 4, 4A, 5, 5A).

SOME CRITERIA TO BE MET BY A BILINGUAL OPAC

Strictly speaking, bilingual or multilingual OPACs have yet to appear. As stated by Paula Goosens: "Multinational OPAC's do not yet exist, although on a smaller scale some multiregional OPAC's are operational or under development."[12] Neither are bilingual OPACs numerous. Quite a number of OPACs, however, offer multilingual log-on procedures which then provide database menu displays, commands, and messages in the language selected by the user.

In order that an OPAC be considered bilingual, it must allow the user to search in the language of his/her choosing. The authority control with reciprocal references must be available in the same file. The ideal situation would include one bilingual subject headings list or thesaurus for searching in either language with retrieval under subject headings or terms used both in the "other" language or in the language used for searching. The least that can be expected is multilingual authority files which include equivalent forms from one language to the others. Moreover, searching in any language must allow retrieval of the whole collection and not be limited to items matching the language of the search.

TWO BILINGUAL ONLINE CATALOGUES

Due to the official bilingual status of Canada, one might expect to find numerous bilingual OPACs. But we have encountered only two: the Canadian Workplace Automation Research Center ISIR/SIRI catalogue, which is closer to a specialized database, partially matches the pattern described above; the Canadian version of the Dortmunder Bibliotheksystem (DOBIS), developed by the National Library of Canada, closely meets the bilingual criteria.

The Canadian Workplace Automation Research Center, an agency that comes under the federal ministry, Communication Canada, has developed an online bilingual catalog of its specialized collection (17,000 items) on information regarding workplace automation, the ISIR/SIRI database. Although it is not a general public catalog, the bilingual system (MINISIS) is accessible to local and remote users as a database. French language items are catalogued in French and English language items in English with descriptors assigned in the language of the item. In the case of bilingual items, separate records are prepared with bilingual descriptors. The thesaurus has 5,700 terms, one third of which are in French, and can be accessed online. The descriptors are displayed in the order of entry into the database. The printed thesaurus, however, displays English and French descriptors in one alphabetical order.

The Canadian version of DOBIS is an integrated library management system which has been developed by the National Library of Canada and the Canada Institute for Scientific and Technical Information. Operational since Fall 1979, it now contains 5.1 million records. After sign-on, all searching functions are immediately accessible. Documents can be searched by LC card number, ISBN, ISSN, call number, miscellaneous numbers, names, titles, and subjects.

It is easy to learn to use the system. The screen display layout is uniformly divided into three parts: (1) screen title (current function and error messages); (2) communication area; (3) instructions to operator and area for operator response. DOBIS does not require the user to know the MARC formats. The dialogue with the system combines menus and commands in a way which requires a minimum of reference to the user's manual. A direct SDS screen is available anytime when using the searching function.

Since DOBIS is used not only by the staff of the National Library of Canada but also by other federal government libraries, namely the Canada Institute for Scientific and Technical Information and their searchers and patrons, it can be considered a "public" catalogue.

DOBIS is bilingual. Users can converse in either French or English. The system is built around Canadian MARC which permits differentiation of the language of the document and of the subject headings by its special control field 17 and its common subfield $1. The system handles the full ALA (MARC) character set which includes the diacritical marks used in French.

> Relationships between records in the bibliographic file (preceding/succeeding, parent/analytic, parent/supplement, etc.) and between authority records in the name or subject files (see/ see from, see also/see also from, English form of name/French form of name, etc.) are accomplished by control number linkages and type of linkage codes rather than by the repetition of information in both records.[13]

Currently, the two OPACs described above provide subject access in some sort of parallel bilinguism. In DOBIS and to a lesser degree in ISIR/SIRI, there is a beginning of a correspondence between the two languages, the one through authority control and the other through the thesaurus; but the integration stops short here. As far as searching is concerned, the catalogue user defines and refines his/her search statements successively in the two languages.

PRESENT AND FUTURE BILINGUAL OPACs

The best bilingual searching would retrieve all records through the use of one language. Such a system would take subject headings or terms from a thesaurus and then retrieve all records in the other language by means of a special module invisible to the user that would establish the concordances between the two languages. But this module is not yet available in the databases or in the OPACs of multilingual countries or agencies. Paula Goossens suggests, however, an example taken from the NEWWAVE database of the Koninklijke Bibliotheek, Brussels, which incorporates LCSH in three languages (English-French-Dutch); but she concludes that ". . . no real multinational cooperative program for subject indexing is revealed. Thus for the moment a multinational OPAC cannot offer the much desired subject heading search facility."[14]

A decade ago, authority control in unilingual catalogues appeared, to say the least, unjustifiable. Burns then stated: "The real key to the effective bilingual structuring of data displays, in online systems and printed products alike, will be the authority control system."[15] Nowadays, as online searching tests the use of subject headings or other controlled vocabulary, it appears that some form of controlled vocabulary is a prerequisite for implementing bilingual or multilingual OPACs.

Future online library catalogues, the so called third generation, will have characteristics similar to bibliographic databases and will call for sophisticated processes including "switching languages" and multilingual thesauri. Authority control already provides a way to switch to a preferred form. The experimental OKAPI MARK 2, at the Polytechnic of Central London, includes "lists of 'synonym classes' or 'subject terms' "[16] which handle nouns, phrases, abbreviations, irregular plurals, and alternative spelling.

Another way to provide subject access to the searcher would be to provide a built-in automatic translation module similar to the one found in multilingual thesauri software. Multilingual thesauri are by definition confined to special areas of the universe of knowledge whereas OPACs thesauri should help the general user with a wide variety of information needs. The built-in translation module is an enormous endeavour that cannot be envisioned within the near future.

DIACRITICAL MARKS AND THE TERMINALS: AFTERTHOUGHT AS A POST-SCRIPTUM

As stated by Joseph R. Matthews, "the majority of operational online catalog terminals do not use the full ALA character set"[17] and do not display diacritical marks. To accommodate both English and French alphabets, the system must generate the corresponding codes; and the terminals must display the accented letters. Fortunately, diacritics are now supported on newer terminals; they complement the standard character set. The QUERTY keyboard layout is then slightly modified to accept the accents or accented letters.

If these special characters are not available, compromises are used: diacritical marks are either simply ignored and the meaning guessed by the context, or an explanation is given to avoid a misinterpretation. For instance, tâche (job, occupation) and tache (stain): "Tache, Evaluation des" "Tache (Nettoyage)." Another way is to put the accent before the accentuated letter: "ˆTaches, Evaluation des." This is a better but not a satisfactory solution to the problem. Accents in French are no embellishment; the meaning of a word is often determined by the accent. For instance, the word "peche" has no meaning, but "pêche" means "peach" and "fishing." "Pêchê" means "sin"! Lack of accents in a key word search could yield unwanted noise.

English is the only major European language lacking accents and diacritical marks. Other languages, on the other hand, require these signs to distinguish between homographs, homophones, singular, plural, etc. We dare say that omitting an accent in French is, indeed, a spelling error!

NOTES

1. Paula Goossens, "Across the Language Barriers in Multinational OPACS", in *Les Bibliothèques, tradition et mutation*: mélanges offerts à Jean-Pierre Clavel à l'occasion de son 65e anniversaire: avec un frontispice original de Raymond Moretti (Lausanne: Bibliothèque cantonale et universitaire, 1987), 401-416.

2. *Règles de catalogage anglo-américaines/*élaborées par the American Library Association, the British Library, le Comité canadien de catalogage, the Library Association, the Library of Congress; rédigées par Michael Gorman et Paul W. Winkler; version française établie par Paule Rolland-Thomas avec la collab. de Pierre Deslauriers (Montréal): ASTED, 1980)
The 1982, 1983, and 1985 revisions have also been published in French.

3. *Répertoire de vedettes-matière*, 9e éd. (Québec: Bibliothèque de l'Université Laval, 1983), 4 v.
Between editions, updates are published on COM.

4. *Canadian MARC Communication Format: Bibliographic Data* (Ottawa: Canadian MARC Office, 1988-), looseleaf.
Canadian MARC Communication Format: Authorities (Ottawa: Canadian MARC Office, 1980-), looseleaf.
Also published in French.

5. *Canadian Subject Headings*, 2nd ed. (Ottawa: National Library of Canada, 1985.
Two indices: English-French, French-English at the end of the volume.

6. Barrie A.F. Burns, "Authority Control in Two Languages", in *Authority Control, the Key to Tomorrow's Catalog*; Proceedings of the 1979 Library and Information Technology Association institutes, ed. by Mary W. Glukas (Phoenix: Oryx Press, 1982), 128-157.

7. Ibid., 131.

8. Karen Markey and Anh N. Demeyer, *Dewey Decimal Classification On-line Project: Evaluation of a Library Schedule and Index Integrated Into the Subject Searching Capabilities of an Online Catalog* (Dublin, OH: OCLC, 1986).

9. Karen Markey, "Findings of the Dewey Decimal Classification On-line Project", *International Cataloguing*, 15 (April/June 1986), 15-19.

10. Goossens, "Across the Language Barrier", 409.

11. Nancy Williamson, "Classification and Online Catalogues: recent research and Future Prospects"; Paper Presented at IFLA Conference, Sydney, 1988.

12. Goosens, "Across the Language Barrier", 401.

13. Louis J.S. Forget, and William L. Newman, "Evaluation of the DOBIS System for Use in Canada/Evaluation du systéme "DOBIS" à l'usage canadien", *The Canadian Journal of Information Science/Revue canadienne des sciences de l'information*, vol. 2 no. 1 (1977), 61-78.

14. Goosens, "Across the Language Barrier", 412.

15. Burns, "Authority Control", 137.

16. Steven Walker, "OKAPI: Evaluating and Enhancing an Experimental Online Catalog", *Library Trends* vol. 35, no. 4 (Spring 1987), 631-645.

17. Joseph R. Matthews, *Public Access to Online Catalogs*, 2d. ed. (New York: Neal-Schuman, 1985), 44.

FIGURE 1. All subject headings assigned on a subject analysis work sheet in both French and English.

SUBJECT ANALYSIS REPORT

D.D.N. — N.D.D. 7548740			VERIF. LEVEL — NIVEAU DE VÉRIF.
MISCELLANEOUS — DIVERS		TITLE — TITRE Répertoire numérique détaillé du fonds Armand Frappier	☑ CANADIANA ☐ CIP ☐ NL NN

TYPE	SOURCE	SUBJECTS — MATIÈRES
		Frappier, Armand, 1904- Archives -- Catalogues
		Microbiologie -- Recherche -- Québec (Province) --
		Histoire -- Sources -- Bibliographie -- Catalogues
		Institut Armand Frappier -- Archives -- Catalogues
		Frappier, Armand, 1904 - Bibliographie
		H 1100 H 1100 -- Archives -- Catalogs ☐ VERSO
		H 1095 Microbiology -- Research -- Quebec (Province) -- History -- H 1095 H 1095 Sources -- Bibliography -- Catalogs.
		H 1105 Institut Armand Frappier -- Archives -- Catalogs. H 1100
		Frappier, Armand, 1904- -- Bibliography. ☐ VERSO

CLASSIFICATION	016.576'07'20714

151

NOTES — [ ] CATALOGUING SOURCE — SOURCE DE CATALOGAGE

GEOGRAPHIC AREA — AIRE GÉOGRAPHIQUE n-cn-qu

CHRONOLOGICAL COVERAGE — SUBDIVISION CHRONOLOGIQUE

DATES & DEFAULTS (NL) — DATES ET IMPLICITES (BN) PROTECTION IN EFFECT / PROTECTION EXISTE [ ] LC [ ] CRII [ ] IIVM

FIXED FIELDS (MONOG.) — ZONES FIXES (MONOG.) INTELLECTUAL LEVEL — NIVEAU INTELLECTUEL

FORM OF CONTENTS / FORME DE CONTENU Bibliogr. Catalog

LITERARY TEXT — TEXTE LITTÉRAIRE BIOGRAPHY — BIOGRAPHIE

FIXED FIELDS (SERIALS) — ZONES FIXES (PUBLICATIONS EN SÉRIE) TYPE OF MATERIAL / TYPE DE PUBLICATION

NATURE OF CONTENTS — FORME DE CONTENU

LEADER FIELDS — ZONES GUIDES ENCODING LEVEL — NIVEAU D'INTÉGRALITÉ [✓] FULL / INTÉGRALE

SINGLE COPY — EXEMPL. DISTINCT STATUS TYPE / TYPE DE STATUT [✓] CATALOGUED / CATALOGUÉ **OUTPUT PRODUCTS (NL) / PRODUITS DE SORTIE (BN)** [ ]

[ ] REPORT INVALID HEADINGS / SIGNALER VEDETTE(S) INVALIDE(S) [ ] NOTIFICATION REQUIRED / AVIS DE MODIFICATION INITIALS / INITIALES [✓] INPUT COMPLETED / SAISIE COMPLÉTÉE

DATE 8182 7788 M. J. T.

```
Searching
Document numbers
Complete    7548740   not rep   printed   monogra   ISBD A2   full   authenticat

SUBJECTS:
   RVM      Frappier, Armand, 1904-  Archives Catalogues
   RVM      Microbiologie Recherche Qu/ebec (Province)
            Histoire Sources Bibliographie Catalogues
   RVM      Institut Armand Frappier Archives Catalogues
   RVM      Frappier, Armand, 1904-  Bibliographie
   LCSH     Frappier, Armand, 1904-  Archives Catalogs
   LCSH     Microbiology Research Quebec (Province)
            History Sources Bibliography Catalogs
   LCSH     Institut Armand Frappier Archives Catalogs
   LCSH     Frappier, Armand, 1904-  Bibliography
CLASSIFICATION NUMBERS:
            016.576/07/20714 19
            CD3649*
```

FIGURE 1A. The terminal display format. RMV stands for *Répertoire de vendettes-matière*; LCSH stands for *Library of Congress Subject Headings*.

FIGURE 2. Subject headings taken from the *Répertoire des vendettes-matière, Library of Congress Subject Headings*, and *Canadian Subject Headings*.

SUBJECT ANALYSIS REPORT
RAPPORT D'ANALYSE DOCUMENTAIRE

National Library of Canada / Bibliothèque nationale du Canada

D.D.N.—N.D.D. 7625550	TITLE — TITRE L'âge au futur		VERIF LEVEL — NIVEAU DE VÉRIF

CANADIANA ☑ CIP ☐ NL BN ☐

MISCELLANEOUS — DIVERS

TYPE	SOURCE	SUBJECTS — MATIÈRES	
		Prédiction sociale	
		Personnes âgées -- Québec (Province) --	
		" -- Québec (Province) --	
		Prévision sociale -- Québec (Province)	
		Québec (Province) -- 1960-	
		Québec (Province) -- 1960-	
			VERSO ☐
		Aged -- Quebec (Province) -- Social conditions.	H1100
		Aged -- Quebec (Province) -- Economic conditions.	H1100
		Social prediction -- Quebec (Province).	H1140
CSH		Quebec (Province) -- Social conditions -- 1960.	H1140
CSH		Quebec (Province) -- Economic conditions -- 1960.	H1140
			VERSO ☐

CLASSIFICATION	305.2'6'09714

154

NOTES ☐ CATALOGUING SOURCE — SOURCE DE CATALOGAGE

GEOGRAPHIC AREA — AIRE GÉOGRAPHIQUE | n-cn-qu

CHRONOLOGICAL COVERAGE — SUBDIVISION CHRONOLOGIQUE

DATES & DEFAULTS (NL) — DATES ET IMPLICITES (BN)

PROJECTION IN EFFECT
PROJECTION EXISTE | ☐ LC | ☐ CSH | ☐ IVM

FIXED FIELDS (MONOG.) — ZONES FIXES (MONOG.)

INTELLECTUAL LEVEL — NIVEAU INTELLECTUEL

FORM OF CONTENTS
FORME DE CONTENU | Statis.

LITERARY TEXT — TEXTE LITTÉRAIRE | BIOGRAPHY — BIOGRAPHIE

FIXED FIELDS (SERIALS) — ZONES FIXES (PUBLICATIONS EN SÉRIE)

TYPE OF MATERIAL
TYPE DE PUBLICATION

NATURE OF CONTENTS — FORME DE CONTENU

LEADER FIELDS — ZONES GUIDES

ENCODING LEVEL — NIVEAU D'INTÉGRALITÉ | ☑ FULL
INTÉGRALE

SINGLE COPY — EXEMPL. DISTINCT

STATUS TYPE
TYPE DE STATUT | ☑ CATALOGUED
CATALOGUÉ

OUTPUT PRODUCTS (NL)
PRODUITS DE SORTIE (BN) | ☑

☐ REPORT INVALID HEADINGS
SIGNALER VEDETTE(S) INVALIDE(S)

☐ NOTIFICATION REQUIRED
AVIS DE MODIFICATION

☐ INPUT COMPLETED
SAISIE COMPLÉTÉE

DATE | 8104 | INITIALS
INITIALES | M.J.T. | Sep 16 1988

NL-777 (r. 85/07)

FIGURE 2, PART 2 (continued)

TYPE	SOURCE	SUBJECT — MATIÈRES		

RESEARCH — RECHERCHE

Aged -- Economic conditions -- Q.P.

Aged -- Social conditions

Retirement

| 305.26 | Aged -- Q.P. -- Social cond. -- Cong. |
| 306.38 | Family -- Soc. asp. -- Q.P. |

Retirement Q.P.

```
Searching
Document numbers
Complete   7625550   not rep printed   monogra   ISBD A2   full      authenticat

TITLES (cont.):
       actifs? / Jean Carette ; [conception et r'ealisation, Carole
       Kearney]

SUBJECTS:
RVM    Personnes ^ag'ees Qu'ebec (Province) Conditions sociales
RVM    Personnes ^ag'ees Qu'ebec (Province) Conditions 'economiques
RVM    Pr'evision sociale Qu'ebec (Province)
RVM    Qu'ebec (Province) Conditions sociales 1960--
RVM    Qu'ebec (Province) Conditions 'economiques 1960--
LCSH   Aged Quebec (Province) Social conditions
LCSH   Aged Quebec (Province) Economic conditions
LCSH   Social prediction Quebec (Province)
CSH    Quebec (Province) Social conditions 1960--
CSH    Quebec (Province) Economic conditions 1960--
```

FIGURE 2A. The terminal display format for the headings selected from the three lists referred to under Figure 2.

```
Searching
Names
Full information      Authority 258859          NLC      authenticat
                                                 auth     AACR2

CONTROL NUMBERS:
   NLC    n.a.      a: 0053-K-4111F
NAMES:
   fore   n f  a: Alexandre, le Grand, 356-323 av. J.-C.
NOTES:
   cat src n.a. : CaOONL nnn CaOONL
   auth ct n.a. : nlc
   wrk cat n.a. : Gautier, de Ch^atillon. The Alexandreis.
   fnd /nt n.a. : Petit Robert 2. Dates.
   fnd /nt n.a. : Grand dict. Larousse encycl. Alexandre III le Grand.
CROSS REFERENCES:
   eng equiv n.a.       n.a.       n.a.       n.a.     :
      Alexander, the Great, 356-323 B.C.
   seen from ~former ~e.rules g fr lin ref gen :
      Alexandre III, le Grand, 356-323 av. J.-C.
   seen from ~former ~e.rules g fr lin ref gen :
      Alexandre III, roi de Mac'edoine, 356-323 av. J.-C.
```

FIGURE 3. Example of a record for personal name.

Searching
Names
Full information   Authority 2588866   NLC   authenticat
                                              auth   AACR2

CONTROL NUMBERS:
  NLC   n.a.   a: 0053-K-4111E
NAMES:
  fore   n e a: Alexander, the Great, 356-323 B.C.
NOTES:
  cat src n.a. : CaOONL nnn CaOONL
  auth ct n.a. : nlc
  wrk cat n.a. : Gautier, de Ch^atillon. The Alexandreis.
  fnd /nt n.a. : LCNA 1977-1985. Dates.
  fnd /nt n.a. : Britannica Micro. Alexander III the Great. Dates.
CROSS REFERENCES:
  fre equiv n.a. :   n.a.   n.a. :
    Alexandre, le Grand, 356-323 av. J.-C.
  seen from ¬former ¬e.rules g fr lin ref gen :
    Alexandros, ho Megas, 356-323 B.C.
  seen from ¬former ¬e.rules g fr lin ref gen :
    Alexander III, the Great, 356-323 B.C.
  seen from ¬former ¬e.rules g fr lin ref gen :
    Alexander III, King of Macedonia, 356-323 B.C.

FIGURE 3A. Example of a record for personal name.

```
Searching
Names
Full information      Authority 244181          NLC    authenticat
                                                auth   AACR2

CONTROL NUMBERS:
  NLC    n.a.       a: 0052-D-8656E
NAMES:
  cor,pl  e e  a: Brussels (Belgium)
NOTES:
  cat src  n.a.  : CaOONL fre CaOONL
  auth ot  n.a.  : nlc
  fnd /nt  n.a.  : LCNA (1977-1985)  AA2.  (Avec subdivisions)
  fnd /nt  n.a.  : Atlas du monde contemporain.  (Bruxelles)
CROSS REFERENCES:
  fre equiv  n.a.  n.a.    n.a.    n.a.    :
    Bruxelles (Belgique)
```

FIGURE 4. Example of a record for geographic name.

```
Searching
Names
Full information      Authority  244187          NLC       authenticat
                                                 auth      AACR2

CONTROL NUMBERS:
   NLC    n.a.         a: OO52-D-8656F
NAMES:
   cor,pl  f f  a: Bruxelles (Belgique)
NOTES:
   cat src  n.a. : CaOONL  fre CaOONL
   auth ct  n.a. : nlc
   fnd /nt  n.a. : Atlas du monde contemporain.
   fnd /nt  n.a. : LCNA (1977-1985)  AA2 (Avec subdivisions)  (Brussels, Belgium
                   )
CROSS REFERENCES:
   eng equiv  n.a.        n.a.      n.a.      n.a.     :
              Brussels (Belgium)
```

FIGURE 4A. Example of a record for geographic name.

```
Searching
Names
Full information    Authority   19092        NLC      authenticat
                                             auth      AACR2

CONTROL NUMBERS:
   NLC   n.a.     a: 0002-D-5530F
NAMES:
   cor,dir f f  a: 'Eglise catholique
NOTES:
   cat src  n.a. : CaOONL fre CaOONL CaOONL
   auth ct  n.a. : nlc
   gen s.a  n.a. : la subdivision 'Eglise catholique aux diff'erents sujets, p.e
                   x. Asc'etisme---'Eglise catholique ; Guerre, 1934-1945 (mondia
                   le, 2e)---'Eglise catholique.
   eg/note  eg   : Christianisme.
   use/sop  n.a. : UTILISATION EN VEDETTES-MATI'ERES:  Peut ^etre subdivis'ee g'
                   eographiquement.

CROSS REFERENCES:
   eng equiv n.a.        n.a.       n.a.       n.a.    :
           Catholic Church
```

FIGURE 5. Example of a record for corporate name.

Names
Full information   Authority   75520   NLC   authenticat
                                                    auth   AACR2

CONTROL NUMBERS:
   NLC   n.a.   a: 0002-D-5530E
NAMES:
   cor,dir e e   a: Catholic Church
NOTES:
   cat src   n.a. :   Ca00NL eng Ca00NL Ca00NL
   auth ct   n.a. :   nlc
   lcl use   n.a. :   Its   The Code of Canon Law : a text and commentary. Ca00P
   fnd /nt   n.a. :   LCNA 1977-June 1984.
   use/scp   n.a. :   SUBJECT USAGE: May be subdivided geographically.
CROSS REFERENCES:
   seen from   ^ former   ^e.rules n.a.   ref gen :
   fre equiv   n.a.   n.a.   n.a. :
      'Eglise catholique

FIGURE 5A. Example of a record for corporate name.

Title Words as Entry Vocabulary to *LCSH*:
Correlation Between Assigned *LCSH* Terms and Derived Terms from Titles in Bibliographic Records with Implications for Subject Access in Online Catalogs

Carolyn O. Frost

STATEMENT OF PROBLEM

While title keyword access in an online library catalog is not an effective replacement for controlled searching, it can complement a subject heading search. Many online catalogs presently allow users to search with keywords in titles as well as with subject headings. Searching with title keyword retrieves all records with titles matching the user's search terms, but not records on similar subjects with different title terms. To retrieve the latter, the user can search further using the subject heading terms assigned to the title matches; but this involves a second search path and an interruption of the search strategy. In many systems, the user is required to exit the keyword title mode in order to enter the mode allowing a subject heading search.

There are times when the user enters a term which matches not only a word in the title, but also a word in the subject heading as well. In some cases, the title term or terms may completely match the subject heading vocabulary. When this occurs, the common language of the title and subject vocabulary could be exploited to provide direct links to displays of other works which have been assigned the same subject terms. In addition, links from invalid to

---

Carolyn O. Frost is Associate Professor, the School of Information and Library Studies, University of Michigan.

valid terms could be provided if the user's title term matched a "see" reference term in *LCSH*. In the future, access could also be provided to related terms, since the impending implementation of the machine-readable *LCSH* into online catalog system designs will direct users from one subject heading term to broader, narrower, or other related terms which can then be used to refine or to extend a search. These links, which connect related subject terms, could be extended to title terms as well, if the title term were identical with a subject heading.

Example: a user enters the term *witchcraft* in a title keyword search. This term matches a title keyword in a bibliographic record: "The art of witchcraft." The term also matches the subject heading "Witchcraft" in *LCSH*. The system can then display:

> a. all the books that the library has which contain this title word:
> *The art of witchcraft*
> *Modern witchcraft*
> *Witchcraft and sorcery*
> b. all the books in the library indexed under the subject heading "Witchcraft":
> *The black arts*
> *Sorcery in the Middle Ages*
> *The art of witchcraft*
> *Modern witchcraft*
> *Witchcraft and sorcery*
> c. authorized terms which can be used to broaden or narrow the search, or to find related terms:
> BT Occultism
> NT Amulets
> Charms
> Magic drawings
> Voodooism

If we assume the desirability of this type of link, a major question remains in determining its feasibility. Will there be enough correlation between subject headings and title keywords to justify the inclusion of this linkage capability in the design of an online system?

To address this and related questions, sample bibliographic records from the University of Michigan Library catalogs were examined to determine degrees of match between title keywords and terms in corresponding subject headings. In many respects, the questions raised and the subsequent analyses are related to the issue of controlled and uncontrolled vocabulary.

THE UNCONTROLLED VS. CONTROLLED VOCABULARY DEBATE

Svenonius observes: "the question of the effectiveness of controlled vocabularies in information retrieval has been raised repeatedly in the literature of library/information science" and "that this is so suggests that its answer is neither obvious nor trivial, but depends on a number of variables."[1] For information retrieval in the context of library catalogs, however, the concept of controlled vocabulary for subject terms has been well established since the beginning of this century. While some still question the need for controlled vocabulary and for authority control in online catalogs with keyword access, the two systems have successfully co-existed, but on separate planes. However, if title keywords could be linked to matching subject heading terms, the advantages of a controlled vocabulary search could be gained by title-keyword searchers in many instances. Most notable among these advantages are: subject heading terms leading to broader, narrower or related terms; references leading from unauthorized to authorized terms; and collocation of materials on the same subject but with titles expressed in different terms.

Viewed in this light, the comparison of controlled vs. uncontrolled vocabulary can be reexamined and applied to bibliographic records to assess the value of providing links between title keywords which are identical to subject heading terms. This study will not address the question of whether the subject heading term or the title term is more relevant to the subject matter of the document. Instead, it will focus on the degree of similarity between subject heading terms and title terms.[2]

PREVIOUS RESEARCH

While debate continues in the literature of information science over the relative merits of uncontrolled and controlled vocabulary, studies on the effectiveness of controlled vocabularies have focused primarily on specialized thesauri used in online database searches of the journal literature rather than on subject headings used in library catalogs. A number of studies have examined the correlation between assigned index terms and title terms. For the most part, these studies were concerned with the effectiveness of title words for indexing purposes. Some of these studies examined titles in printed indexes and compared them with terms from their associated subject headings. Montgomery and Swanson examined entries in *Index Medicus* to determine the extent of match between words in the title and with words identical to or synonymous with the corresponding subject heading. The intent was not to evaluate retrieval effectiveness of controlled and uncontrolled terms but to determine the extent to which human indexing operations can be simulated by machines.[3] Each title was examined for identical terminology with the corresponding subject heading including synonymous terms as determined by medical dictionaries and drug indexes. Subheadings were not included.

The findings revealed an extraordinary 86% degree of match. From this the researchers concluded that

> if a computer were provided with the title of each of these articles, the *Index Medicus* subject heading list, and a synonym list or thesaurus group of each subject heading, it could then be programmed to determine which subject headings should be assigned to each article.[4]

The Montgomery/Swanson results contrast sharply with those of a parallel study by O'Connor of three other indexing systems in the medical literature. The results ranged from 13% to 68% and led the researcher to the general conclusion that "any proposal to replace a medical subject index produced by subject specialists with an automatic index based on 'thesaurus' processing of titles should be viewed with great caution."[5]

Bloomfield matched words in a thesaurus with words in a title and abstract. His study took all the words of a title and abstract as found in six articles in *Physics Abstracts, Chemical Abstracts,* and *Nuclear Science Abstracts* and searched for each word in thesauri made up of the subject index for each journal. The comparison looked at three categories of match: (1) words that matched identically and words that matched the first word of a multi-word heading; (2) words that were represented in the subject index by *see* references, either from a single word match or the first word of a multi-word *see* reference; and (3) words that did not match any words in the subject index. The findings revealed that an average of 20 percent of the words from the title and abstract matched words in the thesauri. Bloomfield concluded that "it is impractical to use the words of the title and the abstract as input for matching against a simulated computer memory storing a full scale thesaurus." He decided that this was the case because in writing abstracts authors include "many of the peripheral ideas associated with the main thesis."[6]

METHODOLOGY

Objectives and Research Questions

The primary purpose of this study was to consider the value of title terms as entry vocabulary to controlled lists. The study's focus is on the user who has entered a word which appears in the title. How likely is it that this term will also appear as a subject heading, as part of a subject heading, or as a truncated part of a subject heading?

The study did not consider the presence of such matches to be indicators of the effectiveness of derived (keyword-title) vocabulary as a sole source of subject search terms. The assumption will be that human judgement and controlled vocabulary are still a necessary part of indexing retrieval. The general research question addressed by the study was: What degree of match exists between the controlled vocabulary of subject terms and the derived terms within the title?

Sample Determination and Data Gathering

The sample was extracted from the University of Michigan Library's shelflist. Excluded were works in the literature classification categories, non-book materials, and local or specialized subject headings (e.g., MeSH). After the removal of the excluded categories, the total sampling population was 1,740,647. A sample of 2,401 records was chosen to give a 95% confidence level and an error rate of 2%. The records from the sample yielded 4264 assigned subject headings. The number of cards in the Library's public catalog is estimated to be 10 million, representing a collection of approximately 6 million volumes.

The heading analysis included topical, geographic, and name subjects. Of the 2401 records in the sample, 120 records had no subject headings; and an additional 13 were otherwise ineligible for analysis. A total of 2268 eligible records were analyzed and coded for degree of match of the title with subject headings. Each record was also coded for its Library of Congress Classification category as determined by the assigned call number.

Categories of Analysis

In this investigation, several categories of similarity between keyword title and subject terms were identified, and these categories correspond to the levels of match addressed by the questions below:

- To what extent are title words exactly the same as a subject heading?
- To what extent are title words the same as the main heading component of a subdivided heading?
- To what extent are title words the same as individual words in the main subject heading?
- To what extent are title words the same as individual words in a topical or geographic subdivision of a subject heading?
- To what extent do words in the title match *part* of the word(s) in a main subject heading?
- To what extent do words in the title term match *part* of the word(s) in a subdivision?

Since each record was coded for its Library of Congress Classification category, the study was able to compare patterns of match among subject discipline groups.

FINDINGS

Each record was ranked according to its highest level of match. For example, if a record contained a title with keywords matching an entire subject heading as well as part of a subject heading, the record was counted only as an exact match of an entire subject heading. Thus, occurrences of more than one category within a single record, as well as multiple instances of the same category of match, were not counted.

Exact Match — Entire Heading

In an exact match, the entire subject heading was represented by keyword title terms in direct order. The complete subject heading could consist of a main heading without a subdivision or a main heading with subdivisions. For example,

> Title: Auditing theory and practice
> Subject: Auditing
> Title: Images of good and evil
> Subject: Good and evil
> [multiple title words were counted as an exact match only if they occurred in the direct order of the subject heading and not as inverted terms]
> Title: Wages in the United States in 1931.
> Subject: Wages — United States

In eleven percent of the records, keywords from the titles exactly matched a complete subject heading. Within disciplines (according to Library of Congress Classification categories), the range of match was from 2% to 23%. As expected, the scientific and technical disciplines contrasted sharply with the disciplines in the humanities and in history.

The highest percentages of exact matches occurred in the disciplines in science and technology: 23% for Q (Science), 18% for R

(Medicine), and 19% for T (Technology). For these disciplines, the combined rate of exact matches was 20%. The social sciences, G (Geography and recreation), H (Social sciences), J (Political science), K (law), and L (Education), had a combined percentage of only 8% for exact matches. The highest degree of exact matches (14%) was found in the B's (Psychology, Religion). The second highest (10%) was the H category and the third, L (8%).

The humanities were not represented in full, since the literature categories, with heavy percentages of records without subject headings, were not included in the sample. As expected, the categories of music (M) and art (N) contained small percentages of records with exact matches, 3% and 5% respectively.

The LC Classification categories comprising the historical disciplines—C (Auxiliary sciences of history), D (General and Old World history), and E-F (American history)—as a group had only a 4% rate of exact matches, the same percentage as the two disciplines in the fine arts. Within this group, the range of percentages varied sharply: the classification category of E was 2%, while the category of C, which included archaeology, was 24%.

Exact Match—Main Heading Component of Subdivided Heading

In this category, the title keyword matches only the main component of a subdivided heading. Sometimes, most notably in the case of form subdivisions, the refinement of the subject results in a heading which is not likely to have occurred to the user.

> Title: Music ho!: a study of music in decline
> Subject: Music—Philosophy and aesthetics
> Title: Art censorship
> Subject: Art—Censorship—Chronology
> Title: Radiation biochemistry
> Subject: Radiation—Physiological effect

We expected the percentage of matches in this category to be considerably larger than in the previous category, since subdivisions did not have to match. However, only twelve percent of the records contained titles with keywords matching a main heading component of a subdivided heading; the percentage is almost identical to the 11% match on complete headings.

In contrast with the previous category of exact matches where the science and technology disciplines enjoyed the highest rate of match, the leaders in the category of main heading matches were the social science disciplines (16%). Next in line were the science and technology disciplines, where the combined rate of match was 13%. For the historical disciplines, the combined rate of match was 12%, while the humanities disciplines were a very distant fourth with 5%.

Some of the categories which had the lowest degree of match on complete headings had the highest rate of match on main headings. All of the highest percentages of match in this category were found in the social science or historical disciplines. The E category had a 17% match rate; and the rates of match in the categories of F, L, H, and J all exceeded the matches found in any of the science categories – Q 15%, R 14%, T 11% and S (agriculture), a mere 6%. The remaining social science disciplines had percentages in this category not far behind the sciences: D 10%, G 13%. The humanities disciplines of music and art had rates of 6% and 4% respectively. Since the social sciences placed so high in this category, we looked to see if the occurrences of names of places or groups were a factor. This did not prove to be the case. Within the highest ranking category of E, only 7% of the matches on main headings were names of places or groups. This contrasted sharply with F, where 89% of the matches in this category were names of places or groups.

Exact Match – Main Heading Keyword

The retrieval value of a match on the main heading keyword can vary, depending on the distinctiveness and the number of the matching words.

Title: Child psychology
Subject: Child study
Title: Public finance
Subject: Finance, Public
Title: Optimization theory
Subject: Mathematical optimization

Of all the categories of match identified in this study, this was the most frequent. Thirty percent of the records contained titles matching a main heading keyword. In contrast to the other two categories of match, the highest scoring discipline was fine arts (57%) and the lowest was science (18%). The humanities, music (37%) and fine arts, had a combined rate of match of 50%. We assumed that the high percentage could be attributed to the frequency of titles containing personal names or proper words, e.g., "The sketches of Vincent Van Gogh." An analysis of the records in the two humanities disciplines substantiated this assumption: 42% of the matching words in M and 59% in N were indeed proper names. Wiberly's study of subject terms in the humanities led him to conclude that "because a majority of the terms . . . are precise, namely, singular proper terms — the names of persons or single creative works — subject access is far more straightforward than has been generally recognized." He concludes, as does Line, that "because the basic subject matter of the humanities consists of events, individuals, and artistic products, the hard core of the field is made up of easily indexed and retrievable elements."[7] A preliminary study by Frost of index terms for German language and literature appearing in an issue of the *MLA* (Modern Language Association) *International Bibliography* revealed that 80% of the titles indexed contained names of literary works or authors.[8]

The two next highest rates of match for keywords (30%) were found in the historical and social science disciplines. Within the historical disciplines, the range was from 24% (C) to 42% (E). In the E's, a noteworthy 88% of the records in this match category were names of persons or groups; and this was true for 57% of the records in this category in the C's. In science and technology, the rate of match was 23%, with Q at the low end of the range (18%) and S at the high end (36%).

Exact Match — Subdivision Keyword

A match on subdivisions can be useful if the subdivisions are topical or geographic.

Title: Surveillance
Subject: Police patrol — Surveillance
Title: Michigan athletics
Subject: College sports — Michigan

A match on a subdivision keyword can be especially meaningful if, in addition to the term matching the subdivision, there is also a term matching the main heading, e.g.,

Title: Pottery techniques of native North America
Subject: Indians of North America — Pottery

Throughout the sample, subdivision matches occurred infrequently. In only 5% of the sample was the highest level of match on a subdivision keyword (or entire subdivision). For all disciplines, percentages in this category were relatively low, ranging from 12% (E) to 1% (B). In the social science disciplines, the combined rate of match was 6%; for the historical disciplines 5%, for science and technology 5%, and for the humanities, 2%.

In summary, a review of all the previous match categories shows that half of the records (53%) contained at least one word which matched an entire word in a subject heading. The next categories of match deal with partial (truncated) matches of words.

Truncated Match — Main Heading Keyword

The value of a truncated keyword can vary according to degree of truncation and the importance of the retrieval term.

Title: Primary metals
Subject: Metal trade — United States
Title: Successful investing
Subject: Investments

For 14% of the sample, the highest level of match was on part of a word in the main subject heading. Of these matches, 27% were singular/plural variants, (e.g., "catalog"/"catalogs"); and 28% were foreign language cognates (e.g., "Sonata"/"Sonaten").

The highest rate of match (18%) was in science and technology.

Second was the historical group (13%), followed by the humanities (12%). Within the humanities were both the highest ranking individual discipline, music (22%), and the lowest, art (6%). The social science disciplines had a combined rate of match of 10%, ranging from a low of 7% (education) to a high of 17% (geography).

The two highest-ranking individual disciplines were music (22%) and science (21%). In science, this rate is partially attributable to a high frequency of foreign language cognate words; 41% in this category in the sciences were cognates (higher than the overall average). In music, 61% of these matches were due to singular/plural variants, e.g., "opera," "operas."

Truncated Match – Subdivision Keyword

Considerations in the retrieval value of a truncated match on the subdivision keyword are essentially similar to those for truncated matches on a main heading keyword.

> Title: The cost of lighting
> Subject: Electric utilities – Costs

For only 1 percent of the sample, the highest level of match was on part of a subject heading subdivision. Within disciplines, there was very little variation; the combined rates of match were 1% for both the scientific disciplines and the social sciences, .5% for the humanities, and .6% for the historical disciplines.

No Match

The "no match" categories included words which had synonymous meanings, words which were only distantly related, words which were not at all related, and words which were in different languages and had no cognate stems in common. (Non-English headings which fit one of the matching categories were counted as a match.)

For 27% of the sample, there were no words from the title which matched any part of the subject heading. The rate of non-matches was highest in the history group (36%) with a range from 18% for E to 43% for D. Next highest was the social sciences group, with a rate of 28%, followed by the humanities (26%). As expected, the discipline group with the lowest percentages of non-matching headings was the science and technology group (18%). The highest percentages for individual disciplines in this category were in D (43%), J (34%), and H (29%); and the lowest were in the sciences: R (16%), and T (17%).

Foreign Language Titles

Two-thirds (66%) of the non-matches were foreign language titles. This was most true for the humanities, which had 84% of its non-matching titles in foreign languages as compared with rates of 72% for history, 63% for the social sciences, and 52% for science.

Combined Rate for All Categories of Match

If we combine all categories with some level of match, it is possible to determine the extent to which keywords in a title would match at least *some* part of a subject heading or subdivision. Seventy-three percent of all records had some degree of match.

As expected, the discipline group with the highest degree of combined match was the science and technology group: 82%. Not too far behind were the humanities (74%) and the social sciences (72%). The lowest percentage of combined match was for the history disciplines (64%).

The rates of combined match range from 57% (D) to 84% (R). As expected, all of the disciplines in the sciences had a high degree of combined match (T 83%, Q 81%, S 75%), but the combined match in some of the social science and historical disciplines was also very high: L (83%), E (82%), and F (80%). These were followed by G (76%), H (71%), B (68%), and J (66%). In the humanities, the rates of combined match were 76% for N and 70% for M.

CONCLUSIONS

In over half (53%) of the bibliographic records, a title term would match at least one word in the subject heading; and in slightly under a quarter of the records, there would be a match of a complete main heading. The rate would increase if multiple instances of a match within a single bibliographic record were taken into account. If truncation is counted, there is at least a partial match in almost three-fourths of the records. It is not obvious whether this degree of correlation justifies the design of a mechanism to link title and subject keywords. To be of greatest value, the linking mechanism would need to be capable of combining individual words from the title to effect a match with a subject heading (e.g., to make the title "Haitian art" compatible with "Art, Haitian") and would also need to allow truncation. Further analysis of the data is needed to determine the effect of multiple title-subject matches within individual records. Additional research could help estimate the retrieval value of displays which would result from the link to subject headings. It is likely that the advantages resulting from title keyword-subject heading would benefit a wide range of disciplines. While the science and technology disciplines had the highest rate of combined match for all categories (88%), the humanities and social sciences were not substantially lower (74% and 73%). In some categories of match (main heading and main heading keyword), these two discipline groups were ahead of the sciences.

NOTES

1. Elaine Svenonius, "Unanswered Questions in the Design of Controlled Vocabularies" *Journal of the American Society for Information Science* 37 (Sept. 1986): 331-340, p. 331.

2. Indirectly, the study does look at one indicator of relevance of title terms. If we assume that assigned headings are indicators of subject content, then assigned headings can serve as a criteria by which we can measure, in part, the relevance of the title keyword.

3. Christine Montgomery and Don R. Swanson, "Machine-like Indexing by People" *American Documentation* 13 (October 1962): 359-366, p. 359.

4. Ibid, p. 363.

5. John O'Connor, "Correlation of Indexing Headings and Title Words in Three Medical Indexing System". *American Documentation* 15 (April 1964): 96-104, p. 100.

6. Masse Bloomfield, "Simulated Machine Indexing, Part 2: Use of Words from Title and Abstract for Matching Thesauri Headings", *Special Libraries* 57 (April 1966): 232-235, p. 235.

7. Stephen E. Wiberly, Jr. "Subject Access in the Humanities and The Precision of the Humanist's Vocabulary". *Library Quarterly* 53 (October 1983): 420-433, p. 420, 421.

8. Carolyn O. Frost, Unpublished Paper, 1975.

APPENDIX I

Levels of Match Between Keyword Title and Subject Heading Words

n = 2268

	All	Sci./tech.	Soc. sci.	Human.	Hist.
Match on entire hdg.	11%	20%	8%	4%	4%
Match on main hdg.	12%	13%	16%	5%	12%
Match on main hdg. keyword	30%	23%	30%	50%	30%
Match on subdivision	5%	5%	6%	2%	5%
Truncated match -main hdg.	14%	18%	10%	12%	13%
Truncated match - subdiv.	1%	1%	1%	.5%	.6%
All matching categories	73%	82%	72%	74%	64%
No match	27%	18%	28%	26%	36%

Subject Searching in Law Library OPACs

Alva T. Stone

SUMMARY. Law libraries that introduce online catalogs to their publics often experience the same kinds of problems and benefits as other types of libraries. Nevertheless, certain issues for OPAC subject searching can be particularly challenging for law libraries. This paper addresses those issues, especially the impact on subject access of the design of *shared* OPACs and the special problems regarding subject searches on government agency names and titles of laws. Difficulties with law-related subject headings are also discussed. Finally, keyword and call number searching are examined from the law library perspective.

Do subject searches in the online public access catalog (OPAC) pose any special problems for law libraries?

The discussion which follows seeks to answer this question by focusing on three areas of concern. First, there are special considerations for law libraries that share their online catalogs with other libraries. (This is not uncommon among academic law libraries, which may share an online system with the campus "main" library.) The second focus will be on particular types of subject searches that are likely to cause problems for the law library user. Related to this are the barriers to access that result from inconsistent *LCSH* terminology or inadequacies in its syndetic structure for law-related subject headings. Finally, this paper will address the two most widely discussed alternatives to the subject heading approach, keyword and call number searching, as they apply to the law library environment.

The illustrations used below are from a LUIS catalog, the public

Alva T. Stone is Head of Cataloging, College of Law Library, Florida State University, Tallahassee, FL 32306. The author wishes to acknowledge Steve Ifshin of NOTIS Systems Inc. for the technical assistance he provided, and Michele Dalehite and Elaine Henjum of the Florida Center for Library Automation, for their helpful comments.

catalog component of the NOTIS system. Some of the system features and capabilities (or lack thereof) will not necessarily mirror those of other brands of OPACs. Nevertheless, the concerns expressed may be universally applied; they are factors to consider whether the law library is in the initial stage of selecting an online system, in the intermediate stage of modifying it for local implementation, or in the later stage of requesting system enhancements from the OPAC vendor.

SHARED SYSTEMS

If the law library does not share its system, then one factor to consider is the OPAC's introductory and help screens. Can these be changed to make them more relevant for the specialized clientele of law libraries? For example, the "vanilla" version of the LUIS screen that introduces subject searches gives the following instruction:

TO SEARCH BY SUBJECT: EXAMPLES:
TYPE s = followed by a subject term   s = television
or first part of subject term   s = shakesp
                                             s = symbolism in art

While it is quite probable that the law library would have subject entries under TELEVISION – LAW AND LEGISLATION, the example of SHAKESPEARE is questionable, and the final heading, SYMBOLISM IN ART, is extremely unlikely to result in any law library "hits." Fortunately, a NOTIS library can modify the examples on the LUIS introductory screens although the assistance of a programmer is required.

The examples are not likely to be changed to law-related subjects if the law library's entries are integrated in a campus-wide catalog. In that case, the more important questions are: how easy is it to distinguish the law library entries from those of the main library? And, can the OPAC user limit his search results to only the law library materials?

At Florida State University the Law Library was established as an autonomous processing unit, with its own catalog records (code "FL"), which may differ from those of the main library and its branches (code "FS"). The system, however, utilizes a union index regardless of the processing unit. Thus, when a subject search in LUIS results in the display of an index screen, it is readily apparent (by the "FL" code) which of the titles belong to the Law Library, as shown below:

LUIS SEARCH REQUEST: S = DRUG TESTING -UNITED
   SUBJECT/TITLE INDEX – 4 TITLES FOUND, 1-4 DISPLAYED
DRUG TESTING -UNITED STATES
1 drug testing: protection for soc   (1987)FL law:HV5823.5.U5 D7 1987
2 faas refusal to cooperate with d   (1987)FS main,doc:Y4.G74/7: F31/71
3 police drug testing   (1987)FL law:HV7936.D78 P76 1987
4 proficiency standards for drug t   (1987)FS main,doc:Y4.G74/7: D84/23

In another campus-wide NOTIS installation, the law library was not set up as a separate processing unit; LUIS users identify the law library titles by the "law" location that precedes the call number (see example above). However, according to the previews of completely redesigned NOTIS indexes (called the Merged Headings Index) to be introduced soon, both the call numbers *and locations* are expected to be dropped from the subject index displays in LUIS. When that happens, if the law library has not been designated as a separate processing unit, the LUIS user will need to request 'amplification' (an expanded display) or to view each bibliographic record individually to determine law library holdings.

At present one cannot qualify a LUIS subject search in a shared system so as to retrieve only the law library entries. This is an enhancement in development which NOTIS Systems, Inc. plans to test in 1989. Since it is not known whether the qualifier will correspond to the call number location or to the processing unit, the law library may be well advised to establish itself as a separate processing unit as well as a separate location. (It should be noted that in some systems the main and law libraries share a single bibliographic record while providing an ability to narrow the search by location. This type of design carries its own complexities since it requires a high level of cooperation between autonomous libraries in the maintenance of the shared records.)

Regardless of whether the libraries' bibliographic records are shared or separate, another important issue must be addressed by law libraries that share an online *authority* file with the campus main library. Who will be responsible for the authority work that lays the foundation for the online displays of cross-references from variant and related search terms? (At this writing, the generation of "search under" and "search also under" references in LUIS is still being tested, but their display within staff mode indexes is expected in 1989.)

Here are a few of the policies and procedures that the law school library and the main library should agree upon: Will Library of Congress subject authority records be transferred to the local system for all headings that have been used on bibliographic records or only the authority records that include 4xx and/or 5xx fields? Can "original" (non-Library of Congress) subject authority records be created, or existing records be enhanced with locally-added cross-references? Will both libraries be allowed to add new or updated authority records? When Library of Congress changes a (1xx) subject heading, how will the main and law libraries coordinate the corresponding corrections to their respective bibliographic records?

At some institutions with a shared system, the main library has chief control over the online authority file, although the law library may provide input regarding the creation/update of records or may add authority records for headings that have been used only on law library bibliographic records.[1] At Florida State University, it was decided that both the main and the law library would be allowed to create new or updated authority records. (Actually, changes affecting fields other than the 1xx field are now done automatically via a text-matching and overlay program developed by the Florida Center for Library Automation for use with Library of Congress's weekly *Subject Authorities* tapes.) The two libraries have also agreed to generally accept the Library of Congress authority records without local improvements. Corrections to a bibliographic record can be made only by the library which owns the particular title, but the two libraries make frequent use of electronic mail to inform each other about bibliographic records that need correction as the result of subject heading revisions.

While this discussion might seem to digress into a technical processing concern with authority work, it is important to understand the impact on subject access for the end user. For example, if the main library changes its subject entries under WIRE-TAPPING to the new form WIRETAPPING but fails to notify the law library to correct its entries, the user is not well served by the resulting split files in the OPAC. Likewise. when the law library is the first to use the new subject heading DRUG TESTING, it should take responsibility for adding the authority record and for verifying the presence of scope notes in the local system to distinguish it from DRUGS — TESTING, a different heading that already appears on some main library records.

SPECIFIC SEARCH PROBLEMS

The foregoing comments deal with subject retrieval issues in shared systems. Now let's look at specific types of subject searches which are likely to be problematic for law library users. Two such types are names of government agencies and titles of particular laws.

An inexperienced user may not stop to think that a government agency is subordinate to the country (or state, or city, etc.) which the agency serves. Hence, the patron might search for IRS documents by requesting the author entries under "Internal Revenue Service," a search that yields this guide screen display in LUIS:

```
LUIS SEARCH REQUEST: A = INTERNAL REVENUE SERVICE
   AUTHOR/TITLE GUIDE — 25 ENTRIES FOUND
   1   INTERNAL REVENUE SERVICE    = UNITED STATES   + A
   4   INTERNAL REVENUE SERVICE    = UNITED STATES   + C
   6   INTERNAL REVENUE SERVICE    = UNITED STATES   + F
   8   INTERNAL REVENUE SERVICE    = UNITED STATES   + G
   11  INTERNAL REVENUE SERVICE    = UNITED STATES   + I
   20  INTERNAL REVENUE SERVICE    = UNITED STATES   + M
   22  INTERNAL REVENUE SERVICE    = UNITED STATES   + R
   25  INTERNAL REVENUE SERVICE    = UNITED STATES   + T
```

This type of "wraparound" indexing for subordinate parts of corporate names could be one of the more user-friendly features in LUIS, if it weren't for the fact that only main entries are indexed in this way. (The same entries are retrievable, along with many added entries, by conducting the traditional search, A = UNITED STATES INTERNAL REVENUE SERVICE.) If one is interested in retrieving entries for materials *about* the IRS, the "wraparound" technique does not come into play:

> LUIS SEARCH REQUEST: S = INTERNAL REVENUE SERVICE
> NO SUBJECT HEADINGS FOUND. FOR POSSIBLE REASONS, TYPE h

The help screens do not explain that a subject search for the name of a government agency requires keying the name of the country or other political jurisdiction as the first element. In fact, in our library's LUIS catalog, the "corrected" search string S = UNITED STATES INTERNAL REVENUE SERVICE does result in a guide screen that displays "13 headings found." Needless to say, patrons and staff who use this type of search for government agencies as authors find it hard to understand and difficult to remember that the same form of name will not work in a subject search. (The upcoming LUIS merged headings indexes will resolve this inconsistency by removing the search capability from author searching rather than by expanding the capability to subject and added entry index fields.)

Uniform titles for laws can be easily retrieved when they are entered directly under their own names. For instance, the BERNE CONVENTION FOR THE PROTECTION OF LITERARY AND ARTISTIC WORKS is the uniform title for an international treaty that has been used as a subject heading. However, most laws apply to only a single jurisdiction; and the subject heading therefore takes the form of a name-plus-title. Staff members using terminals logged in the NOTIS cataloging mode can search for these headings by keying a slash in the place where the MARC subfield "t" would be found (e.g., S = CANADA/CANADIAN CHARTER OF RIGHTS AND FREEDOMS). But this technique does not work in the LUIS public catalog. The only subject search that retrieves the heading in LUIS is a search on the name alone. In the Florida State University online catalog the S = CANADA search results in a guide display that lists 751 headings spanning across 49 screens! The subject heading CANADA/CANADIAN CHARTER OF RIGHTS AND FREEDOMS shows up on the 34th screen in a section of name/title headings that follow all the CANADA headings with subject subdivisions but precede all the CANADA headings with alphabetical extensions (i.e., phrases or subordinate names). To illustrate:

    CANADA
523   – TREES -SEED -IDENTIFICATION
524   – WATER-SUPPLY
527   CANADA /CANADIAN CHARTER OF RIGHTS AND
      FREEDOMS
533   CANADA /FOREIGN INVESTMENT REVIEW ACT
535   CANADA ADVISORY COUNCIL ON THE STATUS OF
      WOMEN
536   CANADA AGRICULTURE CANADA RESEARCH
      BRANCH

This type of convoluted arrangement resembles the structure imposed by the old filing rules. That structure was seldom understood by library patrons (or even, we must admit, by filing clerks). Its use was therefore abandoned in manual catalogs a few years ago in favor of a simpler, strictly alphabetical, word-by-word arrangement.[2] Is there some reason why this step backward is advisable in an online environment?

The relative positioning of these name/title subject headings will change in LUIS after the NOTIS merged headings version is fully implemented. Titles of laws used as subjects will continue to display under the jurisdiction's name alone, but the index entries themselves will fall in the section of entries that precede the subject headings with subdivision; the subfield "t" portion of the heading will be alphabetically arranged within 245-field titles of books having that country (state, etc.) as subject. For example, materials *about* the Social Security Act would be found in the index as shown here:

    UNITED STATES
      • RIGHT AND THE POWER <1976> (FL)
      • SECRET PROCEEDINGS AND DEBATES O <1838> (FS)
      • SOCIAL SECURITY ACT
         • AMENDMENTS TO THE SOCIAL SECURIT <1985> (FL)
         • FORMATIVE YEARS OF SOCIAL SECURI <1966> (FS)

- LEGISLATIVE HISTORY OF TITLES I- (FL)
- SOCIAL SECURITY IN THE UNITED ST < 1971 > (FL)
- SPEKTRUM AMERIKA < 1964 > (FS)
- SPIRIT OF THE REVOLUTION < 1924 > (FS)

While this type of arrangement may be rationalized for personal name/title subject headings (e.g., personal names followed by the titles of literary works or musical compositions), it hardly seems logical for titles of laws. We might be able to convince some searchers that books about the tragedy *Hamlet* are necessarily also about Shakespeare; it would be a much farther stretch of imagination to presume that books about the Social Security Act treat the same subject as books about the United States. No, it makes more sense to arrange all types of subject headings alphabetically word-by-word, without regard to punctuation or (unseen) MARC codes. Indeed, it might be advantageous to have UNITED STATES /SO-CIAL SECURITY ACT follow closely after UNITED STATES — SOCIAL POLICY and just in front of UNITED STATES SOCIAL SECURITY ADMINISTRATION.

There is, however, a positive development on the horizon for LUIS users. After the new index is in place, LUIS users will be able to input a specific search based on the *title* portion of the subject heading alone and retrieve the desired entries in a 'rotated' heading display. To illustrate, a search constructed as S = SOCIAL SECURITY ACT will yield this response:

```
      SOCIAL SECURITY ACT
         • UNITED STATES
1           • AMENDMENTS TO THE SOCIAL SECURIT < 1985 > (FL)
2           • FORMATIVE YEARS OF SOCIAL SECURI < 1966 > (FS)
3           • LEGISLATIVE HISTORY OF TITLES I- (FL)
4           • SOCIAL SECURITY IN THE UNITED ST < 1971 > (FL)
```

No discussion of specific search problems would be complete without a critical examination of the controlled vocabulary used for subject access. In most American OPACs, subject vocabulary is taken from *Library of Congress Subject Headings* (*LCSH*). The word "control" is significant — it implies that headings will be consistent, and thus predictable, and that there will be adequate pointers (i.e., cross-references) from variant and related terms.

Many law-related headings in *LCSH* are not consistent in word choice. For instance, compare GOVERNMENT ATTORNEYS (or ATTORNEY AND CLIENT) to PATENT LAWYERS (or WOMEN LAWYERS). Other headings are not consistent in their word ordering; for example, the inverted heading EMPLOYEES, DISMISSAL OF makes "employees" the entry word, whereas the heading RECRUITING OF EMPLOYEES does not. *LCSH* seems to be particularly out-of-control for headings where non-legal topics are made legal by the addition of "law" in a phrase or subdivision. To be fair, the Library of Congress has not been insensitive to this problem. In 1978-79, the Library of Congress responded to the suggestions of many law catalogers by revising numerous subject headings that contained the subdivisions − LAW, − LAWS AND REGULATIONS or − LAWS AND LEGISLATION to the single standard form − LAW AND LEGISLATION.[3] However, no changes were made to headings that had already been established in phrase forms (AGRICULTURAL LAWS AND LEGISLATION, FORESTRY LAW AND LEGISLATION, DAIRY LAWS, and FARM LAW, to name just a few). In online catalogs that sort topical headings with subdivisions in one alphabetical list followed by another section of phrase headings that begin with the same word, the user may not make the correct guess when constructing his search string.

Here's an illustration of the problem. A user looking for books on laws relating to insurance might search S = INSURANCE − LAW; the response from a LUIS catalog will be "no entries found." In this case the correct guess would have been to use the search S = INSURANCE LAW. Unfortunately there is no "use" reference in *LCSH* leading from INSURANCE − LAW AND LEGISLATION to INSURANCE LAW, which means that the desired "search under" pointer will not display in LUIS. However, if the user does find the index listing for INSURANCE LAW, he should also see "search also under" references to no less than 25 narrower or related headings: INSURANCE, AGRICULTURAL − LAW AND LEGISLATION; INSURANCE, AUTOMOBILE − LAW

AND LEGISLATION; INSURANCE, AVIATION—LAW AND LEGISLATION; etc.

Law libraries would benefit from cross-references that link the *subdivided* legal subject headings with related subdivided strings, but Library of Congress has a policy of not repeating at the subdivision level the cross-references already established between the main topics. For example, the following reference,

> INSURANCE, PROPERTY—LAW AND LEGISLATION
>> search also under
>>> INSURANCE, CASUALTY—LAW AND LEGISLATION
>>> INSURANCE, FIRE—LAW AND LEGISLATION
>>> INSURANCE, FLOOD—LAW AND LEGISLATION
>>> INSURANCE, MORTGAGE GUARANTY—LAW AND
>>> LEGISLATION

is *not* authorized by *LCSH* because the established links between the main headings are presumed to be sufficient:

> INSURANCE, PROPERTY
>> search also under
>>> INSURANCE, CASUALTY
>>> INSURANCE, FIRE
>>> INSURANCE, FLOOD
>>> INSURANCE, MORTGAGE GUARANTY

There are two reasons to question this presumption. First, there is no evidence to show that the typical OPAC user will be likely to look upward (or on a previous screen) from INSURANCE, PROPERTY—LAW AND LEGISLATION to notice the related topics listed under the lead term INSURANCE, PROPERTY. Secondly, such a reference structure gives more weight or value to the concept of insurance, whereas in truth the legal aspects of a topic are usually the chief emphasis of works to which the subdivision —LAW AND LEGISLATION is assigned.

This problem is compounded when, as often occurs, an additional subdivision appears in the string. Users who search for material about laws concerning the *taxation* of insurance, for instance, will not encounter any references under INSURANCE—TAXATION—LAW AND LEGISLATION that point to narrower subject headings which are also subdivided by —TAXATION—LAW AND LEGISLATION (i.e., INSURANCE, CASUALTY; INSURANCE, GROUP; INSURANCE, HEALTH; INSURANCE, LIFE; and INSURANCE, PROPERTY). Because the cross-reference structure fails in satisfying this subject need, the user may have to make an exhaustive, tedious search through all the headings that begin with the word INSURANCE.

ALTERNATIVES TO SUBJECT HEADINGS

On the other hand, our user's needs might be met by a keyword search that uses Boolean operators to combine the terms TAXATION—LAW, and INSURANCE. Indeed, the difficulties which law libraries have in subject retrieval of government agency names *and* titles of laws might be overcome if the OPAC has keyword/ Boolean search capabilities. All of the examples given above—INTERNAL REVENUE SERVICE, CANADIAN CHARTER OF RIGHTS AND FREEDOMS, and SOCIAL SECURITY ACT—are search terms that yield the desired results when entered as keyword searches.

The keyword/Boolean search can also be helpful when the user's terminology itself does not mesh with the headings or references established in *LCSH*. The relatively new concept of "animal rights" is a case in point. ANIMAL RIGHTS was proposed as a new subject heading at the Library of Congress, but it was rejected due to its apparent incongruity: in the law, rights are only associated with persons. (Consider some of the established headings that contain the inherently legal term—CIVIL RIGHTS, RIGHT TO COUNSEL, or PRIVACY, RIGHT OF. It would be nonsensical to apply such concepts to animals, although their advocates might argue for animal RIGHT TO LIFE legislation!) Nevertheless, the phrase "animal rights" has entered popular usage, and a keyword search in the OPAC would help the user find books on the subject.

Here is another law-related phrase that has been even more widely used but still has not been authorized as a valid heading in *LCSH*. The phrase "legal reasoning" undoubtedly does not meet two basic criteria for Library of Congress acceptability as a new heading: the topic must be discrete *and* identifiable. Legal reasoning may not be discrete from other types of reasoning (although its context is different) and the topic certainly is difficult to define. *Black's Law Dictionary* does not recognize "legal reasoning." However, the phrase has been used (though not defined) in other standard reference sources and was the subject of an entire chapter in a recently published legal encyclopedia.[4] What does Library of Congress do with books that purport to be about "legal reasoning"? Usually the subject heading LAW — METHODOLOGY or LAW — PHILOSOPHY is assigned, but sometimes LAW — INTERPRETATION AND CONSTRUCTION or even SEMANTICS (LAW) is used. However, none of these subject headings has a "UF Legal reasoning" line in *LCSH*, which means that the online catalog user will find no "search under" directional signals to these headings when the search S = LEGAL REASONING is entered. Before concluding that the library has no materials on this subject, the user might attempt to identify works that bear the *title* "legal reasoning." In the FSU Law Library such a search would result in the retrieval of these five entries:

LUIS SEARCH REQUEST: T = LEGAL REASONING
   AUTHOR/TITLE INDEX — 5 ENTRIES FOUND
   1 FL:LEGAL REASONING *GOLDING MARTIN P (MARTIN PHILIP) <1984
   2 FL:LEGAL REASONING AND LEGAL EDUCATION
   3 FL:LEGAL REASONING AND LEGAL THEORY *MACCORMICK NEIL <1978
   4 FL:LEGAL REASONING SEMANTIC AND LOGICAL ANALYSIS *BRKIC JOHN <1985
   5 FL:LEGAL REASONING THE EVOLUTIONARY PROCESS OF LAW *ZELERMYER WILLIAM <1960

But see how much more effective a keyword/Boolean search would be for retrieving materials on this subject:

LUIS SEARCH REQUEST: K = LEGAL ADJ REASONING
   KEYWORD SEARCH INDEX — 16 ENTRIES FOUND, 1-16 DISPLAYED
   1 FL:An artificial intelligence approach to *Gardner Anne von der Lieth <1987
   2 FL:Legal reasoning and legal education <1986
   3 FL:Tactics of legal reasoning *Schlag Pierre <1986

4 FL:Computing power and legal reasoning <1985

5 FL:An introduction to law and legal reasoning *Burton Steven J <1985

6 FL:Laying down the law the foundations of legal reasoning research an <1985

7 FL:Legal reasoning semantic and logical analysis *Brkic John <1985

8 FL:Legal reasoning *Golding Martin P (Martin Philip) <1984

9 FL:How to brief a case an introduction to legal reasoni *Delaney John <1983

10 FL:Justice law and argument essays on moral and lega *Perelman Chaim <1980

11 FL:Moral and legal reasoning *Stoljar S J <1980

12 FL:Legal reasoning and legal theory *MacCormick Neil <1978

13 FL:Introduction to law and legal reasoning *Fischer Thomas Covell <1977

14 FL:On legal reasoning *Aarnio Aulis <1977

15 FL:Legal reasoning the evolutionary process of law *Zelermyer William <1960

16 FL:An introduction to legal reasoning *Levi Edward Hirsch <1949

Most law students trained in searching the WESTLAW and/or LEXIS databases should be aware of the advisability of considering synonyms or variant words when devising keyword searches. Their hands-on experience with truncation and Boolean operators transfers favorably to the OPAC, where a search constructed as K = (LE-GAL OR LAW$ OR JUD$) AND REASON$ retrieves not only all the titles shown above but also three editions of a work entitled *Reason in Law* and other works with "judicial reasoning" in the title.

Critics of OPAC keyword searching point out that the feature is costly to operate, that it slows down response time, and that it's too difficult to teach users the skills needed for its effective use. Some attention is now being given to another subject-oriented access point in the OPAC record—the call number. Would law library patrons benefit from the capability of searching by classification number?

If the law library uses the Library of Congress classification scheme, any affirmative answer would have to be qualified. One potential problem stems from the basic structuring of the K (Law) class, from the fact that the first order of division into subclasses is by jurisdiction (KD for British law; KE for Canadian law; etc.)

rather than by topic. This means that a researcher interested in "animal rights" in any or all the developed nations would have to search under KF390.5.A5 for U.S. laws, under KE452.A5 for Canadian laws, under KD667.A5 for UK laws, under KJV325 for France, and so forth. This is analogous to the situation with Library of Congress classification for the Visual Arts, where the first order of subdivision is by form rather than by historical period or style. In that case the user who identifies the class number N6923.B9 as dealing generally with the artist Michelangelo might not realize the OPAC may also have entries indexed under NB623.B9 (about Michelangelo's sculptures), under ND623.B92 (on his paintings), NA1123.B9 (his architecture), or NC1055.B9 (his drawings)!

These difficulties might be overcome in a highly sophisticated system which integrates the subject terms within the different subclass schedules into a sort of superguide to the class numbers so that the user will have all the pointers he needs for all the contexts of a subject. Libraries that have OPACs with the call number searching feature but no class schedule or classification index mounted online might wish to keep copies of the printed schedule(s) near the public terminals. It should be quite a challenge, however, to attempt to develop generic help screens that instruct the patron on use of the schedules!

The Library of Congress class schedules for Law, like those for Literature, make extensive use of form division tables. Hence, a span of two, five, 10 or 20 numbers may be appropriate for a given topic. Works about the general U.S. laws on immigration, for example, are classified under KF4801-4820. If the OPAC allows for a range of call numbers to be searched and retrieved, here is the breakdown of the number and formats of the materials on U.S. immigration law that would be identified at the FSU libraries:

2 titles	KF4801	Bibliographies
6 titles	KF4802	Periodicals
3 titles	KF4805.8	Compiled legislative histories
2 titles	KF4806.5-599	Particular acts
1 title	KF4808.7	Summary of federal legislation
2 titles	KF4812	Reports, regulatory agency decisions
1 title	KF4814	Digest of court or agency decisions
3 titles	KF4815	Looseleaf services

1 title	KF4818	Casebook
5 titles	KF4819.A2	Collected papers and essays
5 titles	KF4819.A3-49	Official reports
28 titles	KF4819.A7-Z	Treatises. Monographs
8 titles	KF4819.3	Compends. Outlines. Minor works
4 titles	KF4819.6	Popular works

But what happens if the OPAC does not recognize a range of numbers? When the search CL = KF4801-4820 is executed in NOTIS staff mode, the hyphen is *not* recognized as having special meaning; the system therefore starts dropping elements from the right of the command text until it can make a "fuzzy match," a match on a portion of the call number as input:

CALL NUMBER INDEX – 2 ENTRIES FOUND
1 FL: KF 4801 N34 1985
2 FL: KF 4801 S68 1986

Should this defect in system design be carried into the OPAC (the call number search is a LUIS enhancement slated for 1989), we can easily imagine the worst-case scenario: the user might conclude that the library has only these two books on U.S. immigration law. Some other user might retrieve the index entries for the remaining 69 titles, but only if he has the endurance for searching each of the twenty possible numbers separately, one at a time. Even then, half of those searches would result in no hits (e.g., KF4803, KF4804, etc.) and the bulk of the libraries' materials, the 50 titles classed under KF4819-4819.6, would not be displayed until the user's 19th search!

Some OPACs with call number search capability have the feature which allows the user to enter the call number index at any point and then browse up/down into higher/lower call numbers. The problem illustrated above clearly shows that if law libraries are to reap the maximum benefits of call number searching, then either this call number "browsing" feature or the ability to search a range of numbers must be present.

CONCLUSIONS

By and large, law libraries with OPACs have experienced the same benefits and problems regarding subject searches as other types of libraries. This paper has addressed a few specific questions that are of greater concern to law libraries and some broader questions as viewed from the law library perspective.

Several specific considerations relate to law libraries (usually law school libraries) that share a single online catalog with other libraries. The system's design should allow the OPAC user to easily distinguish the titles belonging to the law library. For this purpose, the law library's code or location ought to appear in the index displays as well as on the individual title's bibliographic record. It is also desirable to offer the OPAC user the option of qualifying his search to retrieve only the law library entries. Responsibility for authority control in a shared online catalog is extremely important. The law library and main campus library must cooperate in establishing the policies and procedures to be followed for online subject authority records and the corresponding forms used on bibliographic records. Otherwise, the OPAC user may not benefit from the online display of cross-references that lead him to desired subject headings or (worse yet) may be confronted with split files because some entries continue to be indexed under an obsolete form.

Law library users are more likely to conduct subject searches on names of government bodies or titles of laws, and both of these can be problematic in the online environment. Permutation or "rotating" of subject headings is a system design feature which improves access to titles of laws used as subjects, as it allows retrieval when the OPAC user has searched on the subfield "t" portion of the heading alone. If this feature could be extended to subfield "b" data as well, the problem of retrieving entries for works about government agencies might be resolved.

The broader question of the use of *LCSH* in online catalogs was discussed in the context of law-related subject headings. Although in recent years Library of Congress has established new headings in the form [Topic]—LAW AND LEGISLATION, over 50 "law" headings in phrase form remain valid without counting the many headings with "LAW" as a parenthetical qualifier. This inconsistency is significant in OPACs which index the subdivided headings differently. If the OPAC indexing were to disregard punctuation (or some subfield codes), or indeed, if there were more "used for" references in *LCSH* for the subdivided variant, it would matter less that these phrase forms are used because *access* to the headings would not be thwarted. Law libraries might consider enriching the local version of subject authority records by adding references that link related headings of the [Topic] — LAW AND LEGISLATION types. Such "subdivision-to-subdivision" references are explicitly prohibited in Library of Congress's practice.[5] Public libraries may complain that the level of specificity in *LCSH* is too great for their needs; the problem described above suggests that for *special* libraries the syndetic structures in *LCSH* may not be specific enough!

As in other types of libraries, law libraries with OPACs capable of keyword/Boolean searching will usually benefit from this mode of access. It was shown that the keyword search capability may overcome some problems caused by an imperfect index design or associated with choice of term or word order in *LCSH* in addition to expanding access to subject-rich fields such as book titles. Since most American law schools now require their students to gain "hands-on" experience in searching WESTLAW or LEXIS, the OPAC user in a law library may actually be better prepared for keyword searching than patrons in other types of libraries where searching in online databases (Dialog, ERIC, etc.) is more frequently done only by library staff.

Although call number searching is generally touted as a helpful enhancement for subject access, the law library might restrain its enthusiasm somewhat, especially if it uses the Library of Congress classification scheme. In that case, the OPAC user may be satisfied with his search results only if his interest is confined to a single jurisdiction (say, the United States), and if the OPAC has a call number index "browse" feature or allows for a range of class numbers to be searched and retrieved.

Searches by call number or by keywords, improvements to law-related subject headings and cross-references, and better system design to resolve user problems related to specific searches or multiple libraries sharing a single system — these are just a few of the issues affecting the utilization of OPACs in law libraries. It is hoped that the discussion and illustrations given here will assist the law library in the process of selecting an online system and perhaps stimulate current law users to focus on some of these issues in requesting enhancements from the OPAC vendors.

NOTES

1. Hunn, Nancy O. and J. A. Wright. "The Implementation of ACORN Authority Control at Vanderbilt University Library," *Cataloging & Classification Quarterly.* v. 8, no. 1 (1987), p. 83-84.

2. American Library Association. Filing Committee. *ALA Filing Rules.* Chicago, American Library Association, 1980.

3. Library of Congress. Processing Services Division. *Cataloging Service Bulletin.* no. 4 (spring 1979), p. 12.

4. The term "legal reasoning" is included in the definition of LEGAL PHILOSOPHY in *The Oxford Companion to Law* (Oxford, Clarendon Press, 1980), p. 746. Journal articles about legal reasoning are indexed by *Current Law Index* under the caption REASONING. And the *Encyclopedia of the American Judicial System* (New York, Scribner's, 1987) contains an entire chapter on p. 875-889, "Legal Reasoning," by Lief H. Carter.

5. Library of Congress. Subject Cataloging Division. *Subject Cataloging Manual: Subject Headings.* Washington, D.C., Library of Congress, 1985-. sect. H370.

A Subject Cataloging Code?

Lois Mai Chan

From time to time, the need for a subject cataloging code has been voiced in professional literature; one of the more recent calls appears in an article published in the December 1987 issue of *American Libraries*.[1] Before the profession embarks on the task of developing a code, several questions should be considered: (1) What is a subject cataloging code? (2) Do we need a subject cataloging code? (3) Is it economically feasible to develop such a code at this point in time? and (4) Who will develop it?

The definition of a code is the first question that needs to be raised. A code, by definition, is "a system of principles or rules."[2] A cataloging code, if we take the *Anglo-American Cataloguing Rules, Second Edition* (AACR2) as a prototype, serves two functions: to provide a set of principles which form the theoretical foundation and conceptual framework of the system and to give instructions on the implementation of these principles in the form of specific rules. In considering the development of a subject cataloging code, a related question is what kind of a code are we considering, is it to be a code totally based on theoretical and logical foundations without regard to present practice, or is it to be a code based on current practice, i.e., Library of Congress subject cataloging policies? The first alternative is tantalizing but will pose enormous problems in implementation. The second alternative appears more amenable but will still bring with it many difficulties in terms of resolving problems inherent in current practice.

The second question is, do we need a subject cataloging code? The need has been stated by many over the years and the reasons need not be repeated here. What has not been made clear is the

Lois Mai Chan is Professor, University of Kentucky, Lexington, KY 40506.

199

scope and the depth of the code being discussed. Will it be a subject headings code that provides rules for establishing headings only? Or will it be a subject cataloging code which covers the application of subject headings also? If so, is it to be a code modelled after AACR2? Mary K. Pietris, Chief of Subject Cataloging Division of the Library of Congress, expresses the view that with the availability of the *Subject Cataloging Manual*, there is now no longer a need for a subject headings code.[3] The manual provides guidelines for establishing Library of Congress subject headings and detailed instructions for applying them, in most instances far more detailed than any code can or needs to provide. The guidelines included in the manual may be viewed as rules and "rule interpretations" rolled into one. What is lacking, however, is a statement of principles, as stated in the first function mentioned above. Pietris promises that these will be forthcoming as part of the *Subject Cataloging Manual*.

Thirdly, is it economically feasible at this point in time to embark on the development of a subject cataloging code? This is perhaps the most crucial question, and the answer to it will probably be the ultimate determinant of whether a subject cataloging code is to be developed. The complexities of subject headings and their application will make the development of AACR2 seem child's play. An enormous amount of time and energy will have to be expended on this undertaking, particularly if we wish to involve the profession at large for broad-based participation. If we are thinking in terms of a code on a similar scale of AACR2, we must first ascertain that we are ready to commit the resources required by such an undertaking.

It would be quite unfortunate if I have given the impression that I am against developing a subject cataloging code. In fact, quite the opposite is true. What I have doubts about is the development of a subject cataloging code comparable to AACR2, apart from the *Subject Cataloging Manual*, particularly with regard to the second function of a code stated above, namely, to provide a set of specific rules for application. Many of these rules would most likely either duplicate the LC guidelines in the *Subject Cataloging Manual* or contradict them. The former would be unproductive, and the latter could be counter-productive. In my *personal* opinion, what is most needed and economically feasible would be the development of a set of principles comparable to the "Statement of Principles"[4] resulting from the International Conference on Cataloguing held in Paris in 1961 which formed the basis of Part I of AACR2 and many other cataloging codes. Such a set of principles is needed to provide a theoretical and, in part, perhaps even logical basis and a conceptual framework for subject cataloging. If we decide to continue subject cataloging practice along the course of the Library of Congress Subject Headings system, these principles may point out future direction for its continuing development. The LC subject cataloging guidelines embodied in the *Subject Cataloging Manual* may then be gradually revised and further developed in accordance with the principles, and together, the principles and the LC guidelines can fulfill the function of a code comparable to AACR2, without the need for yet another set of instructions in the form of "rule interpretations." Even if the profession should decide that it would be desirable and economically feasible to develop a full subject cataloging code on the scale of AACR2, such a set of principles should be developed first as the foundation and guiding principles of the rules.

One further question remains: who will develop the code? There appear to be two alternatives: (1) outside of the Library of Congress or (2) by the Library of Congress. The first approach has a precedent in the Code Revision Committee established for the development of AACR2. The second approach would be along the line of the development of the *Subject Cataloging Manual*. In the latter case, the "sections for the *manual* that describe the basic philosophy of assigning headings and of creating new headings" promised by Pietris may be used as the basis of the statement of principles mentioned earlier. It would be unfortunate if either group takes on the responsibility without participation from the other. Such an undertaking should involve the profession at large as well as the Library of Congress. The question is, then, who will take primary responsibility for the overall planning and code development? Three criteria should be considered in determining the vesting of responsibility: (1) available resources, (2) efficacy and efficiency, and (3) implications for implementation. In applying these criteria, the experiences in the development of AACR2 could be used as a point of reference.

REFERENCES

1. William E. Studwell, "The 1990s: Decade of Subject Access: A Theoretical Code for LC Subject Headings Would Complete the Maturation of Modern Cataloging," *American Libraries* 18:958,960 (December 1987).

2. *Webster's Ninth New Collegiate Dictionary*, Springfield, MA: Merriam-Webster, 1983.

3. Mary K.D. Pietris, "LC: New *Manual*, Not Code, Needed," *American Libraries* 18:958 (December 1987).

4. International Conference on Cataloguing Principles, Paris, 1961, "Statement of Principles," in *Report of International Conference on Cataloguing Principles*, ed. A.H. Chaplin and Dorothy Anderson (London: Organizing Committee of the International Conference on Cataloguing Principles, National Central Library, 1963), pp.91-96.

A Reference Librarian's View of the Online Subject Catalog

Constance McCarthy

SUMMARY. This paper suggests that the cataloging community may be setting its goals too low in its approach to online subject access. Truly effective subject retrieval for online catalog users will not be possible until the Library of Congress gives a higher priority to consistency in the assignment of subject headings. In recognition of the intellectual complexity of *LCSH*, the paper proposes the appointment of subject specialists to monitor the assignment of subject headings at the Library of Congress.

Why do library catalogs get so much more respect from reference librarians than they do from catalogers? Is it because catalogers, who create them, are more aware of their shortcomings and inadequacies? Or perhaps reference librarians actually see the catalog daily fulfilling an important function for its users and realize that, although imperfect, it is a superb instrument for the advancement of knowledge? For whatever reason, catalogers sometimes seem not to acknowledge the dignity and intellectual achievement of the catalogs that they helped produce.

For example, as libraries implemented online catalogs, catalogers were known to propose that incorrect book location information *could* be allowed to remain in the card catalog rather than incur the expense of changing records which would shortly be replaced. Public services librarians were appalled at the very thought. Minimal level cataloging has arrived and with it minimal information for users of those books. Reference librarians, experienced in finding value in every part of the catalog record, remain dubious. Many contemporary catalogers appear to believe that much information in

Constance McCarthy is Assistant Head, Reference Department, Northwestern University Library, Evanston, IL 60208.

the bibliographic record is unused while reference librarians want even more information added. But it is about subject headings that the views of catalogers and reference librarians differ most dramatically. Catalogers seem to feel that too much is expected of the subject headings they assign. Reference librarians, knowing the needs and expectations of the public, hope for much but are often disappointed.

In recent years, the Library of Congress, in response to online catalog use studies which show the popularity of subject searching,[1] has become more responsive to the difficult task of providing better subject access. Pauline Cochrane has referred to this change in attitude and practice as a "paradigm shift."[2] The Library of Congress now assigns more subject headings to most books, and terminology is somewhat closer to colloquial usage. Improvements have been made in "see also" cross references to move towards a more rational, more thesaurus-like use of terms. However, the access vocabulary provided through "see" references remains miserly although greater generosity in this area could make a far greater difference to the average catalog user than any number of enlightened changes in the subject headings themselves. Meanwhile, the need for more accurate and consistent assignment of subject headings by catalogers at the Library of Congress is seldom mentioned. Little attention is paid to the *serviceability* of the headings, either to the user or to the literature indexed by them.

Elsewhere, I have discussed the "reliability factor"—the degree to which the catalog is successful in bringing together under one subject heading all books on the same topic.[3] In that article, my examples were subject headings assigned to reference books. I sought to demonstrate that it is often impossible to locate the majority of the good reference tools on a topic by consulting a single subject heading and its cross references. In this paper, I will discuss that same concern in a broader context[4] in the hopes of posing a rudimentary challenge to the apparently prevailing view within the cataloging community that little can be done to improve this aspect of subject cataloging. At this important decision point about the future nature of online subject catalogs, I want to suggest that good subject recall is only possible if the right subject headings are put into the record in the first place.

CATALOGER AND LIBRARY USER:
APPROACHES TO SUBJECT ACCESS

In thinking about ways to achieve the best subject retrieval for library users, it may be worthwhile to compare the mental process of a cataloger deciding which subject heading to assign with that of a library user deciding which term to enter into an online catalog. The cataloger has a book in hand and must decide how best to name its subject matter. The library user has an *idea* in mind and must imagine what name the library has given to this idea. The cataloger, in deciding on a name, has access to a more or less familiar list of subject headings, *Library of Congress Subject Heading (LCSH)*, and to its system of underlying rules. The user, in bringing to consciousness words for the idea she has in mind, may be completely ignorant of the concept of established vocabularies and descriptor lists. Even if *LCSH* is available, the user may not begin to suspect the detail, the complexity, and the sheer number of subject headings in the system.

In addition to their different awareness of the controlled vocabulary concept, there is yet a more basic difference in the mental framework of cataloger and user. The cataloger, book in hand, attempts to *describe* it by means of subject headings and chooses — in obedience to the rules — the most specific headings that will encompass the subject of the entire book. In the language of database evaluation, the cataloger strives for *precision*.

The user, choosing a subject term, hopes to find all the books in the library which deal substantially with that topic. The user is interested in *recall*.[5] Although it might be argued that the user's interest calls for less specificity in subject heading assignment, I do not believe this necessarily to be the case as long as the level of specificity is consistent for all items and as long as adequate cross references are supplied. The user's primary interest in recall does not exclude an interest in precision. "All the books" on a topic may be only one book or no books: and the user will not often be well served by the automatic presentation of a group of titles on a broader topic. She should, however, have the opportunity (usually not now available) to see the name of the broader topic displayed as a cross reference so that she can choose it if she wishes. Rather than the lack of books in the database at the right degree of specificity, the more serious problem for the user is likely to be (a) that she will not find the right subject heading or (b) that if she finds the right heading, it will not include all the books on her topic because catalogers (thinking primarily in terms of precision and often apparently ignoring recall) have not assigned the same subject headings to all of them.

SUBJECT ACCESS: A SIMPLE MODEL

Subject access can be represented as a sphere, with an outer layer consisting of the "see" and "see also" references and an inner core made up of the subject headings actually assigned to the books. The conflict just described between the interests of the cataloger and those of the user has, it seems to me, a solution at each level. For the outer layer, the solution is a radically improved syndetic structure. The best suggestions I have seen are proposed by Marcia J. Bates.[6] It is important to note that Bates wishes to maintain standard *LCSH* subject headings as the access points to the records but to surround them with a vastly enriched entry vocabulary (the "Side-of-the-Barn Principle") and to link them within a strong structure of "see also" references. This approach avoids the effort and expense of making extensive changes to *LCSH* itself.

At the inner core, the subject headings themselves as assigned to the books form the heart of the system, without which all the rest would be valueless; but they are seldom discussed or evaluated by OPAC designers and theorists, who appear to believe that books grow their own subject headings. The solution to subject access problems at this level is to give more attention to recall by making sure that all books on the same topic have the same subject heading.

SOME PROBLEMS WITH CURRENT SUBJECT ACCESS

Unfortunately, bringing together under subject heading all books on that subject is not a priority at the Library of Congress. If any reader doubts this, I suggest doing some trial searches of conceptual topics in the catalog of any large library. If no suitable example comes to mind, consider this cluster of subject headings which all relate to ethnic groups in the U.S.: **Ethnology — United States; Minorities — United States; Immigrants — United States; United States — Emigration and Immigration**; and **United States — Ethnic Relations**. There are many other related subject headings, but a perusal of the books assigned to these will suffice.

To begin with the most serious problem, at the inner core of the subject access system, people looking for all the books on one of these topics as defined by the Library of Congress will not find them under any one heading. Many books on any of the five subjects can be found under more than one of the headings, and there is no certainty that a book which is clearly devoted to one of the subjects will be found under its proper heading. In some cases, wrong headings have been chosen — sometimes, it would appear, under the influence of the book's title. Most often though, the cataloger has assigned one or more correct headings but neglected to bring out another aspect of the book with other headings. For example, a book about American immigrant leaders may have "ethnology-ethnicity" headings but no "immigrant" headings. Formerly, there was a reluctance to assign "too many" headings; but this is apparently no longer the case. Rather, it would seem that catalogers are simply unaware of alternative headings which have previously been used for books on the subjects under consideration.

Another "inner core" problem is less serious because most online catalogs can at least partially surmount it: the problem when the headings, although correctly assigned, are separated from each other by overenthusiastic application of subdivisions or by the peculiarities of subdivision arrangement. The library user who sees the subject heading **Minorities — United — States — Economic Conditions**, for example, has no way of knowing that other subtopics will be found elsewhere ("outside" the United States as it were) — like **Minorities — Education — United States**. However, when online catalogs do not require any particular order of subject heading parts, this may no longer be a difficulty. The computer may also improve access to many other books by showing the user titles previously segregated by such form headings as **Addresses, essays, lectures; Collections: Congresses**; and **Miscellanea**. A subdivision problem which cannot be corrected by the computer, however, without additional information in the catalog record, arises from the fact that

Minorities — Education — United States does not include **Minorities — Education — California** or **Minorities — Education — Midwest.** The user who wants all the books on the education of minorities in the United States must scan the complete file on the education of minorities everywhere in the world for United States place names as subdivisions. The specificity principle, of course, creates this problem; and it occurs throughout the catalog for all places which are parts of other places. Still, the user could wish the online subject catalog to be versatile enough to permit retrieval of all books on a topic by country, including all its smaller geographic components.

The next step is to consider the outer sphere problems which confront the user who is just beginning a subject search. A user who decided to look under — for example — **Ethnics** or **Ethnic Americans** would find no "see" reference from these terms to any other heading. Many reasonable terms in the user's vocabulary lead to dead end searches.

Another "outer sphere" problem, but one amenable to solution by the computer, is the lack of scope notes for users. The subject heading **Ethnic Groups**, for example, is an example of a "false friend." Users finding this term might well assume, in the absence of a scope note, that they had retrieved all the books in the library on their topic and never go on to find the "chief" headings, **Ethnology, Minorities,** and **Immigrants.**

What is the end result? A library user, hoping to find the best recent literature on these topics, will not find it — at least not without having first been hindered by the very system that should help perform this task. Those library users who have completed what library researchers usually define as "successful" subject searches (that is — those who have managed simply to find a subject heading) have no way of knowing what they have *not* found, and — as often as not — what they have not found may contain the most important information on the topic.

What can be done to improve the user's chance of a truly successful search? First, the steps already taken by the Library of Congress — more generous assignment of subject headings and improvements in the cross reference structure — are of great value. In addition, I believe it would be useful to look at subject access in a different way.

A SUGGESTION: SUBJECT HEADING MANAGEMENT

It is hardly necessary and perhaps impossible to do an evaluative study of subject access in terms of recall to demonstrate the problems described in this paper. Probably no one disputes their existence. The informal response of the cataloging community is that consistency in subject heading assignment, given the size of the database and the number of catalogers, is probably unfeasible; and that if it were feasible, it would be too expensive.

To reference librarians, this is like saying that the size and complexity of the postal service is such that it is too expensive to assure that all letters are delivered to the right addresses. The very purpose of the system is undermined. Reference librarians wish that subject headings could provide access to the bibliographic database exactly as a good index does to a book, by gathering together all references to a topic (paragraphs in the first case, entire books in the second) under a single heading.

Certainly perfect reliability is impossible. The database *is* enormous; the complexity almost beyond comprehension. Consistent subject access could never even begin to approach the nearly perfect accuracy of present-day name authority work. Furthermore, judgments as to its reliability would necessarily be subjective. But it would make the catalog a greatly more serviceable instrument for library users. Would the effort be worthwhile? How could it be accomplished?

In their attitudes about how "good" the bibliographic database is and how important excellent access to it can be, catalogers differ from the "consumers" of their product. Sometimes catalogers, in their seeming fixation on flaws in descriptive cataloging and in name authority work, devote themselves to ever more scrupulous exactitude to achieve perfect purity in these areas while apparently regarding topical subject headings as little more than a helpful way of describing the book after the user has located it through a known item search.

But the database, regardless of catalogers' opinions, is magnificent! *LCSH* is itself an astonishing resource in its attempt to provide a name for every aspect of human knowledge and to add clarifications by the careful distinctions of its scope notes. Impressive erudition and research have gone into developing even its current rudimentary syndetic structure. Why do catalogers not use this great resource to its fullest to improve user access to the database?

Actually, even a reference librarian can understand the formidable difficulties in achieving consistent subject access. Furthermore, catalogers wishing to demonstrate the hopelessness of my proposed efforts could line up in their defense various studies of indexer inconsistency from the days when online database searching was still relatively new.[7] These studies show a high degree of variability in index term choice by indexers working from a thesaurus. Not only did they find *inter*-indexer inconsistency; individual indexers were inconsistent in their own choice of terms over time. These important studies should be reviewed today as more attention is directed to subject access. The studies show that two trained people, looking at the same document, have almost a 50% probability of using different subject terms to describe it.

What the studies do not show, however, is what would have happened if those indexers had looked at the other titles already assigned those subject terms, had consulted the other index terms given to the additional titles found under the first term, even perhaps had looked at the matter from outside the database by going to the documents themselves. Such work, routinely done in an attempt to bring books on the same topics together, would surely improve the assignment of subject headings. As long as it is not, indexer inconsistency studies merely confirm what we already know: without special efforts, subject terms will not be assigned consistently to books on the same subject.

It seems to me that the best way to undertake such a special and sustained effort would be for the Library of Congress to appoint subject specialists with the responsibility to oversee the assignment of books to subject headings: to ride herd, as it were, on titles straying from their proper flocks. These same subject specialists might also find time to go back and, by splitting files, to rescue the books previously given old, broad subject headings before the approval of new, more specific ones. They could write additional scope notes for public use and would manage the "see" and "see also" references within their subject areas.

Such an endeavor would signal a new way of thinking about subject access. The Library of Congress and the library community would then be actively shaping subject access to the wealth of information in books. The intellectual challenge would be great; the expense would be large; but *it would be worth it*!

NOTES

1. Karen Markey, "Users and the Online Catalog: Subject Access Problems," in *The Impact of Online Catalogs*, ed. by Joseph R. Matthews. (NY: Neal-Schuman, 1986): 35-69.

2. Pauline Cochrane, "A Paradigm Shift in Library Science," *Information Technology and Libraries* (2) 1: 3-4, 1983.

3. Constance McCarthy, "The Reliability Factor in Subject Access," *College & Research Libraries* 47 (January, 1986): 48-56.

4. The degree of subject heading dispersion in the catalog has not been widely studied or discussed. A book by John M. Christ, *Concepts and Subject Headings: Their Relation in Information Retrieval and Library Science*. (Methuen, N.J.: Scarecrow, 1972); p. 141-142, documents the many different subject headings assigned to sociological books on the topics of role and culture. A recent article by Joseph W. Palmer, "Subject Authority Control and Syndetic Structure—Myths and Realities," *Cataloging and Classification Quarterly* 7 (Winter, 1986): 71-95, on the failure of libraries to maintain the syndetic structure of their catalogs has examples of subject heading dispersion, which occurs especially when obsolete headings are not changed.

5. "Recall" can be defined as the proportion of the total number of relevant documents in an online data base that are retrieved in a search. "Precision" is the proportion of the retrieved documents that are relevant. Recent descriptions of these evaluative concepts are given in: Stephen P. Harter, *Online Information Retrieval: Concepts, Principles, and Techniques*. (Orlando, FL: Academic Press, 1986): 155-161; Jennifer E. Rowley, *Abstracting and Indexing*. (London: Clive Bingley, 1982): 49-51.

6. Marcia J. Bates, "Subject Access in Online Catalogs: A Design Model." *Journal of the American Society for Information Science* 37 (November, 1986): 357-378.

7. Many of these studies from the 1960s and 1970s are cited and described in: Susanne M. Humphrey and Nancy E. Miller, "Knowledge-Based Indexing of the Medical Literature: The Indexing Aid Project." *Journal of the American Society of Information Science* 38 (May, 1987): 184-196, an article which reports on a project now underway at the National Library of Medicine to develop a system to assist MEDLINE indexers. Bates also cites some of these studies. Bates, p. 360.

Subject Access in Online Catalogs: Developments in France

Suzanne Jouguelet

During the 1980s, French libraries have chosen interactive integrated systems with cataloging, circulation, and eventually acquisitions.[1] These systems are both foreign (Dobis, Geac, Clsi-Libs 100, Als, Tobias, Sibil) and French (Libra, Iris, Brigitte, Opsys).

The initial emphasis depends upon the type of library. For example, cataloging was the first module implemented at the Bibliothèque Nationale and the Bibliothèque Publique d'Information which do not loan items while circulation within a library network was most important for the Bibliothèque Municipale de Lyon with its main library and 13 branches. But integration of the various modules often subsequently occurs. Lyon, after having installed circulation, brought up the acquisitions and cataloging modules.

The concept of a public interactive online catalog is much more recent in France than in the Anglo-Saxon countries, but since about 1984 the quality of public online access has become one of the major selection criteria. It is no longer necessary to demonstrate the advantages of the online catalog: up-to-date information, more numerous and more precise search strategies (for example, keyword subject searching), boolean operators, etc.

In contrast with data base searching, use of an OPAC is direct, without intermediaries, and without prior training. This computerized tool allows decentralized information access, first in the library and its branches and now directly by users from their homes. In France, MINITEL has made distributed access possible. MINITEL, which will soon celebrate its tenth birthday, has multiple uses: al-

---

Suzanne Jouguelet is a librarian at the Bibliothèque municipale de Lyon, Lyon, France.

213

lowing data base searching, providing a cheap computer terminal, serving as a transactional tool. Users have become accustomed to it by consulting its most popular file, the electronic telephone book. In mid-1988, there were 3,600,000 MINITEL installations in France and 7,000 accessible information sources.

In the book trade, the data base of *Livres Disponibles* (*Books in Print*), named Electre, is accessible by MINITEL; it contains 275,000 in-print books available by title, author, and subject. MINITEL provides access to more and more library catalogs, for example, the Médiathèque de la Villette in the Cité des Sciences et de l'Industrie or public libraries in the Rhône-Alpes region such as Valence and Villeurbanne.

It is thus within this French context in evolution that we will study subject access in online catalogs.

Subject access: the studies on searching show the importance of subject searching.

Online catalogs: we will concern ourselves only with library catalogs and will not consider data bases.

Clearly, one of the factors for successful subject searching is the quality of the indexing. It is fitting, therefore, to first examine *subject indexing in France*.

Beginning in the 1980s, after a history of very individualistic subject indexing, libraries turned towards the use of subject authority lists, precisely because of the new need created by the computer for a common language to facilitate record distribution and sharing. Library of Congress subject headings, translated and modified by the Université Laval in Québec, were chosen by the Bibliothèque Publique d'Information in 1976 and by the Bibliothèque Nationale in 1980. But it is not our intention to deal with this history in detail.

Let us instead describe the current state of affairs. The French authority list is called RAMEAU (Répertoire d'Autorité Matière Encyclopédique et Alphabétique Unifié = Unified Encyclopedic and Alphabetical Subject Authority List) after having been called LAMECH (Liste d'Autorité de Matières Encyclopédiques, Collective et Hiérarchisée = Encyclopedic, Collective, and Hierarchical Subject Authority List). RAMEAU is a joint enterprise of the Ministère de la Recherche et de l'Ensignement Supérieur (Direction des Bibliothèques, des Musées et de l'Information Scientifique et

Technique) and of the Bibliothèque Nationale. The Bibliothèque Nationale has maintained the subject authority list since 1980.

This authority list is a tool to help with indexing. Since it is derived from *Library of Congress Subject Headings*, it is precoordinated and universal in nature. RAMEAU is available online; it is also published two times per year in microfiche. Supervision of the data base, distribution of its products, and support for its network of users has been assigned to a national unit for coordinating subject indexing, the Cellule nationale de coordination de l'indexation matière.

Who are its users?

1. The Bibliothèque Nationale is both the producer and a user of RAMEAU. Its subject authority file, a subunit of its cataloging system, contains about 100,000 headings, including proper names established by the Bibliothèque Nationale. The integration of subject authority records and bibliographic records makes online control of indexing possible.

2. The Bibliothèque Publique d'Information and several important public libraries, for example, Lyon, Grenoble, Rennes.

3. An increasing number of university libraries under the prodding of the Direction des Bibliothèques which wishes to promote at the same time as computerization a common subject access language with a view towards a union catalog. This same group encourages university libraries to do all their current cataloging and eventually their retrospective cataloging on the various networks (OCLC, Libra, Sibil, Bibliothèque Nationale). Cooperation among libraries should foster the realization of a national union catalog. The common subject indexing language would be RAMEAU.

4. The network of pedagogical documentation centers with a multimedia data base on education, "Mémoire de l'Education," in part indexed by RAMEAU.

RAMEAU participants make use of the data base not only as an aid to subject indexing but also to create new or modified terms in the authority file. The libraries in the network make suggestions online for new terms or for modifications. The Bibliothèque Nationale validates these proposals to assure the intellectual coherence of the authority file.

Searchers use ALEXIS, a software used for linguistic applications based upon natural language searching. This language will be used in MINITEL as a new way to search the business portion of the telephone directory (the yellow pages) in natural language. ALEXIS provides keyword searching including Boolean operators and adjacency searching.

The author of an article on LAMECH (the former name of RAMEAU) gave the following humorous example as an introduction to ALEXIS:

> Without having to redo the search equation, you could choose to "navigate" from the term "abominable snowman" in one or another of the following directions:
>
> Man — Fall of Man — Good and Evil — Temptation, etc . . .
>
> Snow — Precipitation (Meteorology) — Cloud Physics, etc. . . .

By the term "navigation" is meant the ability to go from one term to another by using the semantic links between the two pieces of information.

ALEXIS also includes a spelling checker.

France has yet another indexing system, derived from an authority list entitled, *Choix de Vedèttes matières à l'intention des bibliothèques = Choice of Subject Terms for Library Use* (2nd edition, 1987). This system was chosen by the Cercle de la Librairie, publisher of *Livres Disponibles = Books in Print*, for its MINITEL data base, ELECTRE. Many public libraries have adopted it. It is also a precoordinated system, but less rigidly so. In addition, it differs from RAMEAU by its size — 12,500 common noun entries.

In principle, the indexing system in an online catalog is less constraining than in a data base where thesaurus use is indispensible for a successful search. But as we shall see in examining search strategies, it nonetheless plays an important role.

First, let us make the general comment that searching varies from library to library. Even if libraries use the same online system, they may divide their holdings differently. This is the case for the Mediathèque de la Villette, the Bibliothèque municipale de Lyon, and the Bibliothèque Publique d'Information which all three use the Geac online catalog.

For searching purposes, La Villette divides its holdings among three service areas: public reference, children's services, and special reference. The Bibliothèque Municipale de Lyon with its network of branch libraries divides its holding by location. Lastly, the Bibliothèque Publique d'Information with only one location divides its searches by material type—books, serials, audiovisual. The Maison du Livre, de l'Image et du Son in Villeurbanne, which uses the Opsys system, allows searching according to patron category—adults, adolescents, children, everyone.

Searching by successive menus is the most frequent search type. In Geac, for example, subject searching follows the classic model. If the patron uses the exact search term as chosen by the cataloger and retrieves only one entry, a brief record for the item immediately appears.

Example of a Subject Search in the Geac Catalog at the Bibliothèque Municipale de Lyon

Sujet : ABSINTHE			I référence
Référence : Absinthe			
Auteur : DELAHAYE , Marie-Claude			
Titre : Absinthe : Histoire de la Fée verte			
Support : Livre			
Localisation	Prêt	Cote	Etat
4 ARRDT / 4 ADULT	LIVADU	394 – I DEL	Sur place

On the other hand, if a perfect match does not occur or if several entries in the index match the search term, the system displays the corresponding part of the index.

Sujet : AUTISME	RECH. SUJET	
	Corresp. 9 sujets	
	Référ-ces ds le	
	catalogue général	Votre bit
1. Autisme	6	1
2. Autisme infantile Précoce	9	
3. Autisme . . Récits	1	
4. Autisme . . Thérapeutique	2	1

The patron can then browse forwards or backwards in the subject index, which provides automatic right truncation.

If no subject corresponds to the search term, the system displays a list of alphabetically adjacent subject terms.

Example: Subject search "IDEAL"

Les réponses proches sont les suivantes:
1. — Iconographie. . .
2. — Idées politiques, etc. . .

If several titles match the chosen subject, the patron can select from an author/title list of the corresponding items. Twelve citations can appear on the screen at the same time. It is possible to browse forwards and backwards in the list of displayed items.

Function keys allow the user to return to this list and also to the index. The ability to back up allows for flexible searching as does a function key for returning to the previous screen.

The citation is available in several formats: brief citation with local information, full citation, and the full MARC record in staff mode.

The integration of the online catalog with the circulation module gives the user the circulation status (on loan and expected back at a certain date, on shelf, etc.) and will eventually allow him to reserve the item. With an integrated acquisitions module, the system also displays on-order items with the appropriate status.

Here is an example of a subject search in another system, Opsys:

GEOLOGIE		demande : Géologie
ligne	n b	Concepts trouvés
1	24	Géologie
2	1	Géologie : Afrique
. . . .		
8	2	Alpes Maritimes : Géologie
. . . .		
21	8	Terre : géologie

In this system, a subject search is implicitly a keyword subject search. Librarians in staff mode can do hierarchical searches, that is, subject searches by the first element in the subject chain.

To follow up on the previous search, typing in 21 brings up the following screen (the column to the right is the call number for the library where the terminal is located):

Huit ouvrages trouvés:
1. — La merveilleuse aventure de la terre   **500 MER**
2. — Notre planète la terre / Keith Lye   **550 LYE**

Automatic truncation is not provided; an explicit indicator (*) is needed. By choosing a line number, the user gets the complete record.

Keyword searching increases the number of access points and helps overcome the faults of a precoordinated indexing system by retrieving the subject word wherever found in the subject heading string. As we saw in the previous example, keyword searching in this system is implicitly provided for subject searching. In other systems, subject searching and keyword searching are separate; and the user must specifically designate a keyword search in the author, title, or subject indexes. Only one keyword may be used, and the library can define a stop list.

On the keyword searching menu, the system asks for the type of search: in the title fields, in the personal and corporate author field, or in the subject fields. Unlike the general subject searching mode, truncation is not automatic; the symbol (*) is necessary.

Several examples follow:

Example of the help screen for keyword searching at the Bibliothèque Municipale de Lyon

---

"Tapez un mot exprimant le sujet qui vous interésse.

Ex. : LYON pour obtenir la liste de tous les documents dont le sujet comporte le mot LYON

Tapez le début d'un mot suivi du signe # pour obtenir les sujets comportant des mots de même racine.

Ex. : pour obtenir la liste de tous les documents dont le sujet comporte les mots Electricité, Electronique, Electrotechnique

---

Votre mot : Montagne	Corresp. 32 sujets	— votre bibl.
1. — Animal .. montagne	2	1
2. — Cézanne, Paul (1831-1906)		
"La Montagne Sainte Victoire"	1	1
3. — Chemin de fer de montagne . . France	3	2
. . . .	. . . .	. . . .
10. — Montagne .. Amémagement		
. . . .		
13. — Oiseaux de montagne		
14. — Sauvetage en montagne		

To get around cumbersome menu-driven searching, command-driven searching with chained commands is possible. For example, in the keyword subject search for the term "mountain," menu-driven searching requires five screens:

1. Summary
2. Selection of keyword searching
3. Selection of keyword subject searching
4. Access to the search screen to type in the keyword
5. The keyword index for the word "mountain"

By chaining the commands (MOT/MSUJ/Montagne), the trained user arrives directly at the index screen with considerable time savings. But command-driven searching is not available in all systems.

Cross references, both unused forms ("see" references) and related forms ("see also" references), are provided to a greater or lesser degree depending upon the library and its system; but they are tied closely to the degree of linkage between the bibliographic file and the authority file. For the libraries which have integrated authority files, for example, the Bibliothèque Nationale, the Bibliothèque Publique d'Information, and the Médiathèque de la Villette, the unused forms ("see" references) are integrated into the subject index; and the searcher is sent to the used form. For related references ("see also" references) in the online system of these libraries, the function "REN" provides access to the "see also" references. The following example gives the results of a search for the subject "géologie" in the online catalog of the Bibliothèque Nationale.

Example of a subject search for "Géologie" at the Bibliothèque Nationale

Sujet : Géologie		29 notices
Auteur	Titre	Date
1. Mathon, Claude-Charles	"La biosphère a	
	un passé	1984
2. Bellair, Pierre	"Elements de géologie"	1979
3.		

Choisissez un des n à gauche ou bien
IND : retour à l'index   AVT : suite de cette liste
REN : liste des renvois   SOM : nouvelle recherche

If the user types "REN," the list of "see also" references appears:

Sujet : Géologie
      1 — Alluvions
      2 — Création
      3 — Cristallographie
      . . . .

The REN function is also available at the brief record and full record levels.

Another way to access materials by subject is to use the classification numbers. Many libraries integrate this search with other number searches (shelf location, ISBN, etc.). The Bibliothèque Publique d'Information, an open stack library, provides an interesting example of subject access through classification. This library offers two distinct searching strategies: by subject and by shelf location (simplified Universal Decimal Classification), but it has also integrated classification into subject searching. The system gives the classification location for the subject, which makes it possible for the patron to go immediately to the shelves. The location directions are given in capital letters in the subject index.

Example of a subject search for "Sri Lanka"

1. – Sri Lanka (Rep.)	25 sujets
2. – SRI LANKA (HISTOIRE)	
3. – Sri Lanka/Antiquités	
4. – Sri Lanka/Bibliographie	

2. Sri Lanka (Histoire)		
	Orientation	
Etage : 3ème	Bureau : 9	Cote 954-5

This is an example of an interesting link because with the subject heading the user can go directly to the classification number and through it to the shelf location.

Boolean searching is not yet heavily used in French online catalogs except for the implicit "and" in the author-title search. Even when possible in the online system, it often degrades response time. Boolean searching is available, however, at the Médiathèque de la Villette where subject searching is heavily used (60-65% of all searches, a normal percentage for a science library); but it is difficult to judge its usefulness. It seems as if certain patrons use this search strategy just to "try it out" because it puzzles them. In addition, the public finds it difficult to manipulate the Boolean operators (and, or, not).

In the majority of French online catalogs, the integration of the different modules (circulation, online catalog, acquisitions) allows the user to find out about document availability and eventually to reserve wanted items. The public is also aware of materials on order.

The systems described in this paper allow for flexibility. The beginner has function keys and a menu-driven approach with numerous help screens which the library itself can define. The skilled user can chain commands and arrive quickly at the sought after information.

Unfortunately, there are also limitations: no automatic spelling correction, no chaining of keywords, no combining of keywords and classification, no searching by multi-word expressions.

It is common to distinguish data bases from online catalogs by saying that online catalogs are available without intermediaries, without a searching manual, without previous training. These statements are all true, but only partially. In truth, users often encounter difficulties in using online catalogs.

The Bibliothèque municipale de Valence, an Opsys system user, did a study on searching and on the reasons for search failures by using a program on Opsys which provides a list of unanswered queries. Subject searching is most frequently used (over 50% of all searches), but only 23% of the subject searches retrieved anything according to the study made during February-March 1988. Typing and spelling mistakes play a large part. The study found eight incorrect ways to type or to spell "psychanalyse" and almost as many for "graphologie." Opsys does not provide automatic truncation, and the indexing language requires using the singular. Subject searches with plural forms therefore failed.

Users tend to use phrase searches, for example, "French Banking System," "Schools in Morocco," "Life after Death," "How to Lose Weight," "French Cities," "Non-renewable Resources." They also use many complex subjects: "Corporations and Society," "Space and Satellites," "Reading and Freedom," "Don Juan and Don Juanism." But this system does not have Boolean searching. In addition, searching by dates is rarely successful.

Heavy use of cross references is necessary in an attempt to predict the subject terms that the general public will use when approaching the online catalog. A lack of understanding of how to use the online catalog is also apparent. Not everyone instinctively knows what is meant by a subject search as is proven by the use of obvious titles as subject search keys.

This undertaking at the Bibliothèque de Valence is interesting because it attempts to understand the user's logic while librarians are more prone to consider the initial steps in the process, for example, indexing strategies. But both ends of the chain are essential for successful searching.

It is very probable that more sophisticated analysis on the use of online catalogs in France will soon appear. Libraries are beginning to master their systems and will soon be able to devote more time to studying user behavior. The Bibliothèque Publique d'Information has just conducted a study to compare its online catalog and its CD-ROM catalog, Lise. It will be enlightening to compare the usage of the two systems.

In this article, we have talked about librarian indexing strategies and about patron searching. It is clear that the search language is their meeting point and that its capabilities determine in large measure the success of the search. Alexis, the search language for thesaurus generation discussed above, can serve as an example of the direction to take since it was developed within the perspective of natural language queries.

The primary goal is to allow the user to get an appropriate response even if the question is not formulated in the same terms as at the point of indexing.

NOTE

1. Robert P. Holley translated this article from French into English. All screen displays from the various online catalogs have intentionally been left in the original French as transcribed by the author.

Subject Access in Online Catalogs: An Overview Bibliography

Doris Cruger Dale

INTRODUCTION

In reviewing the literature which deals with subject access in on-line catalogs, it quickly became evident that the topic is of great interest to librarians.[1] During the past ten years and especially since 1982, there has been a wealth of information published on this subject. The first item in this review is dated 1978 and the latest three articles appeared in one issue of *Information Technology and Libraries* in 1988. Almost 40 percent of the items were published in 1984 and 1985, and 9 items were published in 1987. Slightly over 50 percent of the items were published in six journals, with the greatest number appearing in *Information Technology and Libraries* and *Library Resources & Technical Services*.

This review is divided into three sections. The background section includes general discussions of the topic and surveys of the literature on the subject. The second section includes material on research and development from the great number of research studies that have been carried out using a variety of methodologies. Individual libraries have also contributed a great deal of development work.

The last section deals with the future, and there are only a few studies in this section. Most of the research studies also include recommendations for future implementation and research.

Doris Cruger Dale is Professor, Department of Curriculum and Instruction, Southern Illinois University, Carbondale, IL.

Although an attempt has been made to locate all the material on this topic, some studies have been omitted because they dealt with subject access in other types of catalogs or dealt solely with the Library of Congress subject headings. Some studies surely have been missed, as neither a bibliography nor an online catalog can include everything written on the subject although readers and users of catalogs do expect such completeness.

BACKGROUND

For an introduction to the subject, the librarian should first read Pauline Atherton Cochrane's continuing education course in *American Libraries* and then follow this up with some of her other articles and books. Her selected papers, published in 1985, bring together some of her most important work in this field. Mandel and Markey are two authors who have written prolifically on the subject of online catalogs, and their works provide an overview of this topic. Classification as a retrieval tool is beginning to be widely discussed. Two particularly thought-provoking articles are those by Jarvis, who recommends integrating pathfinders into online catalogs, and Simonds, who believes that the national standard for subject access should be changed.

Arret, Linda. "Can Online Catalogs Be Too Easy?" *American Libraries* 16, no. 2 (February 1985): 118-20.

The author bases her conclusions on research and a year-long training program with the Library of Congress Information System online. Users want two things: to feel in control and to be able to learn and relearn a system easily. They also want better subject searching. Keyword searching does not bring with it an increased feeling of success, and menu systems have their own problems. Users can solve their search problems with restricted vocabularies. Searchers do want instruction by humans. This results in the highest measure of learning, success, and satisfaction.

Carson, Elizabeth. "OPACS: The User and Subject Access." *Canadian Library Journal* 42, no. 2 (April 1985): 65-70.

After a brief survey of previous studies on subject access in an online public access catalog, the author repeats the finding that user requests do not match the headings assigned by experts. In an online catalog users expect improved subject access through additional access points, subject term display, search delimiters, and key words. LCSH's are considered inadequate. Some online systems make classification numbers available as access points, but this fails to satisfy the demand for access to the contents of the book. The variations among OPACs are so extensive that it is difficult to compare them. Perhaps in the future, matching the capabilities of computers with user needs will be better understood.

Cochrane, Pauline A. *Improving LCSH for Use in Online Catalogs: Exercises for Self-help with a Selection of Background Readings.* Littleton, Colo.: Libraries Unlimited, 1986. 348 p.

This book deals first with the improvement of *Library of Congress Subject Headings* and second with its use in an online catalog. The first part of the book includes discussions and exercises. Three of the six sections include material on *LCSH* in the online catalog. The second part of the book includes 30 background readings from journals and conference proceedings by authors ranging from David Judson Haykin to Berman, Chan, and Cochrane. Six of the articles deal with subject access in an online catalog.

Cochrane, Pauline A. "Subject Access in the Online Catalog." *Research Libraries in OCLC: A Quarterly* no. 5 (January 1982): 1-7.

The major focus in this paper is on *LCSH*. What the Library of Congress does with *LCSH* will have an effect on every library's online catalog. She first reviews subject access via card, COM, and online catalogs and lists some of the advantages and disadvantages of each form. Some recommendations made by researchers are now appearing in online catalogs: access to every word in the subject heading phrase and to every word in a title; limitation by date, language or form; and a browsing capability by call number. Each improvement needs evaluation. Other features suggested include: automatic interaction between searcher and computer, automatic display of some retrieval items, automatic display of logical outlines, and automatic display of limit options.

Cochrane, Pauline A., and Markey, Karen. "Catalog Use Studies — Since the introduction of Online Interactive Catalogs: Impact on Design for Subject Access." *Library & Information Science Research* 5, no. 4 (Winter 1983): 337-63.

The years 1981-1982 marked the beginning of a trend toward experimentation in library catalog design. These years also marked a new era in catalog use studies. To descriptive surveys and questionnaires were added transaction log analysis, systems analysis, protocol analysis, focused-group interviews, and online search and retrieval experiments. Research studies employing each of these methods are discussed in this article along with the limitations of the methodology and the types of research questions that each method can answer. Not all research questions can be answered by a single methodology. Librarians now have a mountain of data but are still without answers to questions relating to ergonomics aspects or costs of online catalogs.

Cochrane, Pauline Atherton. "Modern Subject Access in the Online Age." *American Libraries* 15, nos. 2-7 (February 1984, March 1984, April 1984, May 1984, June 1984, July-August 1984): 80-83, 145-48, 150, 250-52, 254-55, 336-39, 438-41, 443, 527-29.

Billed as "American Libraries first continuing education course," this series tries to help librarians understand the implications of technology on subject access. A brief list of terms used in the discussion and some notes on the online environment are valuable parts of the first lesson. Lesson 2 compares the features of the older and newer ways of subject access. The third lesson begins with a table showing some of *LCSH* weaknesses and continues with comments from ten librarians on two major questions regarding the validity of and changes needed in *LCSH*. In lesson 4, four more librarians respond and three Library of Congress staff members reply. Lesson 5 covers the impact of technological developments on subject access. Lesson 6 concludes by discussing the user.

Cochrane, Pauline Atherton. *Redesign of Catalogs and Indexes for Improved Online Subject Access: Selected Papers of Pauline A. Cochrane*. Phoenix: Oryx Press, 1985 484 p.

This collection brings together 30 works of this author written between 1961 and 1984 and is organized by the five questions which she has been asked many times: Where are we going in the redesign of catalogs and indexes? What do we know about users and catalogs? What can we do to improve subject access? Will classification have a use online? What can be learned from subject access research? Many articles were issued as part of conference proceedings, and some were previously unpublished. The chronological list of selections shows an interesting progression from a concern with classification to the last 10 articles which deal with subject access in the online age.

Dwyer, James R. "The Road to Access & the Road to Entropy." *Library Journal* 112, no. 14 (1 September 1987): 131-36.

Only a portion of this article is devoted to subject access in an online catalog. The author recommends retaining subject vocabulary control. Many catalog users have trouble matching their search terms with those in the controlled vocabulary (*LCSH*). Desirable added features in an online catalog include the ability to see lists of terms, the inclusion of more terms, and the ability to search by any word in the subject field. Users of the catalog also want a deeper analysis of the contents of library books including the ability to search contents notes. Classification inconsistency prevents its effective use for subject searching. "Ideally, authority control should be authoritative, relevant to the database being searched, and accessible to the public."

Hildreth, Charles R. "Beyond Boolean: Designing the Next Generation of Online Catalogs." *Library Trends* 35, no. 4 (Spring 1987): 647-67.

Stating that the online catalog will never be a perfect product, the author points out the unique qualities of this new form. It is interactive, infinitely expandable, and public. Searching activity can be logged for analysis. He states that we have moved beyond first-generation catalogs which were basically circulation control systems, but current development has slowed to a snail's pace with a continuing priority of control over access. The second-generation online catalogs are closer to bibliographic information retrieval systems. Users prefer the online catalog; it is easier to maintain; but there is need for further improvements. Users need to describe what they do not know in order to find it. He suggests several enhancements to improve access.

Hill, Janet Swan. "Online Classification Number Access: Some Practical Considerations." *Journal of Academic Librarianship* 10, no. 1 (March 1984): 17-22.

Presenting her thesis that in the United States call numbers are used primarily for arranging and locating books, the author claims that both DDC and LC are non-theoretical. Because of this, the possibility of using classification in subject searching online has its problems. Some of these are: classification schemes are not easy to use; numbers have not remained static; they are often inconsistently assigned; a book can only be classed in one number; call numbers are accepted from external sources; numbers are not assigned for the purpose of subject searching but to park a book; and classification may not be as well suited to machine searching as might be thought. The future of classification access must take into account these factors.

Holley, Robert P., and Killheffer, Robert E. "Is There an Answer to the Subject Access Crisis?" *Cataloging & Classification Quarterly* 1, no. 2/3 (1982): 125-33.

After discussing some of the criticisms against *LCSH*, the authors present suggestions to improve subject access. These include replacing *LCSH* with PRECIS and using Pauline Atherton's Subject Analysis Project to apply abstracting and indexing principles to monographs. Both of these have theoretical merit, but their chance of adoption is minimal because Library of Congress is unlikely to revise its subject analysis system. They suggest that the Library of Congress system could be better utilized by automated subject searching and the use of machine readable authority files. Benefits include the ability to search by words in subject headings, the use of Boolean logic, free text searching of content notes, an automatic cross-reference structure, and the ability to change subject headings.

Jarvis, William E. "Integrating Subject Pathfinders into Online Catalogs." *Database* 8, no. 1 (February 1985): 65-7.

The author recommends subject searching assistance via the integration of pathfinders into online catalogs. Pathfinders usually provide key titles, subject headings, classification numbers, and secondary indexes to help users find the information they need in the library. Pathfinders could be provided in user manuals, by way of full text display online, by off-line printouts, or could be cataloged as bibliographic entries. An example of a pathfinder online is presented. Jarvis believes that pathfinders could become a significant enhancement to online library catalogs.

Lipow, Anne Grodzins. "Practical Considerations of the Current Capabilities of Subject Access in Online Public Catalogs." *Library Resources & Technical Services* 27, no. 1 (January-March 1983): 81-7.

Three questions are discussed: (1) do we need subject headings if we have keyword searching, (2) are the users' views of online catalogs useful, and (3) what is wrong with user-friendly systems? Although 99 percent of all nonfiction titles use words that describe the contents of the book, assigned subject headings are essential because keyword searching has severe limitations. Users seem to love anything that is online, but the initial enthusiasm lasts only a short time. The online catalog can be uncommunicative and unhelpful;

the user must know how to spell and use the correct punctuation. The computer doesn't know everything even though users think it does. User-friendly systems offer limited service. Library instruction is essential for advanced searches.

Mandel, Carol A. "Enriching the Library Catalog Record for Subject Access." *Library Resources & Technical Services* 29, no. 1 (January March 1985): 5-15.

This paper examines ways of enhancing bibliographic records for better subject access. Records could be enhanced by using classification, keywords, and more subject headings. Subject cataloging at the Library of Congress costs about $15 per title. In light of that cost, does book content indexing belong in the online library catalog? Periodical articles are not indexed in the online catalog, and many special index tools analyze parts of books. Perhaps only some monographs merit fuller content analysis. In an online catalog, records can contain more access points. Should we expect Library of Congress to do this? Enriched online catalog databases need to be constructed, tested, and weighed against cost-effectiveness and need.

Mandel, Carol A. *Multiple Thesauri in Online Library Bibliographic Systems: A Report Prepared for Library of Congress Processing Services*. Washington: Cataloging Distribution Service, Library of Congress, 1987. 94 p.

Mandel examines the issues surrounding multiple controlled-language vocabularies for online systems. She discusses computer support for controlled vocabularies in three functional areas: thesaurus management, subject authority control, and subject searching. The Library of Congress maintains not only the 145,000-term *LCSH* but also several specialized subject vocabularies. A key decision for Library of Congress involves the redesign or replacement of MUMS and SCORPIO. However, no system in use today has made the searching of terms from multiple thesauri in the same file easy for the users of that file.

Mandel, Carol A., and Herschman, Judith. "Online Subject Access — Enhancing the Library Catalog." *Journal of Academic Librarianship* 9, no.3 (July 1983): 148-55.

This paper examines previous research on subject access under the headings: findings and methods, reasons for search failures, failure analysis, free text vs. controlled vocabulary searching, and studies of users' needs. Both research and action are necessary to improve subject access in the future. Records must be enriched because there are not enough descriptive words in the standard records to permit adequate subject searching. This is a costly process. Transaction logs now provide the means to analyze search failures. Online catalogs must help users take advantage of *LCSH*; only about 5 percent of users consult this book. The subject heading list needs to be available online, but for *LCSH* to be useful it needs to be revised or reconstructed.

Markey, Karen. "Integrating the Machine-Readable LCSH into Online Catalogs." *Information Technology and Libraries* 7, no. 3 (September 1988): 299-312.

Four generalizations are presented: users' search terms fail to match the controlled vocabulary; users do not know the source of the catalog's controlled vocabulary; users want to be able to browse through a list of words related to their search terms; and only a fraction of assigned subject headings in an online catalog match Library of Congress subject headings. The potential of *LCSH* online can only be realized if links are provided between the terms users enter and the controlled vocabulary and if links are provided between the subject information in the records and the subject headings in *LCSH*. Search tactics to improve precision need to be offered, such as narrower headings, broader headings, related headings, assigned headings, and free-text terms.

Piternick, Anne B. "Searching Vocabularies: A Developing Category of Online Search Tools." *Online Review* 8, no. 5 (October 1984): 441-49.

Searching online by subject has created different conditions, and there is now a need for controlled searching vocabularies. The author discusses four types which could be useful in online searching by human searchers: enhanced thesauri and enhanced subject heading lists (more entry terms, a rotated display of terms), synonym listings, index term listings from machine-stored indexes, and merged vocabularies. Examples of each type are given, and the advantages and disadvantages are discussed. Controlled vocabularies should be examined closely for their application possibilities in online catalogs.

Simonds, Michael J. "Database Limitations & Online Catalogs." *Library Journal* 109, no. 3 (15 February 1984): 329-30.

The author argues that the MARC database is an inadequate foundation for the online catalog. He states that patrons use subject access far more than previously thought and that they are frustrated with its current limitations. The major problem is the database itself. The MARC record is the current standard, but it does not provide adequate subject access. Improvement in technology will not help. *LCSH* does not provide adequate subject cataloging. Simonds believes the MARC record should have included a field for indexing terms. Boolean searching does not work because the average number of subject headings per item is less than two. He concludes that: "The only hope for adequate subject access is through fundamental changes in the national standard."

Wang, Chih. "The Online Catalogue, Subject Access and User Reactions: A Review." *Library Review* 34 (Autumn 1985): 143-53.

The author reviews previous studies and research on subject access in an online catalog. After defining subject access, the problem of subject access using *LCSH* is discussed along with problems caused by improper design of OPACs. The author then summarizes the literature which covers suggested improvements for *LCSH* and suggested improvements for OPACs. Continuous research and development are needed both to improve *LCSH* and to enhance the capability of online subject searches. The studies and research cited are listed in an extensive bibliography.

West, Martha W. "Classification as a Retrieval Tool." *National Online Meeting Proceedings* (1984): 433-36.

Defining classification as the identification and description of like items, the discrimination of unlike items, and the ordering of these items, the author suggests that: "classification in the form of an expert system based upon classification of descriptors . . . [can be] an effective and powerful retrieval tool" in an online system.

RESEARCH AND DEVELOPMENT

Pauline Atherton's 1978 study is required reading as it is cited extensively in much of the literature published since that time. The research base on subject access is extensive, and the authors of these studies make many recommendations. The Council on Library Resources and OCLC have been responsible for much of the research, and they are to be commended for their support. Major research studies deal with the use of classification in online catalogs. The works by Cochrane, Demeyer, Hildreth, Kaske, Mandel, and Markey are of special significance. The *Dewey Decimal Classification Online Project* was a seminal study on the use of DDC to provide subject access in an online catalog. Chan carried out a theoretical analysis of LCC indicating its advantages and disadvantages if used in a similar way.

Atherton, Pauline. *BOOKS Are for Use: Final Report of the Subject Access Project to the Council on Library Resources*. Syracuse, N.Y.: Syracuse University, School of Information Studies, 1978. 190 p.

After creating an online BOOKS database of 1,979 monographs in the humanities and social sciences, the records were augmented with subject descriptions (about 300 words per title) taken from the book's table of contents and/or index. The cost of selecting terms was $5.00 per title, and selection took 12 minutes per title. Suitable information was found in 90 percent of the books selected from the University of Toronto Libraries. A controlled test of 90 searches comparing online searching of MARC records (8 minutes online) and BOOKS records (4 minutes online) showed that more relevant items were retrieved using the BOOKS database (130 items) than the MARC database (56 items). Benefits included greater access, greater precision, and less costly searching.

Bates, Marcia J. "Subject Access in Online Catalogs: A Design Model." *Journal of the American Society for Information Science* 37, no. 6 (November 1986): 357-76.

A proposed model for the design of online subject catalog access would be incorporated into existing Library of Congress subject heading indexing so as to enhance access without requiring recataloging. Three design principles are presented: uncertainty, variety, and complexity. Design features include an access phase (both entry and orientation), a hunting phase, and a selection phase. An end-user thesaurus and a front-end system mind are presented as examples of online catalog system components to improve searcher success. In order for subject searching to be most effective, methods must be devised to help the searcher enter the catalog, get oriented, explore terminology, generate variety, hunt in powerful ways, and get more information about each book.

Besant, Larry. "Users of Public Online Catalogs Want Sophisticated Subject Access." *American Libraries* 14, no. 3 (March 1982): 160.

The investigators involved in the Public Access Online Catalog Project administered by CRL presented some preliminary findings at a Denver meeting. Besant discusses some findings related to subject access. Questionnaires were distributed to both users and nonusers. A strong preference was shown for subject search augmentation including the ability to search a book's table of contents or index, to view a list of related search terms, to print search results, and to search by any word in the subject heading. The most important indication so far is the need for standards for public access catalogs. The full report has been published in Using Online Catalogs: A Nationwide Survey (New York: Neal-Schuman Publishers, 1983).

Chan, Lois Mai. "Library of Congress Classification as an Online Retrieval Tool: Potential and Limitations." *Information Technology and Libraries* 5, no. 3 (September 1986): 181-92.

Because a study of DDC as a searcher's tool for online subject access indicated that inclusion of a classification scheme in an online catalog could provide enhanced subject access, Chan explored the feasibility of using LCC in a similar way. Her theoretical analysis indicates advantages and disadvantages. Disadvantages are its large size, the difficulty of putting the tables online, the lack of a unified consistent index, only one call number per item, and the fact that numbers cannot be easily manipulated. Advantages are its very specific discrete numbers, diversity and richness in terminology, use of broad terms in the indexes, stability of class numbers, completeness, *LCSH*'s inclusion of LCC numbers, and the effectiveness of known-item searching. Research is necessary.

Cochrane, Pauline A., and Markey, Karen. "Preparing for the Use of Classification in Online Cataloging Systems and in Online Catalogs." *Information Technology and Libraries* 4, no. 2 (June 1985): 91-111.

The authors present the preliminary findings of a research project using selected portions of the DDC Schedules and Relative Index to create a searcher's tool for subject access in an online catalog. Many online catalogs provide access by classification number, but searchers must know the exact class number. In the OCLC project, the addition of classification records provided the following benefits: browsing capability, enriched subject description, up-to-date schedules for editing and shelflisting, and a tailored version of the library's classification practices.

Frost, Carolyn O. "Faculty Use of Subject Searching in Card and Online Catalog." *Information Technology and Libraries* 6, no. 1 (March 1987): 60-3.

Juniors, seniors, and graduate students at the University of Houston were questioned about their use of subject searching in the online catalog. A majority of the 81 students searched by subject; graduate students used subject searching less. Those who failed in their subject searches said they would try an author or title approach or ask a librarian for help. Only 3 percent would give up. Improvements requested were the capability to combine subject terms, inclusion of a summary of the book's content, and the ability to see a list of the terms. A majority of the students were unaware of *LCSH* as the source of the subject terms used in the online catalog.

Frost, Carolyn O., and Dede, Bonnie A. "Subject Heading Compatibility Between LCSH and Catalog Files of a Large Research Library: A Suggested Model for Analysis." *Information Technology and Libraries* 7, no. 3 (September 1988): 288-99.

This study at the University of Michigan Library determined how many subject headings in the catalog matched those in the machine-readable Library of Congress Subject Authority File, how easily conflicting headings could be converted through automated control, and which conversions required human intervention. A sample of 2,401 cards were pulled, data sheets were created for 3,814 topical and geographic headings, and records were analyzed. The average number of subject headings was 1.8 per title. Over two-thirds of the headings had subdivisions. Forty-four percent of the headings matched *LCSH* exactly, and most of these were main headings without subdivisions. Only 31.2 percent of all subdivisions matched. Geographic subdivisions pose the greatest problem in conversion.

Hancock, Micheline. "Subject Searching Behavior at the Library Catalogue and at the Shelves: Implications for Online Interactive Catalogues." *Journal of Documentation* 43, no. 4 (December 1987): 303-21.

This study on subject searching at the City University Library in London was designed as the first half of a "before and after" study. The nature and effectiveness of subject searching at the catalog and at the shelves was studied by means of observing and questioning 95 library users selected randomly during the 1985-86 academic year. Subject searching predominated (72 percent). Some specific item searches developed into subject searches. There was a tendency to search using broad terms. Searchers went to the shelves with only one class number and tended to browse only within that area. Searchers examined 6 items on the shelves and selected 2. We need to know more about how a search develops in order to develop user-related online catalogs.

Hildreth, Charles R. *Online Public Access Catalogs: The User Interface* Dublin, Ohio: OCLC, 1982. 263 p.

The Council on Library Resources sponsored this report on ten operating online public access catalog systems. One difficult aspect of the task was the fact that each of the systems was constantly changing. In the 12 sections of the report, only a portion of section 8 (p. 129-32) is devoted to subject access variations. Limitations on subject access imposed by today's OPACs include the following: the subject headings index cannot be seen, see also references are not displayed, *LCSH* headings must be entered exactly, few provide title keyword access, few provide browsing by call number, limiting features are not always available, and limits are placed on the number of "hits" allowed.

Jamieson, Alexis J., Dolan, Elizabeth, and Declerck, Luc. "Keyword Searching vs. Authority Control in an Online Catalog." *Journal of Academic Librarianship* 12, no. 5 (November 1986): 227-83.

This study at the University of Western Ontario investigated the value of keyword searching versus searching with subject headings from a controlled vocabulary. It built a sub-sample of 251 records. Non-preferred terms were taken from LC's authority records, and 1189 see references were generated; 899 were alternate subject headings. These were coded for synonymous terms and inverted terms. The cataloging records were printed out, and each keyword was searched separately in all MARC fields. In keyword searching for synonyms, only 15.52 percent of the terms were matched. In searching for terms in inverted order, the match rate was 100 percent. Fields 650 and 245 were most productive. Keyword searching cannot compensate for the lack of cross references.

Kaske, Neal K. "The Variability and Intensity over Time of Subject Searching in an Online Public Access Catalog." *Information Technology and Libraries* 7, no. 3 (September 1988): 273-87.

Subject searching in an online public access catalog at the University of Alabama was studied during the spring semester 1987. Transaction logs of 165,083 searches were analyzed by hour of day, day of week, week of term, and month of term to determine degree of variability and intensity of searching (mean number of searches per hour). Subject searches were defined as those using the subject command; these comprised 45.81 percent of the total. The time of greatest subject searching and total searching was from 3:00 to 4:00 p.m.; the second peak was from 7:00 to 9:00 p.m. Monday had the most transactions, but Sunday was the day of most intense searching, including subject searching. The peak for total searching was during the 15th week of the term.

Kaske, Neal K., and Sanders, Nancy P. "On-line Subject Access: The Human Side of the Problem." *RQ* 20, no. 1 (Fall 1980): 52-8.

The OCLC Research Department designed a ten-step research plan to determine "the features of an automated subject retrieval system that would support the present search tactics employed by library users." Two hundred interviews were conducted with users as they searched the subject card catalog. Focused-group interviews were also held. Some findings applicable to the design of online subject access catalogs were: users looked for terms that were too broad or too narrow; users wanted more headings and access to subjects using keywords in the title; the tables of contents and the indexes of books are needed for selection; delimiters are desirable; subject terms need to be displayed and defined; and *LCSH* was not widely used.

Kelm, Barbara. "Computer-sided Subject Cataloguing at the Deutsche Bibliothek in Frankfurt am Main." *International Cataloguing* 13, no. 4 (October-December 1984): 45-7.

In 1966 the Deutche Bibliothek installed the first computer for the purpose of producing a national bibliography. The following aids were developed: the subject heading reference pool (cumulated every six months), the subject heading pool (the standard list), and Biblio-Data (an online information database with updated title and subject headings lists plus access assistance such as keyword lists). Over 100 institutions in Germany and abroad use Biblio-Data even though they are hindered by the numerous changes in the rules. The goal is cooperative subject cataloging and standardization in subject cataloging.

Kern-Simirenko, Cheryl. "OPAC User Logs: Implications for Bibliographic Instruction." *Library Hi Tech* 1, no. 3 (Winter 1983): 27-35.

Transaction logs from three unidentified libraries were examined to analyze searching behavior of online public access catalogs. This method reveals search strategy but cannot accurately assess success. The three OPAC systems analyzed provided a variety of searching options and various types of transaction logs. In system A, 45 percent of 204 searches failed to match items in the file; in system B, 35 percent of 231 searches failed; and in system C, 39 percent of 69 searches failed. Current terminology is of crucial importance. Truncation was rarely used. Subject heading displays would be helpful. Operators need to be demonstrated. Point-of-use instruction would be valuable. Users must be trained before they can exploit an OPAC to its full potential.

Lawrence, Gary S. "System Features for Subject Access in the Online Catalog." *Library Resources & Technical services* 29, no. 1 (January-March 1985): 16-33.

Designers of online catalogs need to know that the requirements of subject access are more complicated than those of access by author or title. Thirteen systems were studied. Tasks were divided into three types, one type being searches for books on specific subjects. Users who searched in the online catalog by subject were not happy with the search results. On the other hand, they were satisfied with the online catalog. The points to be considered in designing online catalogs (what to search, what to search with, how to search, and how to display search results) are discussed in this paper along with examples and suggestions. The author believes that there is no one right approach to improving subject access, but that it can be done.

Lipetz, Ben-Ami, and Paulson, Peter J. "A Study of the Impact of Introducing an Online Subject Catalog at the New York State Library." *Library Trends* 35, no. 4 (Spring 1987): 597-617.

The authors report the findings of an impact study done at the New York State Library. They investigated the use of the card catalog before and after the online catalog was available. They also compared uses of two different subject catalog systems. They counted visitor traffic and interviewed a sample of visitors during three different time periods. The new online subject catalog was accepted. Card catalog use decreased. A larger proportion of visitors used the catalog, but the use of the catalog by the library staff dropped. The proportion of subject searches increased from 27 percent to 43 percent. The change in the catalog brought no improvement in the success rate of searches, nor did it increase general satisfaction for visitors.

Logan, Susan J. "The Ohio State University's Library Control System: From Circulation to Subject Access and Authority Control." *Library Trends* 35, no. 4 (Spring 1987): 539-54.

The Library Control System at Ohio State University went online in 1970 to provide circulation control. It has been gradually enhanced until today it serves as an online catalog. Subject access was added in 1978. When a word or subject is entered, the computer displays an alphabetical segment of the subject index. The user then can see a list of titles and may search by line number to see the location of the title and its circulation status. The subject search was designed so that the user could enter any word and receive some response. By June 1979, subject searches were 9.3 percent of the searches of choice; in 1985/86, 30 percent of the searches were by subject. Inclusion of the syndetic structure in 1981 increased the success rate to 82 percent.

Ludy, Lorene E. "OSU Libraries' Use of Library of Congress Subject Authorities File." *Information Technology and Libraries* 4, no. 2 (June 1985): 155-60.

In September 1984, the Ohio State University Libraries applied the 1981 Library of Congress Subject Authorities File (SAF) to its online public access catalog (Library Control System, LCS). The author discusses the type of headings in the SAF, how subject headings are stored in LCS, how SAF was applied to LCS, the complications caused by subdivisions (especially the more than 500 free-floating subdivisions), and how outdated data is handled. One benefit was that global changes could now be made when an LCS heading matched a SEE reference. Applying the SAF has improved control of subject headings in the LCS online public access catalog. The addition of reference links, scope notes, and suggested class numbers will assist users in subject searches.

Mandel, Carol A. *Classification Schedules as Subject Enhancement in Online Catalogs*. Washington: Council on Library Resources, 1986, 24 p.

In January 1986, thirty librarians were invited to participate in a conference sponsored by Forest Press, OCLC, and CLR, to review the results of the DDC Online Project and to explore the potential for future use of DDC and LCC in online catalogs. The author provides a brief background on the project and synthesizes the formal presentations and discussions which focused on three themes: what subject search enhancements are needed, what is the future role of class number searching, and how can LCC and DDC be used online? Future development should cover subject search features, subject search strategies, DDC as a classification authority file online, refinement of DDC in the online catalog, displaying of related subject terms, and LCC online.

Markey, Karen. "Subject-Searching Experiences and Needs of Online Catalog Users: Implications for Library Classification." *Library Resources & Technical Services* 29, no. 1 (January-March 1985): 34-51.

Research, based on surveys and transaction log analyses, reveals that subject searches are the predominant approach to searching in online catalogs. Computer searching by subject is difficult as is finding the correct subject term. OCLC's Developmental Online Public Access Catalog included in its database headings from the DDC schedules and entries from the DDC relative index as a basis for using classification for subject searches. Because DDC is already in machine-readable form, classification becomes a valuable tool for subject access, for browsing, and for screen display. Preliminary findings of the OCLC project are presented in this article.

Markey, Karen. *Subject Searching in Library Catalogs: Before and After the Introduction of Online Catalogs*. Dublin, Ohio: OCLC Online Computer Library Center, 1984. 176 p.

OCLC's participation in research began in 1979. Some of the results existed only in separate and difficult-to-access reports. The author has integrated three of these reports into this book and added a great deal of new material. Chapter titles indicate the book's scope: transition from traditional to online catalogs, methods for studying library catalog use, implementation of online subject searching, subject access points and library catalogs, importance of subject access in online catalogs, improving subject access in online catalogs, patrons' experiences with online catalogs, and the new dimension of online catalog use. The purpose of this research is to understand the users in order to effect improvement in online public access catalogs.

Markey, Karen. "Thus Spake the OPAC User." *Information Technology and Libraries* 2, no. 4 (December 1983): 381-87.

An OCLC project team conducted focused-group interviews with OPAC users and nonusers plus library staff at six libraries (Dallas Public, Iowa City Public, Library of Congress, Mankato State University, Ohio State University, and Syracuse University). A moderator at each library led a group of 6 to 12 individuals through an open discussion to elicit participants' needs and perceptions of the online catalog in their own words. Data analysis yielded six generalizations: users like the online catalog; some features of the card catalog should be implemented in the online catalog; users have problems finding the right subject heading; users have suggested features to improve subject access; users want access to much more than books; and they want the OPAC to provide new services.

Markey, Karen, and Demeyer, Anh N. *Dewey Decimal Classification Online Project: Evaluation of a Library Schedule and Index Integrated into the Subject Searching Capabilities of an Online Catalog*. Dublin, Ohio: OCLC, 1986.

Widely reviewed, summarized, and discussed in the journal literature, this is the final report of the Dewey Decimal Classification Online Project. An executive summary presented on pages xxv to xliii is followed by the detailed report of 382 pages. The volume concludes with 17 appendixes, a list of references, and an index. The executive summary in this report should be required reading for librarians interested in subject access in online catalogs. Designers of online catalogs should read the whole report.

Markey, Karen, and Demeyer, Anh. "Dewey Decimal Classification Online Project: Integration of a Library Schedule and Index into the Subject Searching Capabilities of an Online Catalogue." *International Cataloguing* 14, no. 3 (July-September 1985): 31-4.

This paper was first presented at the 51st IFLA General Conference in Chicago. The authors describe the Dewey Decimal Classification Online Project, funded by the Council on Library Resources, OCLC, and Forest Press, which focused on how DDC could be used for subject access online. Three research questions were formulated, and two experimental catalogs were developed. Two tables illustrate how subject searching is done in the Subject Online Catalog (with traditional subject searching capabilities) and the Dewey Online Catalog (with additional subject searching capabilities based on the DDC relative index and schedules). Retrieval tests were conducted at four libraries. The final report was published by the CLR in 1986.

Moore, Carole Weiss, "User Reactions to Online Catalogs: An Exploratory Study," *College & Research Libraries* 42, no. 4 (July 1981): 295-302.

A pilot study was conducted at four institutions (Ohio State University, University of Toronto, Guelph University, and Ryerson Polytechnic Institute) to observe user reactions to their fledgling online catalogs. Questionnaires and interviews were used with a small sample of users. The systems were designed for circulation and were not advertised as online catalogs. The majority of use was for known-item searches. Even though the catalogs had none or limited subject searching capabilities, from 20 to 60 percent of the users intended to search for subjects. Known-item searches had a higher success rate than subject searches. There were frequent requests for better subject access. What is not found in the first place is often not found or used at all.

Ross, James. *"Geographic Headings Online."* *Cataloging & Classification Quarterly* 5, no. 2 (Winter 1984): 27-43.

An examination of subject headings in the Washington Library Network (WLN) online system reveals that geographic terms are difficult for the cataloger to verify in some cases. In addition, the searcher often must know both the new and old form of geographic name and the structure of the heading to complete an effective search. The author discusses: agencies contributing data to WLN, changes in geographic subject headings caused by AACR2, the headings for cities and other jurisdictions in Britain, inverted headings, online subject verification in WLN, "indirect" headings with exceptions, and changes of names. Geographical headings need to be established according to consistent guidelines. Keyword searching might help, but it is not always available.

Settel, Barbara, and Cochrane, Pauline A. *"Augmenting Subject Descriptions for Books in Online Catalogs."* *Database* 5, no. 4 (December 1982): 29-37.

This research involved adding words and phrases from the books' index and/or table of contents to MARC records. Rules and procedures for the selection of subject descriptions for the BOOKS record are presented under the headings: begin selection with table of contents, index or both; selection of entries; applying the quota—or knowing when to stop; and formatting selections for computer input. In the experiment, the average number of selections per book was 32.4 and the average time spent on selections was 10 minutes per book. In a controlled test environment, two searches were performed online using MARC and BOOKS records. Ninety queries were searched. Searches in MARC retrieved 56 documents, in BOOKS, 131 documents. MARC searches took twice as long.

Turock, Betty J., and Shelton, Hildred. *"Online Catalog in the Small Public Library: Enhanced Subject Access Via Microcomputer."* *National Online Meeting Proceedings* (1984): 405-11.

The staff members in the Pittsylvania County, Virginia, Public Library, which serves a population of 66,137, collected terms for which the users needed assistance. The users' search vocabulary seldom matched *LCSH*. The librarians developed a thesaurus/bibliography keyed to *LCSH*, written using PFS1 File, and stored on a Apple II microcomputer. One thousand items were entered, and the screen display included eight fields of information to assist the patron: broader subjects, narrower subjects, related subjects, and scope notes. The program is capable of handling natural language terms. When the test stage is over and sufficient data are gathered, the library will place the database on a hard disk and make it available to their patrons.

Walker, Stephen. "OKAPI: Evaluating and Enhancing an Experimental Online Catalog." *Library Trends* 35, no. 4 (Spring 1987): 631-45.

An experimental online catalog named OKAPI (Online Keyword Access to Public Information) was developed at the Polytechnic of Central London. The primary purpose of the experiment was to determine if the online catalog satisfied users and provided effective searching. Specific books can be searched as well as books about something. Raw statistical information was obtained automatically. Data showed that 40 percent of the searches were by subject. The attitude of most users was favorable. Just under 300 queries were identified, and each of these was repeated by the experimenter; 62 percent were judged successful. Most bibliographic records do not contain enough information nor information of the right kind. Catalogs should produce better results.

Williamson, Nancy J. "Classification in Online Systems: Research and the North American Perspective." *International Cataloguing* 14, no. 3 (July-September 1985): 29-31.

The author reports that the IFLA Standing Committee on Classification and Subject Cataloguing is attempting to identify and encourage the research needed on the most effective methods of introducing classification into online cataloging systems. This study has gone through two phases. An exhaustive literature search was carried out. A questionnaire was sent to North American libraries to collect data on the degree of use made of classification in online catalogs. Directions for research are indicated in the form of questions based on these topics: effective use of computers, use of thesauri, classification online with updated schedules, suitable databases for research, and development of appropriate standards.

THE FUTURE

Only four studies are included in this section. The section on research and development should also be consulted for recommendations about future development of subject access in online catalogs. Lawry strongly recommends that users need prior instruction in order to use the new online catalogs successfully because they mistakenly believe that the online catalog will tell them everything they need to know. Richmond believes that there is not much of a future for keyword or Boolean searching or for *LCSH* online. The use of classification online and the use of PRECIS offer greater promise. Svenonius also talks about the use of classification in online systems in the future. She predicts a resurgence of interest in both the theory and practice of classification. And because of this interest in classification for subject retrieval, Wajenberg recommends an expansion of the MARC codes for the Dewey decimal numbers.

Lawry, Martha. "Subject Access in the Online Catalog: Is the Medium Projecting the Correct Message?" *Research Strategies* 4, no. 3 (Summer 1986): 125-31.

The primary focus in discussion of the online catalog is the provision of more subject access. While the card catalog was seen as a fallible human system, users believe that the online catalog will give them all they need to know. Users need to be aware of what the online catalog can do and cannot do. For example, many sources are not in the catalog. Users need prior knowledge and instruction, a guide, and especially a search strategy. Users must bring to their search some knowledge of their research topic by checking an encyclopedia, looking at a general bibliography of the subject, and checking footnotes and bibliographies in a few relevant books. This preamble needs to be an integral part of workshops, classes, and instructional brochures.

Richmond, Phyllis A. "Futuristic Aspects of Subject Access." *Library Resources & Technical Services* 27, no. 1 (January-March 1983): 88-93.

The future in terms of hardware, software, friendliness, and subject access are discussed. A computer language called SMALLTALK is of interest for subject analysis. In SMALLTALK the screens look like pages which are connected in a classified system, which may be called and recalled, and which store and access information in logically organized formats. Another user friendly system is PaperChase (it allows users to search medical literature online without special training). The new media promise access via a wider range of entries; the user will be able to search by whatever term seems reasonable. The author believes there is not much of a future for keyword or Boolean searching, or *LCSH* online. Classification offers greater promise as does the use of PRECIS.

Svenonius, Elaine. "Use of Classification in Online Retrieval." *Library Resources & Technical Services* 27, no. 1 (January-March 1983): 76-80.

The author attempts to answer how classification might be used in the future in online systems. Classification may be used to screen out unwanted documents. Time may be saved. Classification may be used to focus a search by contextualizing search terms (an example would be to consult the DDC relative index) and by enabling browsing. If a database is multilingual, a user's search terms in one language could be switched through DDC to retrieve documents in several different languages. She predicts a resurgence of interest in both the theory and practice of classification.

Wajenberg, Arnold S. "MARC Coding of DDC for Subject Retrieval." *Information Technology and Libraries* 2, no. 3 (September 1983): 246-51.

Based on the increasing interest in the use of classification for subject retrieval, the author recommends an expansion of the MARC codes for the Dewey decimal numbers in fields 082 and 092. The two characteristics of DDC that should be coded are the hierarchy of numbers expressed in the notation and the synthesis of constructed numbers which expresses the relationship of one topic to another. Neither this hierarchy nor synthesis is represented in any way by the current coding. He suggests using the present unused second indicator values of 082 and 092 for this purpose. These codes could then be manipulated to enhance subject retrieval in online catalogs.

NOTE

1. The author would like to thank Betty-Ruth Wilson for her assistance in locating and writing some of the original annotations for articles published in 1984 and 1985. They have been edited and revised for this article.